PRINCE EDWARD ISLAND SAYINGS

Prince Edward Island Sayings

EDITED BY T.K. PRATT AND SCOTT BURKE

UNIVERSITY OF TORONTO PRESS
Toronto Buffalo London

© University of Toronto Press Incorporated 1998
Toronto Buffalo London
Printed in Canada

ISBN 0-8020-0920-4

Printed on acid-free paper

Canadian Cataloguing in Publication Data

Main entry under title:

Prince Edward Island sayings

Includes index.
ISBN 0-8020-0920-4

1. Canadianisms (English) – Prince Edward Island.* 2. English language – Dialects – Prince Edward Island. 3. Prince Edward Island – Quotations, Maxims, etc. I. Burke, Scott. II. Pratt, T.K. (Terry Kenneth), 1943– .

PE3245.P75P75 1998   427.9717   C97-932409-2

University of Toronto Press acknowledges the financial assistance to its publishing program of the Canada Council for the Arts and the Ontario Arts Council.

This book has been published with the help of a grant from the Humanities and Social Sciences Federation of Canada, using funds provided by the Social Sciences and Humanities Research Council of Canada.

Contents

Preface vii
Introduction xi
Dictionaries and
   Other Collections
   Consulted xxix

THEMES

Human Appearance
General 3
Ugliness 3
Hair 7
Eyes 8
Skin 8
Mouth and Teeth 9
Height 10
Size 10
Thinness 11
Legs 16
Clothes 16
Voice 18
Hearing 18

Human Age
Youth 19
Old Age 20
Death 21

Health 23

Character
Laziness 25
Dishonesty 27
Cunning 29
Avarice 30
Arrogance 32
Obstinacy 34
Innocence 35
Eccentricity 36

Intelligence 40

Certainty
Assurance 47
Futility 49
Worth 50
Uncertainty 52

**Foolishness and
Mistakes** 55

Mood
Happiness 57
Misery 58
Anxiety 58
Shock 60
Irritation 62
Anger and
   Contempt 63
Exclamations 64

Social Life
Solitude 66
Company 67
Bad Manners 68

Talking
Silence 71
Chatter 72
Smooth Talk 73
Arguments 74
Nonsense
   Greetings 75
Nonsense Replies 76
Nonsense Farewells
   82

Food
Hunger 83
Eating 84

Drink
Thirst 88
Drunkenness 89

**Bedtime and
Rising** 91

Work
Hard Work 94
Busyness 95

Money
Thrift 99
Poverty 100

Farming and Fishing 102

Weather
Thunder 104
Rain 105

Storm and Cold 106
Darkness 108
Fine Weather 109

Physical Properties
Age of Objects 111
Ease of Job 111
Tightness 112
Touch 113
Heat 113

Dimensions 114
Locations 115
Speed 119

Miscellaneous 120

Bibliography 125

Index 129

Preface

This book is intended as a companion volume to my *Dictionary of Prince Edward Island English*, also published by the University of Toronto Press. In the early stages, the seven-year research program for that dictionary paid as much attention to multi-word sayings as it did to individual words, but as the editing proceeded a difficult decision had to be made. The collected sayings, colourful and interesting as they were, could not be made to fit the format and tone of the envisaged final book. After that dictionary left my hands in late 1986, there came a second difficult choice: whether to carry on with, enlarge upon, and properly present these several hundred abandoned sayings, or simply to get out of the Prince Edward Island vocabulary business altogether. After all, as some contributors to this book might put it, *You get only one shot at a shell bird*. In the end, I and my co-editor, Scott Burke, decided to *thresh another rally*, heartened in due course by the largely enthusiastic reaction to the *Dictionary of Prince Edward Island English*, which came out in 1988. Producing its companion has not exactly proved as slick as a biscuit with butter on it, but here it is at last.

We owe a great debt to the approximately six hundred Islanders who gave us information for this second volume, through questionnaires, interviews, correspondence, and personal contacts. These 'informants,' as they are called, must remain anonymous, but they are the foundation of the work. For helping us to find some of them, and for volunteering special information of other kinds, we thank particularly Donald Anderson, Blair Arsenault, Blaine Bernard, Jim Brown, Amy Bryanton, Mark Burns, Dorothy Chandler, Ethel Conway, Margaret Cousins, George Craig, Cecilia DeLory, Mary Flagg, Margaret Gallant, Michael Hennessey, Betty Howatt, Margaret Kennedy, Frank Lavandier, Frank Ledwell, Clifford Lee, Bernard McCabe, Alan MacRae, Leslie MacLean, Jill Manderson, G. Milligan, Clint Morrison, Elmer Murphy, David Murray, John O'Malley, Dorothy Palmer, Jennifer Shields, Anne Stewart, Basil Stewart, William Stewart, Annabel Veale, Maisie Waddell, Roger Waddell, Mary Warren, and Gerard Woods. An important benefactor has been Dr. David Weale, social historian at the University of Prince Edward Island, who made his personal collection of Island sayings, gathered over many years, freely available. Professor Weale also invited me to address several classes of students in Canadian Studies and Folk History, who then administered our questionnaires to other Islanders as an assignment in these courses. Finally, David Weale's name is scattered throughout the dictionary entries as the source of examples from *Them Times*, first a series of radio broadcasts about the pre-war Island, and then an insightful book.

Students in my linguistics classes cheerfully tackled preliminary versions of some questionnaires, and amplified them in class discussions. Some, whose names are found in the Bibliography, wrote helpful papers. The university at large was highly supportive. I include my colleagues in the Department of English, two Deans of Arts, two Presidents, and the staff of a host of service departments, including the Library, Computer Services, Graphics, Research Development, Central Printing, Personnel, and the Business Office. For favours beyond the call of duty, I would like to name Robert Campbell, Leo Cheverie, Glenda Clements-Smith, John DeGrace, Kay Diviney, Willie Eliot, Elizabeth Epperly, Anna Fisher, Carol Frances, Yogi Gamester, Philip Hooper, Frank Ledwell, Richard Lemm, Geoffrey Lindsay, Frank Pigott, Geoffrey Ralling, Winifred Robbins, Daniel Savage, and Verner Smitheram. It is difficult to imagine a better atmosphere for a long-term research project than that created by these people. I credit also the university's enlightened policies for sabbatical leave and reduced appointment.

A support network beyond UPEI – of academics, lexicographers, and knowledgeable friends – was invaluable. The project profited from the advice, questions, and encouragement of Margery Fee, Manfred Gorlach, Reinhard Hartmann, Tom McArthur, Michael Morrow, and the late George Story; my Irish parents-in-law, Lylagh and Sam Shields; members of the American Dialect Society, the Atlantic Provinces Linguistic Association, the Dictionary Society of North America, the European Association for Lexicography, and Interlex 7 at the University of Exeter, to whose conferences I was permitted to present papers on tricky questions of theory and formating; and especially Michael Agnes, Katherine Barber, and Richard Spears, all practising and experienced lexicographers. Many other scholars, some of whom I have never met, kindly responded to my queries on the electronic bulletin board of the American Dialect Society. The anonymous readers for the publisher were also extremely helpful in their comments.

Dictionary-making is labour-intensive, even given the machines lexicographers now apply to some of the drudgery. To pay the necessary labourers for this project, that is, students working part-time or in the summers over the years 1987 to 1996, I am happy to acknowledge seven awards from the UPEI Senate Committee on Research, and two from the Social Sciences and Humanities Research Council of Canada. The second of these was a substantial three-year grant that effectively did the business, and included computer equipment, supplies, and travel money for research in Halifax and Toronto libraries and for the conferences mentioned above.

Two of the employees were fieldworkers who hunted down informants and administered questionnaires: Connie MacRae and Catherine Meade. Principally, the workers were office assistants who captured and integrated data, checked potential entries against other dictionaries, scanned similar collections of sayings, read Island writings for yet further entries, and did much of the incidental research and filing created by the editing process. Chronologically, they were Francis Handrahan, Gena Stacey, Kirsten MacDonald, Shelley Robbins, and Lisa Tubman. A critical assistant in the final stages was Crystal Fall, who re-processed the entire book into its present, thematic format. The chief and longest-serving research assistants were Mark Jordan, a master of systems organization, who not only did all of the usual tasks, but also administered the most critical survey and analysed the results; and Anthony N. Chandler, who, as editorial assistant in the last years, did much independent and trustworthy manipulation of the text, as well as extensive research checks.

Scott Burke, my co-editor, began as an editorial assistant, the natural extension of his superb work for the *Dictionary of Prince Edward Island English*, but gradually, between spells of qualifying as a lawyer and legislative drafter and taking employment in his field, he moved to the title page, as researcher in off-Island libraries, experimenter with possible layouts, author of the first draft, and adviser on subsequent drafts. There would be no *Prince Edward Island Sayings* without him; as before, it has been a privilege to be his colleague.

Mistakes that remain in the text are Mr. Burke's and mine together, and ours alone. We hope that they do not include the omission of anyone who has made this dictionary possible. To all such we say, thank you for letting us *hoot and holler and wave our donut*.

T.K. PRATT

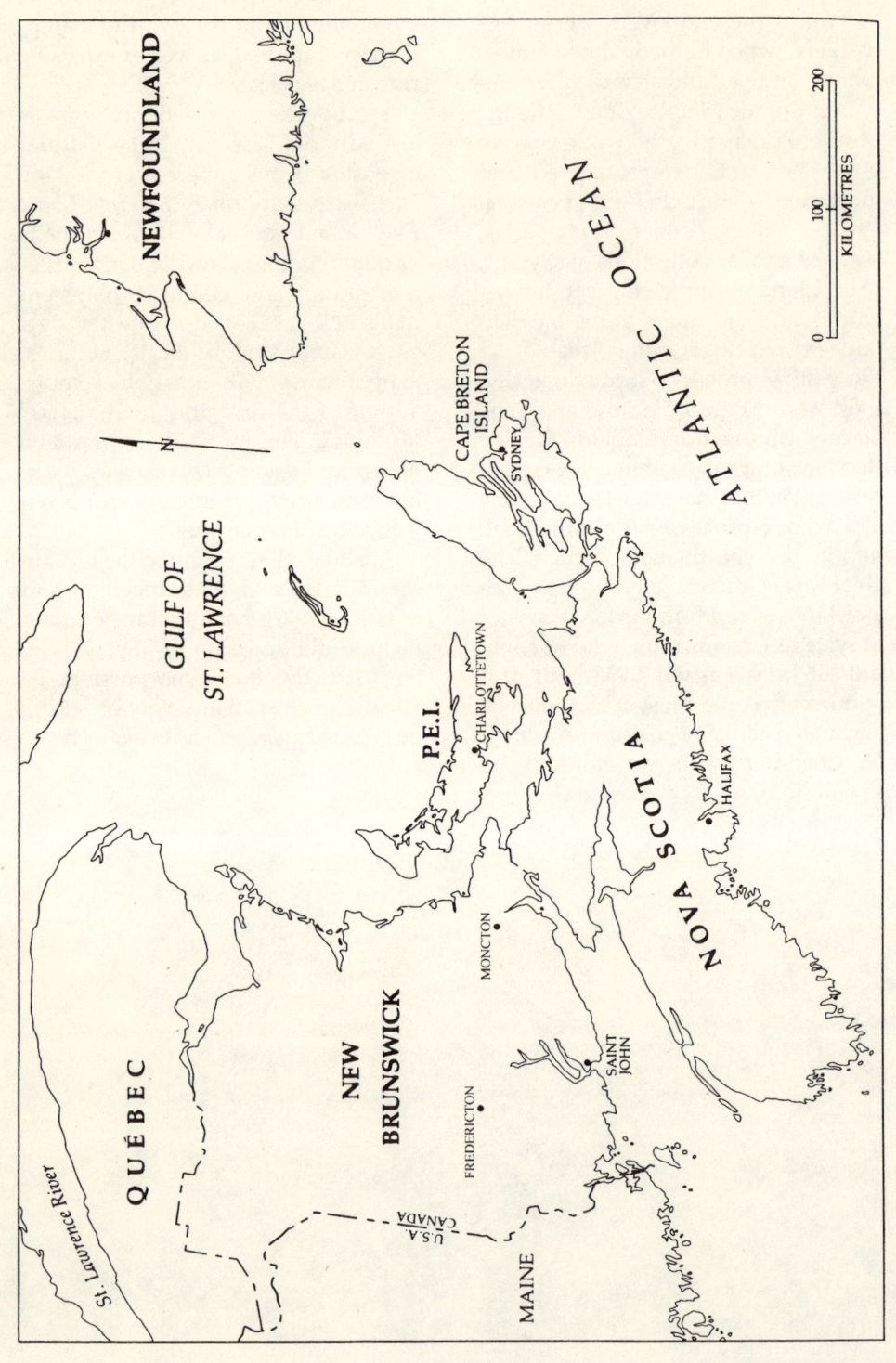

Introduction

What is a thematic dictionary?

This dictionary is intended to appeal to at least five types of reader. Type one is 'the browser,' who is simply led on by a pleasurable sequence of entries to go from page to page, even to read the whole work. Unlike those in a standard dictionary, the entries here are laid out not by the alphabet but in a flow of ideas or themes, as if some Prince Edward Islander were chatting on, *tongue going like a button on a back barn door*, about various preoccupations of the inhabitants. Type-one readers might include visitors to the province, and Islanders in exile reading this book for a taste of home.

Type two is 'the seeker' – someone looking for colourful ways to put an idea or theme, or for ways in which Islanders have expressed such a theme. The editors themselves have used the work in this way to find examples for these opening pages. Such readers would be using the book as they would a thesaurus, since the principal organization is based on meaning. Searches would normally start with the list of Themes in the Contents, and a theme-heading that looks closest to what the seeker has in mind. For example, suppose you want a comment about people's rudeness. Under the general theme of **SOCIAL LIFE**, you would see the sub-theme of **Bad Manners**, and probably turn to that section. Each of the seventy-two theme-sections is short enough for its highlighted sayings to be scanned in a few moments. If *ignorant as a brush fence* seems appealing, you could then read the entry. Within this entry, as it happens, is a cross-reference to a similar saying with a different theme, *homely as a brush fence*. If you looked there too, you would see a wealth of ways to call people ugly – and you can use one of these, if you wish, to be rude in return. Note that many sections end with *See also*, leading via the Index to multi-theme sayings that happen to be entered elsewhere.

The type-three reader – call this one 'the referencer' – is different from the first two. Even more than type two, such a reader might be consulting this book in a library, for, despite the playfulness of its subject, this is a reference book. If you are a referencer, you wish to find out if a certain saying that you already know, in whole or in part, exists within these covers. It might be something Grandmother always said, or a sentence heard on the radio, or a phrase overheard in the street. You may not be sure of what it means, and you have little idea what theme-heading it might be under. But wasn't the word *buttons* in it? If you refer to the Index (page 129), you will see that each saying is listed under each of its main words, in alphabetical order. For example, *To make button holes and sew them on* is included three times, under *button*, *holes*, and *sew*, each time with its page number.

A special kind of referencer, and our fourth category, is 'the researcher.' This reader might be a linguist, folklorist, or social historian – at any rate a specialist of some kind, looking for special data. We certainly include academics among our intended readers; this book is, after all, published by an academic press. Some researchers might be working on similar collections elsewhere, against which they wish to check this one – just as every entry here was checked against the thirty-nine dictionaries listed by title in the section 'Dictionaries and Other Collections Consulted' (following this section). Again, the index is the best first stop. 'Non-Island' sayings (as defined below) that occur from time to time throughout the entries are not indexed.

The final and most formidable type of reader is the native and current Prince Edward Islander. Islanders could be any of the above, of course, but, in addition, they may have strong opinions on what *ought* to be here. Among them are the roughly six hundred people who gave us information, technically called *informants*, who would naturally wish to see if we have done them justice. These, especially, will be looking out for the Island communities mentioned.

All five types of reader, it should be noted, could have been accommodated in an opposite layout, that is, by an alphabetic dictionary with a thematic index. We consider, however, that for our material such an organization, while common, is less reader-friendly. The chief problem with applying the alphabet to sayings, as opposed to words, is that sayings consist of more than one word. No rule of thumb for choosing the precise alphabetic home of every multi-word utterance, or for finding that place unerringly a second time, will be wholly satisfactory, whether the rule uses the first word, the first *main* word, the most *unusual* word, or the *key* (most meaningful) word. Such rules serve editors, not readers: either the rules depend upon advance knowledge or they must alphabetize many words that are trivial or variable – so that different readers will look in different places. Which is the obvious place in the alphabet for *If overalls for an elephant cost five cents they couldn't afford the buttons for a pismire*? Is it *I*, *O*, *E*, or *P*? In fact, the choice of the present editors, in our alphabetic arrangement for office filing, is *A*, because *afford* is what the saying is about; it is the signified and not the signifier. If we had published the book in such an arrangement, this entry would be listed second, after *(to jump) ACROSS the puddle / pond / brook*.

In short, although an alphabetic layout would have been possible, it would be less defensible for a collection of multi-word sayings intended for a varied readership. Certainly the alphabet has been the more normal system in reference books since the invention of the printing press. But, as Tom McArthur has brilliantly demonstrated in his *Worlds of Reference* (1986), such normality may turn out *not to amount to a row of postholes*, a mere five hundred years in the history of civilization. The more venerable thematic tradition has never died, and is rising to prominence again via computer menus. In fact, thematic arrangements can be found in many contemporary wordbooks: learners' dictionaries – McArthur's own *Longman Lexicon of Contemporary English*; terminological dictionaries – McCutcheon's *Descriptionary: A Thematic Dictionary*; dialect collections – Stevenson's *Scoor-Oot: A Dictionary of Scots Words and Phrases in Current Use* and Tabbert's *Dictionary of Alaskan English*; standard phrase books – *The Concise Oxford Dictionary of Proverbs*, *The Macmillan Book of Proverbs, Maxims, and Famous Phrases*, *Picturesque Expressions: A Thematic Dictionary*, and Gulland and Hinds-Howell's *The Penguin Dictionary of English Idioms*; and several other sources. McArthur shows that the editors of such works often arrive independently at highly similar themes and their order: they tend to start, as this dictionary does, with human appearance; then probe into character; then move sideways to moods; from there, they reach out to social life, work, and objects; and conclude with abstractions. This order naturally places *There's more meat on a chicken's forehead* side by side in our entries with *fat as a hen between the eyebrows* – even though the two have hardly a word in common – rather than on widely separated pages.

We must admit, however, that in its finer details, a thematic layout is almost as arbitrary as an alphabetic one. It may be true, as in the present case, that the groupings arise naturally from the data, and are not imposed by an abstract system like A, B, C. It might even be that the result can highlight significant truths. (Does an extraordinary number of ways to criticize thin people, as in the two sayings just quoted, mean that Prince Edward Islanders are less weight-conscious than others?) But such a system means that the editors' categories will change as the evidence comes in. Our **BEDTIME AND RISING**, for example, was, until almost the last minute of editing, **TIREDNESS AND BEDTIME**, while **MISCELLANEOUS** has always been a catchall for sayings that happened not to group themselves conveniently with others. Other editors might have chosen other theme-headings and have put them in a slightly different order. (See the subsections of **WEATHER**, for example, or the placing of sayings such as *There's one room in the attic not plastered* within **ECCENTRICITY** rather than **INTELLIGENCE**.) Within each theme, readers might well see a logic for the flow of ideas that is different from ours. We have changed the logic ourselves more than once, and we are guilty of some forcing. In addition, since some sayings can express more than one theme (for example, *You'll never put air under that* means both 'You've taken far more food on your plate than you can possibly eat' and 'You'll never be able to lift that [heavy weight]'), the choice of place for the main entry versus that for *See also* can be arbitrary.

Finally, thematic organizations are

not only personal but also culture-bound. In former times, reference books would commonly start with **God**, and move in what seemed a natural, descending order to **Angels**, then **Man**, then **Woman** ... But the smoke does not always *go up the chimney just the same*, and *that's a God's fact*.

What is a saying?

For the purposes of this dictionary, a *saying* is a short, prefabricated, relatively fixed popular utterance that stands out from ordinary speech, chiefly by not saying exactly what it means. This final dimension, the *figurative*, may be achieved simply by a little exaggeration (*heavy as a man and a boy*), or by punning on one word (*so crooked that when they die they could be screwed into the ground*), or by some other kind of simple comparison (*stubborn as a calf at a new gate*). On the other hand, the figuration may create a full-fledged *idiom*, a sentence or phrase whose meaning cannot be predicted from any meanings of at least one of its individual words, as in *to kick the cat*, 'to gossip.'

Our requirement, however slight, that a saying be figurative excludes the literal, however expressive. *If you were a fisherman you'd be at sea by now*, a reprimand for sleeping late, is not a saying by this definition, and neither is *She's blowing in the cuttings* for high winds that undo the work of the snow ploughs (not counting the wholly conventional feminine pronoun). In some entries we draw attention to the kind of figuration involved, with labels like *ironic* (*thousands from Tyne Valley alone*), *euphemistic* (*Don't get your water hot*), and *joking evasion* (*out behind the barn*).

Another requirement involves grammar. A saying can be as short as two words, but it must exhibit a certain minimum complexity: *up west* and *from away*, for example, are prepositional phrases. In contrast, many multi-word utterances are essentially one unit, like *basket social* (compound noun), *potatoes and point* (coordinated nouns), and *to bottom up* (phrasal verb). Such cases are not included, for they belong more properly in our word volume, *Dictionary of Prince Edward Island English* (*DPEIE*), even if they were overlooked there, like the many names for the government liquor store: *the power house*, *the brick building*, *the candy store*, and so on. Noun phrases with another grammatical unit embedded in them, as in *a poor day to set a hen*, are included here, however. Note that *DPEIE* itself includes some phrases inside entries (*up at crow piss*), repeated in this volume with the phrase itself now primary.

We have also applied some negative rules. Once, when one of the editors was walking his Maine coon cat on the Charlottetown wharf, a rude sailor, apparently astonished by the animal's size, shouted, 'Does that cat ever shit?' Did the sailor utter a saying? Facetious utterances can often sound like candidates for this book, but if they have seemed (on an admittedly quick and perhaps injured judgment) to have been made up on the spot, they have not been pursued. Another example of a presumed *nonce saying*, as these are called, supplied on a formal questionnaire, is 'so cold in the morning that Grandpa's picture had his hands over his ears.'

Similarly omitted are sayings that appear to be confined to a single household or workplace. One Charlottetown woman made many useful contributions that appear in this work, but we did not use 'No hard times in Miminegash,' after this reply to a query: 'The saying you refer to was one of my late husband's. When I went to work in Summerside in 1930 as a Public Health Nurse, the poverty, [and] the lack of ... nutrition to me was appalling. So I presume a fellow from Miminegash came into my husband's garage one day, and when the hangabouts' conversation got around to the hard times, this fellow came up with, "There's no hard times in Miminegash – we have butter on the plates and two spoons in the molasses dish." The hangabouts immediately latched on to this as a way of expressing good times.' Most social groups, especially families, have pet expressions that only insiders know about. *A fisherman told me the wrong time* is used by one editor's in-laws as a deliberately lame excuse for showing up late, based on its first use in earnest. (Of course the editors can make an error either way, by omission or commission.)

Sometimes submissions to our collection, while not restricted to a group, seem too narrow in their application to be general sayings. An example is *If the doctor looked up your arse, and the nurse looked down your throat, and they didn't see one another, then you had your guts*, which has an unsaid ending: *and you were fit to join the army*. It is a rueful comment on hasty medical examinations for Second World War conscripts. *Put more fire in your speech, or put more of your speech into the fire* has a nice ring to it, but appears to apply specifically to elocution lessons. Finally, *pulling the lazy stick* (also found in Newfoundland) is the name for a specific game of strength in which two people sit on the floor with the soles of their feet touching, and try to raise each other by pulling on a stick between them. None of these submissions appears in this book.

The medical example displays another element that has tended to discourage follow-up research: lack of rhythm. If a supposed saying is both long and lacking a strong rhythmic beat, then it is open to interruption, and so is probably not a (relatively) fixed form. Conversely, *so greedy they would steal the eyes out of your head and come back the next day for the holes* is long but quite rhythmic in the second clause, and it did make the final list.

In our search for genuine examples, it has been helpful to recognize that sayings often fall into definable sub-types. (For further analyses of these, see Pratt, 'The Proverbial Islander,' 1981). Everyone is familiar with the most famous sub-type, the *proverb*, which contains a kernel of apparent wisdom within a figurative husk. Once considered the aristocrat of sayings, the proverb is the only type found frequently in writing. It has also been the subject of considerable commentary, including that of Aristotle, Erasmus, and Nova Scotia's Thomas Chandler Haliburton (in *The Clockmaker; or The Sayings and Doings of Samuel Slick of Slickville*, 1836). Francis Bacon, the seventeenth-century philosopher and Lord Chancellor of England, went so far as to say that 'the genius, wit, and spirit of a nation are discovered in its proverbs' (quoted in *The Macmillan Book of Proverbs, Maxims, and Famous Phrases*). Nevertheless, proverbs seem to have lost their glitter as an adornment to style. While Bacon's age was soaked in the form – Shakespeare, for one example, relied heavily on audience knowledge of proverbs for his puns, allusions, and general word-play – by the time of the more decorous eighteenth century there was a literary reaction against them. In his famous letters of advice to his son, Lord Chesterfield wrote in 1741 as follows: 'There is, likewise, an awkwardness of expression and words, most carefully to be avoided; such as false English, bad pronunciation, old sayings, and common proverbs; which are so many proofs of having kept bad and low company. For example, if, instead of saying that tastes are different, and that every man has his own peculiar one, you should let off a proverb, and say, That what is one man's meat is another man's poison: or else, Every one as they like, as the good man said when he kissed his cow; everybody would be persuaded that you had never kept company with any body [sic] above footmen and housemaids' (*Letters of Lord Chesterfield*, p. 20). New proverbs seem to be coined less often nowadays, even by ordinary people, and when they are, they can become derided as clichés: *The family that prays together stays together*. (The introduction to the *Concise Oxford Dictionary of Proverbs* offers counter-evidence to this point, but there is no space for that argument here.) There are not many proverbs in this collection; in recognition of their special status they have been labelled as such when they do appear. By our definition, they must also be full sentences, like *You might as well expect the tide to wait while you paint the sand*.

Our other sub-types are not automatically identified as such by a label, but may sometimes be referred to in passing as follows: (1) *Proverbial assertion* (*If clues were shoes, they'd be barefoot*); *proverbial exclamation* (*by the end of the stick!*), and *proverbial question* (*Is it cold up there?*). While full sentences, these clearly fall short of being fundamental truisms. (2) *Proverbial exaggeration* (*too lazy to spit*), and *proverbial simile* (*like frosting on a burnt cake*). These are the most common sub-type. They have limited grammatical structures, and are most frequently used for insults. (3) *Proverbial phrase*. Similar to **MISCELLANEOUS** among the theme-sections, this is a category for items that do not fit in the other categories above, yet still have the feel of the proverbial about them. An example is *not sell the catch twice*, that is, 'choose not to repeat oneself.' (4) *Catchphrase*. The least figurative and most internally variable among sayings, catchphrases try to catch the listener's attention by their aptness, but they make little attempt at profundity. They can sometimes be full sentences like *Is your arm broken?*, but typically they are phrases: *well-fed at both ends*, *no good at catching pigs*. (5) *Nonsense*. This last sub-type takes the form of *greetings* (*How's your belly button?*), *replies* (*It's in the pigs' barrel behind the piano*), and *farewells* (*Don't let your antifreeze*). All are a kind of catchphrase, found in this book in their own sub-sections, under the general theme of **TALKING**.

After catchphrases, sayings blur into buried metaphors like *down to earth* (an extraordinary number of metaphors, by the way, go unnoticed in ordinary speech, a phenomenon well documented in Lakoff and Johnson, *Metaphors We Live By*); into conventional set phrases like *How are things?*; and into collocations, which are simply a reflection of the tendency of words to keep company with each other, as *auspicious* seems to demand *occasion*. These vast fields are obviously beyond the scope of this dictionary.

What is a Prince Edward Island saying?

In one sense, any saying – be it a contemporary catchphrase like *Get a life* or an ancient proverb like *Time flies* – is a part of the Prince Edward Island voice if it is used here. In fact, the full range of choices made by and among Islanders could be a powerful probe into the local psyche. Clearly such a huge collection is out of the question. At the other extreme, we could vow to have admitted no candidate that has ever been used anywhere else, in any form. Such a claim would quickly be ridiculed, for no amount of research could ever guarantee, especially in the electronic age, that these volatile and popular utterances are not known in other Atlantic provinces, or in Toronto, Vancouver, Melbourne, or Glasgow, or, for that matter, in an obscure Elizabethan play. In an article entitled 'The Proverbial Islander,' Pratt presented *Faraway cows have long horns* as a model Island proverb, only to discover during the research for this book that it is recorded all over Ireland.

Where then is the middle line? We could draw it by a more accurate – but unsellable – title: *Sayings Undoubtedly Used on Prince Edward Island, and Possibly in Other Atlantic Provinces, or, in a Few Cases, New England, and Not Found (by Us) with the Same Meaning in any Writing Outside This Region, or Attested as Such by Informants Considered to Be Reliable*. In other words, to delineate the concept *Prince Edward Island saying*, we have again employed both positive and negative rules:

1/With one general exception, every item listed has been attested by at least three independent Island informants in the course of the research outlined below. An example of one that did not pass this test is *to eat the Devil out of bolt rope*, supplied by a senior West Prince woman, but confirmed by no one else through two extensive surveys.

2/The general exception to rule (1) comprises fifty-eight submissions that came during the last phase of editing, too late for any survey, though in time for checks against other dictionaries. These entries, like *They went to school for two days; the first was a holiday and the second the teacher wasn't there*, are marked with an asterisk and the words 'Late entry, not surveyed.' A similar set, late submissions thought to be variants of established sayings, is nested within appropriate entries, marked 'Also reported.' In our experience, fieldwork for material of this kind can go on indefinitely, each new survey yielding more possibilities. An ending, if never a finishing, must somehow be made.

3/Sayings that happen to occur in other Atlantic provinces are not excluded, on the grounds that the region has been too long bound together for a boundary to be drawn through the Northumberland Strait. It is not impossible that many 'Atlantic' sayings began in Prince Edward Island; it *is* impossible to say which ones these are. Sayings found in New England must also be admitted, because journeys from Atlantic Canada to the familiar *Boston States* (see *DPEIE*) have been too frequent over the last hundred years for anyone to call a sensible halt at the Canadian border. As it happens, there are only six of these, five of them from Maine. An example that tests the outer limits of our catchment area is *homely as a stump fence*. This simile is recorded here, and in *The South Shore Phrase Book* of Nova Scotia, in Perkins's 'More Notes on Maine Dialect' (1930), and in *The Macmillan Book of Proverbs, Maxims, and Famous Phrases* from an author raised in Maine.

4/ Any saying discovered in writing outside this North Atlantic region has been automatically dropped. However, as with the definition of sayings in general, there can be interesting borderline cases: (a) The recent and delightful *Casselman's Canadian Words* (1995) turns out to contain some of our entries, but we could not exclude any – like *They would squeeze a penny until the water runs out of the Queen's eyes* – that are not attributed either to a specific Canadian region or to the country as a whole. Casselman has knocked out some, to be sure, such as *A farting horse will never tire, and a farting man's the one to hire* (one of our favourites), recorded in Ontario. (b) The *Dictionary of American Regional English* has both winnowed our collection and supplemented it, but this extensive source has not yet been published beyond the letter *O*. It did eliminate, quite decisively, *smiling as a basket of chips* (*basket of chips*, as such, is recorded in various American comparisons in the *Oxford English Dictionary*). (c) Partridge and Beale's invaluable *Dictionary of Catch Phrases, British and American, from the Sixteenth Century to the Present Day* (1985) labels some entries as 'Canadian'; again, unless specifically attributed to the area beyond Atlantic Canada, we have had no choice but to retain them. However, these compilers did eliminate one of our jolliest nonsense greetings, *How's your belly where the pig bit you?* (d) We have made a thorough search for dictionaries, lexicons, articles, and other sources that could make this exclusion rule as solid as possible; these are listed in 'Dictionaries ... Consulted' or the bibliography only if they are cited in the remaining entries for some reason. We have also viewed the complete runs of *Journal of American Folklore* (from 1888), *Dialect Notes* (from 1890), and *American Speech* (from 1925). A note in *American Speech* from 1927, for example, eliminated *homely enough to sour milk* because this simile also occurs in West Virginia. (e) Editorial judgment has necessarily been invoked when an outside item has turned up that is similar to ours but not the same. See, for example, *Wouldn't that boil your britches!* for a close call from Australia and New Zealand, and *to cut the dead man's throat* for one from Scotland. The closest of all is probably *black as the inside of a black cow* which has many American equivalents. On the other hand, we eliminated *If you play with the bull, you'll get a horn in the arse* because *You may play with a bull till you get a horn in your eye* is found in Cheshire, England, and recorded in the *Oxford Dictionary of English Proverbs*. In general we stand on guard against the attitude expressed by one informant that some of our examples are 'only' Island variants. (f) Allusive or indirect references have proved the most difficult. Suppose a journalist, in a story about old rivals having obvious trouble working together for a common goal, finds an analogy: 'After all, Eaton's and Simpson's were not in the habit of sharing marketing strategies.' The comparison *could* be a twist on *Eaton's don't tell Simpson's their business* – itself a probable variant of a New York City proverb, *Does Macy's tell Gimbel's?* It is impossible to say, on the evidence. We have naturally considered that it is better to err on the side of inclusion. In fact, we hold it to be more interesting, not less, that many of our inclusions are shared in some form by other dialects. We realize that the non-uniqueness of Prince Edward Island will be disappointing to some readers.

5/ Although our chief reliance for outside evidence has been on written sources, we have also consulted authoritative observers personally, most notably subscribers to the electronic bulletin board of the American Dialect Society. More casual observations on the distribution of sayings, either from our informants or incidentally, have been noted in the entries, but have not served as eliminators. Such entries, like *crazy as a cut cat* (heard on CBC's 'Basic Black, 27 April 1996), are marked with the cautionary note 'also attested from [outside location].' These can be considered on a danger list, especially if they are within the well-travelled themes of **ECCENTRICITY** and **INTELLIGENCE**. Sayings and idioms have traditionally been given short shrift in dictionaries, while at the same time being subject to much local inventiveness. More research, therefore, needs to be done in many places; we hope that this collection will be seen not as an attempted last word on distribution, but as an interim step.

6/ It will be obvious enough why some entries are marked 'vulgar,' 'coarse,' 'offensive,' and the like. But it will probably not be obvious to some readers why they are included at all. The answer is, briefly, that a lexicographer is a historian, not a moralist, and that Prince Edward Island, while a splendid place to live, is no utopia. Lucy Maud Montgomery has a likeable character use the racist simile *dark as a squaw's pocket* in *Pat of Silver Bush* (1933, p. 61) – which happens to be excluded from this collection for other reasons. Nevertheless we have been extremely cautious ourselves with such sayings, have sought much advice on the whole question, have searched specially for their existence outside our area, and have entertained no borderline speculations.

These, then, are the principles by which entries were chosen for this dictionary from the vastly greater number that came to us through our research. These principles differ from those for *DPEIE*, and this is another reason, in addition to those mentioned in the preface, why the two collections have been separated. The former is 'a record of non-standard words as used, or once used, on Prince Edward Island' (p. xi). Broadly defined, *non-standard* language in any form is the kind that does not have the official sanction of a nation's education or legal systems or of the generally accepted rules for formal writing and publishing. But the distinction between non-standard and standard *words* – not easy to apply at the best of times – does not work well for sayings. By definition, sayings belong to oral, folk culture, that is, to the non-standard camp. (Hence, for example, our use in the headphrases of the informal 'they' for both plural and singular; hence also the fact that not many citations were found in written sources.) Apart from proverbs, none are sanctioned in schools or frequent in good writing, unless in writing that imitates speech, like novel dialogue. The only way in which the distinction *standard/non-standard* can be used here is with regard to sayings that seem to have been given some authority by their presence in national and international collections, such as Partridge's famous *A Dictionary of Slang and Unconventional English* and others mentioned above. We certainly find it helpful to quote parallel information from these collections, but even here our preferred terms are 'common,' 'popular,' 'conventional,' 'established,' 'general,' 'stock,' and so on (whichever seems most appropriate to the case), and only occasionally 'standard.'

How were these Prince Edward Island sayings found?

The research for *DPEIE* was initially directed at both words and sayings, even though the final product was devoted to words only. The lines of investigation included the reading of about nine hundred titles in Prince Edward Island literature, folklore, community histories, diaries, travelogues, reports, and more. After work on the present dictionary began, such reading naturally continued in order to take in more recent writings, such as Bruce, *Down Home: Notes of a Maritime Son* (1988), Hornby, *Belfast People: An Oral History of Belfast Prince Edward Island* (1992), and Weale, *Them Times* (1992). As expected, many more writings were examined than turned out to be relevant; written sources were never likely to prove a highly productive source for local sayings.

Accordingly, the chief, new research for this dictionary has been fieldwork surveys. What is called in the entries *Survey I* is actually five successive questionnaires, 1988–93. The first comprised some four hundred potential entries garnered by the earlier research (which included not only reading, but also incidental observations, correspondence, public appeals, postal surveys, fieldwork interviews, student papers, and folklore tapes). Each of the subsequent questionnaires of Survey I was based partly on its predecessor, that is, on suggestions for new entries from Islanders who filled in the questionnaires or were interviewed. It is often difficult to produce a saying on demand, but the sight or sound of others seems to open a special cache in the memory. Some of these informants were university students in linguistics and folk history, and many others were contacted on our behalf by them. Some students went on to write useful papers on the subject, which are also in the bibliography. In addition, as with *DPEIE*, stories and interviews in local media led to many helpful responses. The project had so much positive publicity on the Island that suggestions for items, contexts, meanings, and distributions trickled in steadily over the years.

About five hundred Islanders had some input into Survey I. A few chose to remain anonymous, and another fifty-eight were unfortunately rendered anonymous by our mistaken notion, in administering the first

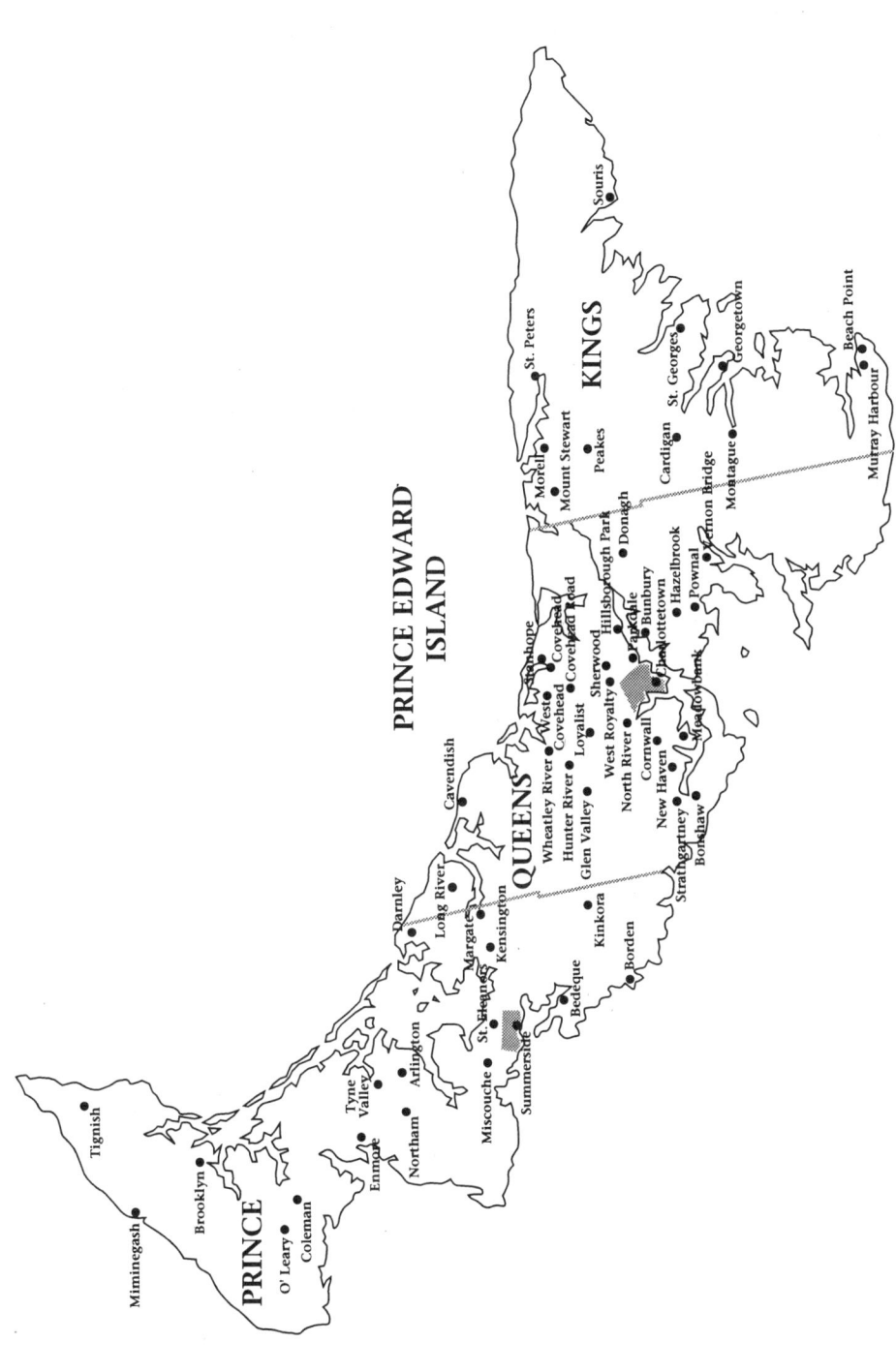

1 Localities of informants for Survey I

questionnaire, that biographical information would not be important. Most Survey I informants kindly supplied their date of birth, gender, education, principal locality, and occupation. To summarize: the youngest was seventeen, the oldest eighty-eight; women outnumbered men by five to three; education levels ranged from grade four to Ph.D. Their various localities, as named in the entries, can be seen on map 1. Finally, a sample of the occupations of these informants, in the order that they happen to reside in our files, includes youth worker, cashier, library technician, waiter, farmer, school principal, clerk, carpenter, nursing administrator, taxi-driver, pharmacist's assistant, mailman, fisherman, editor, civil servant, teacher, homemaker, seamstress, housekeeper, medical worker, artist, businessman, secretary, ferry worker, accountant, telephone worker, airforce pilot, and, as mentioned, university student. Naturally, no one is identified here by name, but local readers might enjoy spotting their neighbours or themselves among the brief biographies.

Survey I was productive, but was clearly haphazard in its selection of informants, and hence no reliable judgment of the Island distribution of any saying was yet possible. A timely grant from the Social Sciences and Humanities Research Council of Canada allowed the work to be put on a more scientific footing. In the summers of 1992 and 1993, a new, carefully designed survey of all sayings confirmed to date was presented to a selected group of Islanders who served for us as a cross-section of the population as outlined in the 1991 Canadian census. This was *Survey II*, technically called a *judgment sample*, whereby Islanders with certain characteristics were deliberately sought out to fill cells in a pre-constructed grid (see page xxiii).

The grid called for equal numbers of men and women. Each informant must have lived most of his or her life in one of five areas, listed across the top in their order from west to east: the three, long-established counties of Prince, Queens, and Kings, from which are removed the two intersecting, urban areas of Summerside and Charlottetown. With reference to the left side of the grid, every informant was considered to be either a young adult (from 18 to 30 years old), or middle-aged (defined for this purpose as 31 to 60), or a senior (over 60). Finally, there were three education levels, primary (grades 1–9), secondary (10–12), and tertiary (beyond grade 12). (In the case of seniors, however, the top grade for each level was set somewhat lower, to reflect the greater difficulty, and hence prestige, of moving beyond grade ten before the educational expansion that followed the Second World War.) As an aid to quick comprehension for those reading the dictionary without the benefit of this introduction, the three education levels are called in the entries 'grade-school-educated,' 'high-school-educated,' and 'college-educated,' although none of these terms is precisely accurate by today's terminology in Canada.

Two deliberate biases made the grid unrepresentative of the population at large. First, despite the fact that the general Charlottetown area is at least two and a half times more populous than that of Summerside, the two were given equal numbers of infor-

		Prince		Summer-side		Queens				Charlotte-town		Kings	
		M	F	M	F	M	F	M	F	M	F	M	F
Young	Education 1–9												
	Education 10–12												
	Education 12+	✗				✗							
Middle-aged	Education 1–9												
	Education 10–12	✗				✗							
	Education 12+	✗				✗							
Senior	Education 1–8												
	Education 9–10												
	Education 11+												

mants. Second, rural Prince Edward Island, defined by us as the three counties without their two main urban areas, was over-represented by about 30 per cent (this definition itself is a simplification of census definitions). These two biases were built in for three reasons: to give Summerside enough informants to make generalizations possible at all; to keep the numbers affordable, since survey research is costly; and to reflect the editors' conviction at the time (mistaken, as it turned out) that Island sayings were more likely to be found out of town. Certain cells were crossed out on the grid, and thus not filled by any informant, both to keep the total number down, and to make the overall distribution as close as possible, given the above distortions, to the broad facts of the Island population. At the same time, the cancellation of certain cells maximized returns from seniors, the less educated, and to some extent the young, again on the notion, which seemed clear from our earlier work, that these groups would yield higher results. In these assumptions we were mostly, though not wholly, correct.

In short, the sample of Prince Edward Islanders for Survey II, like its counterpart in *DPEIE*, was 'a compromise between making statistical sense (so that labels could be attached to given words with some hope of accuracy), and finding the words at all ... [I]rreproachable statistics were not as important as going where the words were to be found' (*DPEIE*, xvi-xvii; there are, however, some critical differences between the two grids, and interested readers should consult the earlier book's different justifications).

Available funding dictated a sample of not much over one hundred informants. The total number of cells created by the above methods was a manageable 114, with sub-groupings as follows:

Prince County (excluding Summerside)	30
Summerside (and area)	18
Queens County (excluding Charlottetown)	30
Charlottetown (and area)	18
Kings County	18
Rural (the three counties)	78
Urban (Summerside and Charlottetown)	36
Men	57
Women	57
Young	38
Middle-aged	34
Senior	42
Primary ('grade-school-educated')	42
Secondary ('high-school-educated')	38
Tertiary ('college-educated')	34

Map 2 shows the rough distribution of these informants across the province, with some localities having more than one informant.

Some informants for Survey II were taken from those who had done one of the early questionnaires in Survey I, but most were selected afresh by a research assistant, normally a UPEI student who knew the area personally and could politely check for the necessary biographical particulars. A further bias of a sort entered the sample at this point, again as in *DPEIE*: '[F]ieldworkers selected informants with a view to their being interested – or at least not uninterested in the idea of talking about unusual "Island" words [in the present case, sayings] ... Once again it was assumed that without such a bias many hours and dollars might be wasted looking for data that simply was not there' (*DPEIE*, xx). The research assistant would deliver the questionnaire, explain the overall purpose, answer any questions, confirm the biographical details, and ask that the checklist be tackled individually. Later he or she would pick it up and bring it to the office for processing and checks.

Whereas Survey I questionnaires left plenty of space for writing between entries, and specifically asked its respondents to challenge the wordings and definitions, and to add comments of any kind, Survey II was a closely spaced 'Checklist,' headed by this instruction only: 'Please use the space after each number to check any saying *you would use yourself*. Go fast; don't stop to think. No other information is asked for. Thank you.' Another key difference in the later survey was that no vulgar or offensive sayings were included, on the well-founded fear, from Survey I, that if such items were present some informants might refuse to participate, and this, quite literally, we could not afford.

In the entries, Survey I lies behind most of the informant quotations. It also contributes the biographies of additional informants, who are listed (in italics) after 'Includes' to amplify

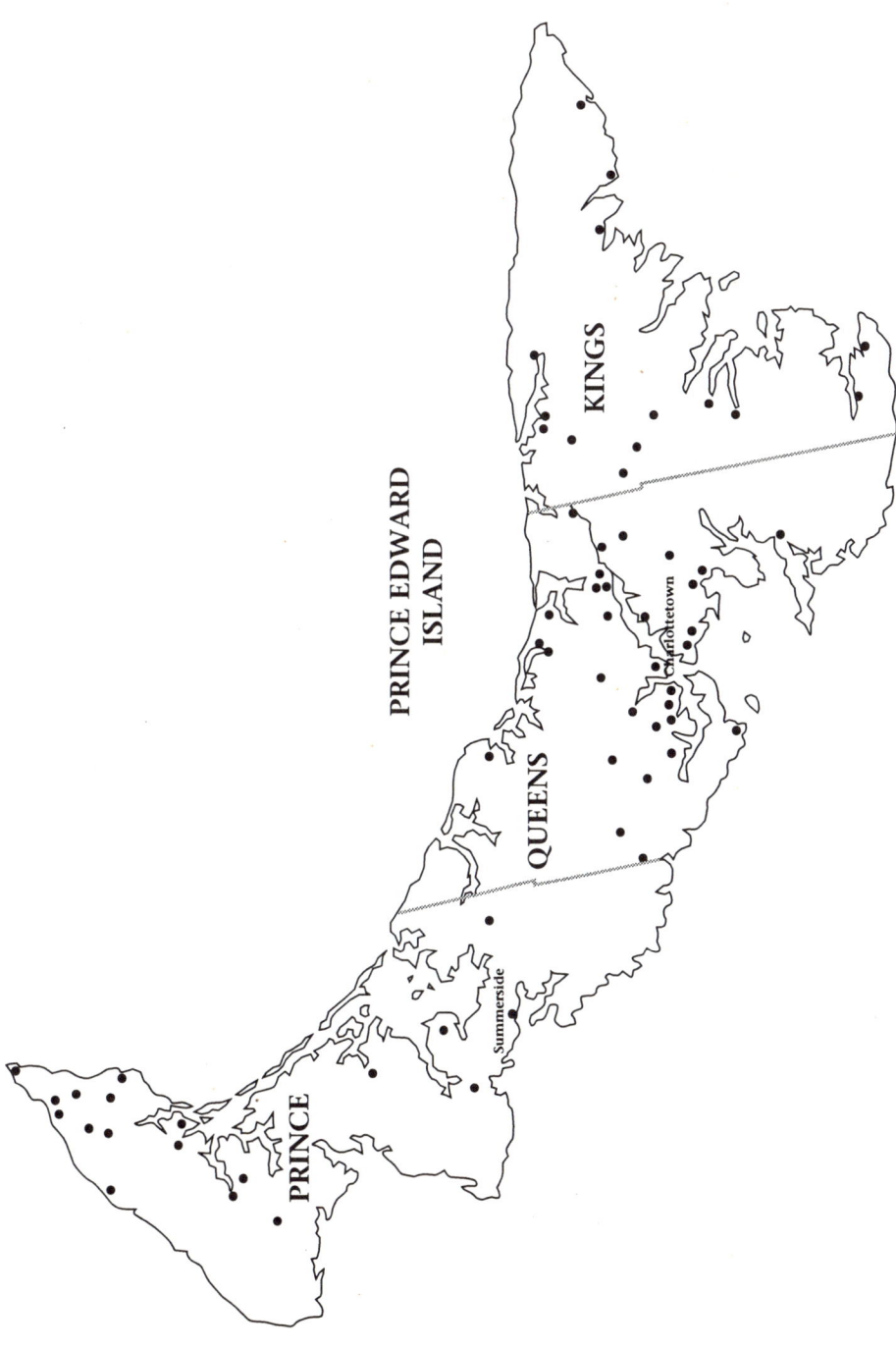

2 Distribution of informants for Survey II

the frequency label, sometimes by showing exceptions. These additions were selected from those who made either no comment or a redundant comment; all, of course, as either users or reporters of others' use, have contributed to our sense of what the entries should emphasize.

Survey II informants, all self-reported users, were the source of the frequency label at the end of most entries. This label might be one word, like 'Rare.' More typically it is several, and can even be as extensive as 'Common in Summerside, widespread elsewhere except occasional in Kings; significantly not young, especially urban, not college-educated' (*Eaton's don't tell Simpson's their business*).

The frequency label always has four possible levels:

Common	50–100% (of informants in given area)
Widespread	30–49%
Occasional	10–29%
Rare	under 10%

However, if the *overall* percentage of users across all areas is under 10 per cent (which translates as eleven users out of 114 or fewer), it is not given any label other than 'Rare.' Maps 3 and 4 give examples of typical distribution patterns, as revealed by Survey II.

When any of the social factors of age, gender, or education are relevant, the label includes one of two qualifiers:

– 'especially' = greater than a 10% difference between the leading category and any other
– 'significantly' = strongly distinctive, as measured by a chi-square test in which $P < 0.05$

For confirmation of Survey II results, we have also made a simple count of Survey I respondents, thus creating *two* polls of overall popularity with (largely) different groups of informants. In no case, happily, was there significant discrepancy between the two. This finding, incidentally, has allowed us to place a short frequency label, preceded by 'probably,' on almost all the vulgar and offensive sayings, even though they were not part of Survey II.

It follows that, while many of our entries are labelled only 'Rare,' this label, as dictated by Survey II, does not necessarily mean that such sayings have only the minimal evidence of three informants for their existence. The fact is that additional users and observers, who have not figured in the calculation, are often silently present from Survey I. For example, the first ten 'Rare' sayings in the collection have total informant counts ranging from eight to twenty-three.

The number of entries made possible by these methods has turned out to be 835, of which 777 were in time to be surveyed. If we were to count the many variants, and the 'also reported,' our list of Prince Edward Island sayings, in other words – to paraphrase Dr. Johnson's rueful Preface to his famous 1755 dictionary of standard English words – our enchainments of the wind, total over 1000. We are well aware that the ultimate interest in what we have managed to tie down for the moment is not the number as such, but how such language features in the life of the province. For this information, the reader is invited to turn to the entries.

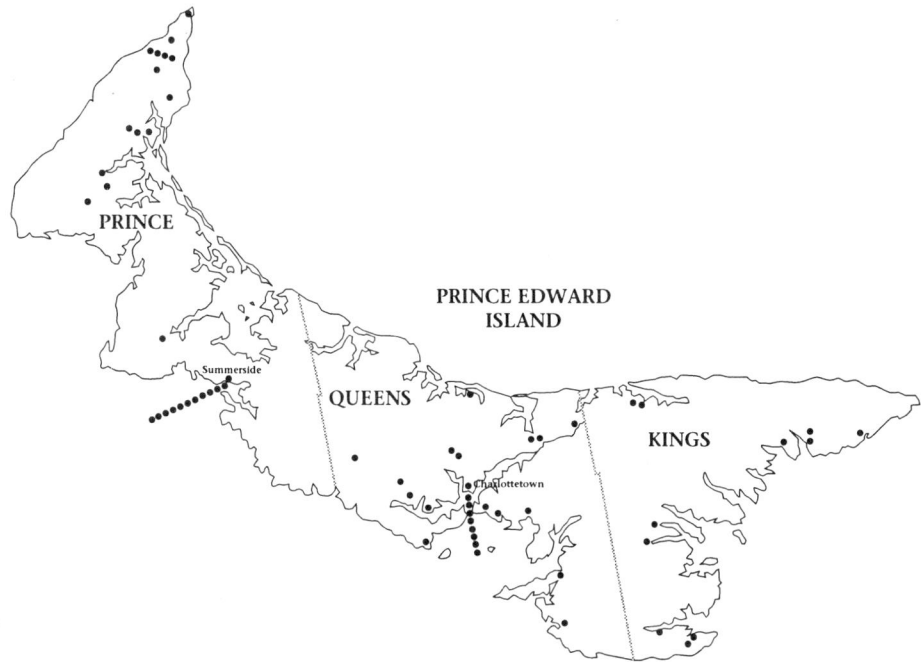

3 Distribution of 'baked in the sun': Common

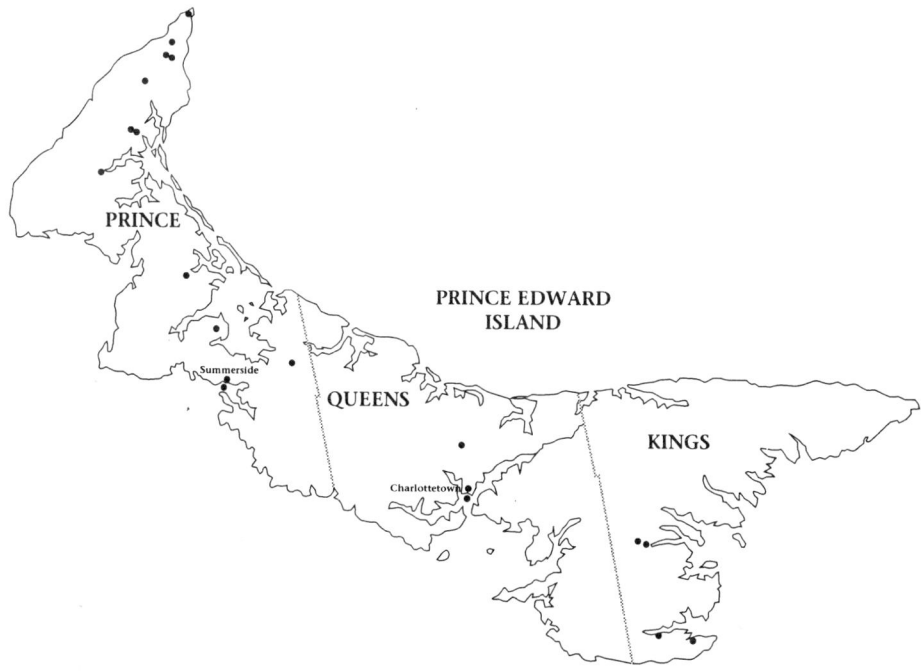

4 Distribution of 'to blow up rain': Widespread in Prince, occasional elsewhere except rare in Queens

Dictionaries and Other Collections Consulted

ASD   *Aussie Slang Dictionary*. Balwyn Victoria, Aus.: Five Mile Press, 1991.

BD   *Brewer's Dictionary of Phrase and Fable*. Centenary edition, revised. Ed. Ivor H. Evans. New York: Harper & Row, 1981.

CCW   Casselman, Bill. *Casselman's Canadian Words*. Toronto: Copp Clark, 1995.

CDEI   *A Concise Dictionary of English Idioms*. Ed. William Freeman. Boston: The Writer, 1969.

CODP   *The Concise Oxford Dictionary of Proverbs*. Ed. John Simpson. Oxford: Oxford UP, 1992.

DA   *A Dictionary of Americanisms on Historical Principles*. Ed. Mitford M. Matthews. Chicago: U of Chicago P, 1951.

DAC   *A Dictionary of Australian Colloquialisms*. Ed. G.A. Wilkes. Sydney: Sydney UP, 1978.

DAP   *A Dictionary of American Proverbs*. Ed. Wolfgang Meider, Stewart A. Kingsbury, and Kelsie B. Harder. New York: Oxford UP, 1992.

DAPPP   *A Dictionary of American Proverbs and Proverbial Phrases 1820–1880*. Ed. Archer Taylor and Bartlett Jere Whiting. Cambridge, MA: Harvard UP, 1958.

DARE   *Dictionary of American Regional English*. Ed. Frederic G. Cassidy and Joan Houston Hall. Volumes I–III. Cambridge, MA: Belknap Press of Harvard UP, 1985–1996.

DAS   *Dictionary of American Slang*. Ed. Harold Wentworth and Stuart Berg Flexner. 2nd supplemented edition. New York: Thomas Y. Crowell, 1975.

xxx   Dictionaries and Other Collections

DCP   *A Dictionary of Catch Phrases, British and American, from the Sixteenth Century to the Present Day.* Ed. Eric Partridge and Paul Beale. 2nd edition. London: Routledge & Kegan Paul, 1985.

DKS   *A Dictionary of Kiwi Slang.* Ed. David Mcgill. Lower Hutt, NZ: Mills Publications, 1988.

DNE   *Dictionary of Newfoundland English.* Ed. G.M. Story, W.J. Kerwin, and J.D.A. Widdowson. 2nd edition with supplement. Toronto: U of Toronto P, 1990.

DPEIE *Dictionary of Prince Edward Island English.* Ed. T.K. Pratt. Toronto: U of Toronto P, 1988.

DSUE   *A Dictionary of Slang and Unconventional English.* Ed. Eric Partridge and Paul Beale. 8th edition. New York: Macmillan, 1984.

EAP   *Early American Proverbs and Proverbial Phrases.* Ed. Bartlett Jere Whiting. Cambridge, MA: Belknap Press of Harvard UP, 1977.

EP   *English Proverbs and Proverbial Phrases.* 1929. Ed. G.L. Apperson. Detroit: Gale Research, 1969.

IPI   *Idioms and Phrases Index.* Ed. Laurence Urdang. Detroit: Gale Research, 1983.

IP   *Irish Proverbs.* Ed. Karen Bailey. San Francisco: Chronicle Books, 1986.

LD   *Longman Dictionary of English Idioms.* London: Longman Group, 1979.

MBP   *The Macmillan Book of Proverbs, Maxims, and Famous Phrases.* Ed. Burton Stevenson. New York: Macmillan, 1948.

ML   *Maine Lingo: Boiled Owls, Billdads, and Wazzats.* Ed. John Gould. Camden, ME: Down East Magazine, 1975.

NDAS   *New Dictionary of American Slang.* Ed. Robert L. Chapman. New York: Harper & Row, 1986.

NDASCE *NTC's Dictionary of American Slang and Colloquial Expressions.* Ed. Richard A. Spears. Lincolnwood, IL: National Textbook Company, 1989.

NDFRRS *NTC's Dictionary of Folksy, Regional, and Rural Sayings.* Ed. Anne Bertram. Lincolnwood, IL: NTC Publishing Group, 1996.

Dictionaries and Other Collections   xxxi

ODCIE *Oxford Dictionary of Current Idiomatic English*. Ed. A.P. Cowie, R. Mackin, and I.R. McCaig. Volume 2. *Phrase, Clause and Sentence Idioms*. Oxford: Oxford UP, 1983.

ODEP *Oxford Dictionary of English Proverbs*. Ed. F.P. Wilson. 3rd edition. Oxford: Oxford UP, 1970.

OED *Oxford English Dictionary*. Ed. J.A. Simpson and E.S.C. Weiner. 2nd edition. Oxford: Oxford UP, 1989.

PPS 'Proverbs and Proverbial Sayings.' In *Frank C. Brown Collection of North Carolina Folklore*, 1: 329–501. Ed. Bartlett Jere Whiting. 7 vols. Durham, NC: Duke UP, 1952.

RH *Random House Historical Dictionary of American Slang*. Ed. J.E. Lighter. New York: Random House, 1994.

SND *Scottish National Dictionary*. Ed. William Grant and David D. Murison. Edinburgh: Scottish National Dictionary Association, [1931]–1976.

SD *Similes Dictionary*. Ed. Elyse Sommer and Mike Sommer. Detroit: Gale Research, 1988.

SDCP *Shorter Dictionary of Catch Phrases*. Ed. Rosalind Ferguson. London: Routledge, 1994.

SSPB *The South Shore Phrase Book*. Ed. Lewis Poteet. Hantsport, NS: Lancelot Press, 1988.

TTEM *Thesaurus of Traditional English Metaphors*. Ed. P.R. Wilkinson. London: Routledge, 1993.

W3 *Webster's Third New International Dictionary of the English Language*. Ed. Philip Babcock Gove et al. Springfield, MA: G. and C. Merriam Co., 1976.

WPI *Words and Phrases Index*. Ed. C. Edward Wall and Edward Przebienda. Ann Arbor, MI: Pierian Press, 1969–70.

YA *You All Spoken Here*. Ed. Roy Wilder, Jr. New York: Viking-Penguin, 1984.

Themes

Human Appearance

GENERAL

to look as if they had been dragged through a barnyard
To present a dirty, dishevelled, or disreputable appearance; parallel to more usual *to look as if they had been through the wars*. A more popular variant on Prince Edward Island is *to look as if they had been dragged through a knothole*, rejected from this collection because of its appearance in Woofter, 'Dialect Words from West Virginia.'
– 'This saying was used often as I grew up on a farm (muddy from head to toe)' (young college-educated Queens man).
– 'Haggard-looking' (middle-aged college-educated Prince woman).
Occasional, except rare in Kings.

They didn't take that off the floor. They didn't pick that up off the street.
Some physical human trait is clearly an inherited feature; based on the standard phrasal verb *to take after* 'to resemble [an older relative] in appearance, manner, or character.' *It wasn't off the ground they licked it* is attested from Ireland; as yet unpublished investigations of *DARE* include *I didn't lick that off the floor* (inquiry in the newsletter of the American Dialect Society, 25.2 [May 1993], 13). Compare *DCP*: 'sucked that out of his (or her) fingers – he (or she) hasn't ... He has mysterious – *or* closely-guarded – authentic information: mostly Londoners' and esp. Cockneys': late C19–20.'
– 'Heard in Georgetown: "He has flaming red hair; he didn't take that off the floor." His father and uncles had red hair' (senior woman).
– 'Referring to the milkman, mailman' (university student).
Rare.

UGLINESS

a face like a dog
A face lacking conventional beauty. The association of *dog* with ugliness is popular slang, as in *NDASCE*: '*dog2* ... an ugly girl.' Compare *OED*: '*dog-faced* ... Having a face like that of a dog' 1607–1873.
Common in Charlottetown, widespread in Prince, occasional elsewhere. *Includes middle-aged high-school-educated St. Eleanor's female nurse, and middle-aged college-educated Charlottetown woman.*

4 Ugliness

*homely as a wet cat
Presenting an appearance that is pitifully uncared for.
*Late entry, not surveyed. Reported by young grade-school-educated Prince man.

a face like a horse / like Pontius Pilate's horse
A large, unlovely face with bulging eyes and prominent cheekbones. No direct connection between Pontius Pilate and ugliness of appearance has been found; as the judge of Christ, he is strongly associated with an evil – and hence, ugly – action. Also attested from Newfoundland and Ireland. Compare *MBP*: 'She's the only gal I love, / With a face like a horse and buggy. Unknown, *Fireman, Save My Child*. (c.1876)'
– '[Interviewer:] I assume then, David, animals feature quite prominently in descriptive language in "them times." [Weale:] Yes, that's true, and you know, around the world folk language is filled with expressions which refer to animals; they're a rich source ... If you wanted to insult someone you might say they had "a face like a horse"' (Weale, 'Them Times' [radio broadcast]).
Occasional; especially senior. *Includes senior West Royalty male telephone worker.*

homely as an ugly fish
Exceptionally plain-featured, with prominent facial bones.
Occasional, except rare in Summerside; significantly senior. *Includes two senior grade-school-educated male farmers of Margate and New Haven, senior high-school-educated teacher, and senior college-educated Charlottetown male editor.*

a face like a skate
A horrifyingly ugly face, about as far along the scale of fish-like loathsomeness as it is possible to go. The *skate* is a large, flat, mottled ray fish with conspicuous eyes, a pointed snout, and spines and prickles in various stages of development on its skin.
– 'Ugly – a face only a mother could love' (senior Parkdale woman).
Rare. *Includes middle-aged high-school-educated Souris female business manager.*

a face like a can / bucket of (squashed) worms
a face like a can of snakes
*Also reported
a face like a sour apple
A highly unattractive face from its excessive wrinkles. No connection is apparently intended to the slang phrase *open a can of worms* 'expose a complicated problem.' Henry Person records 'a face like a pan of worms' in 'Proverbs and Proverbial Lore from Washington,' 183.
Common, except widespread in Prince and Queens; significantly not young, especially male, high-school-educated. *Includes senior Parkdale woman, middle-aged high-school-educated Morell male carpenter, middle-aged college-educated Bunbury male teacher, and young Charlottetown female university student.*

a face like a plowshare
A face with an especially protruding nose. Compare *SD*: 'Nose like a delicate scythe ... Nose like a knife blade ... Nose like a scimitar.'
Rare. *Confirmed by eight informants in Survey I.*

ugly as an axe handle
Unattractive in face or misshapen in body. Also attested from New Brunswick.

Rare. *Includes middle-aged high-school-educated Charlottetown female secretary, and young university student.*

homely / ugly as a brush fence
homely as a board / wire / picket fence
homely as a stump fence
*Also reported
homely as a hardwood stump
So strikingly ill-featured as to draw attention in any surroundings, often because of a short, uptilted nose; parallel to widespread similes *homely as a hedge fence* and *homely / ugly as a mud fence*. See also IGNORANT AS A BRUSH FENCE. The *picket fence* alternate is attested from Newfoundland, and *brush fence* is recorded in New Brunswick (Curtis, *Look What the Cat Drug In!*). The term *stump fence*, as such, is both archaic and widespread in North America (see *DPEIE*), while the saying *homely / ugly as a stump fence* goes to the outer limit of the catchment area for this dictionary. It is recorded in *MBP*, but the source is an author raised in Maine. Similarly Anne Perkins, in 'More Notes on Maine Dialect,' writes: 'It might be said of a woman ... she is "homelier than a stump fence" (120). Compare also *SSPB*: 'homely as a stump fence built in the dark.'
– '*Dads* [a musical play in the Charlottetown Festival] boasts a first-rate cast ... They play beautifully off each other and off the puppets More [the playwright] utilizes as their babies. Those babies, for what it's worth, are homely as a brush fence, but darn if they aren't adorable little scene stealers' (Doug Gallant, 'Fatherhood,' 9).
– '"Ugly as a stump fence" is a well-known phrase, fraught with meaning for any Canadian. For, truly, stump fences are most delightfully and decidedly ugly – like the English bulldog. Now they are scarce in this land ... The stumps were thrown together in rows, their roots piteously pawing the empty air. Tangled and uneven, they lay there like giant molars extracted from the bleeding earth' (Champion, *Over on the Island*, 181).
– 'The stumps ... contributed to the grimness of the landscape ... The saying "homely as a stump fence" is a surviving commentary on these early conditions' (Weale, 'Gloomy Forest,' 11).
[*brush*:] Common in Kings, widespread elsewhere; significantly senior, especially rural. [*picket, stump*:] Widespread or occasional; especially senior. *Includes* [brush] *senior grade-school-educated New Haven male farmer, middle-aged high-school-educated Charlottetown male telephone worker, and middle-aged college-educated Murray Harbour male teacher;* [picket] *senior college-educated Charlottetown male accountant,* [stump] *middle-aged high-school-educated St. Eleanors female nurse, and young college-educated Charlottetown woman.*

homely / ugly as a barn door
homely as Ma's back door
Exceptionally broad-faced and plain.
Widespread in Prince, occasional elsewhere; especially female, not young. *Includes senior grade-school-educated Tignish male farmer, and senior grade-school-educated Miscouche female housekeeper.*

a face like a twisted sneaker
A grotesque face, temporarily or permanently contorted. Compare *TTEM*: 'Face like a twisted sand-shoe (Aus[tralia]).'

6 Ugliness

Rare. *Includes senior high-school-educated Covehead female teacher, and middle-aged high-school-educated St. Eleanors female nurse.*

a face like the east end of a train going west
a face like the south end of a train headed north
An forgettable face having nothing to recommend it to further viewing. Parallel to conventional *face like the back of a bus*. *DARE* records *north end of a chicken flying south*, with variants, as a name for the rump of a cooked chicken, especially in the American south and south midland. Compare SO HUNGRY I COULD EAT THE EAST END OF A HORSE GOING WEST.
Rare. *Includes senior Parkdale woman, and middle-aged college-educated Charlottetown female secretary.*

a face like someone who was chasing parked cars
a face like someone who won the 100-yard dash in a 90-yard gym
1. A flat face or one having a crooked or short nose, as if smashed through the person's stupidity. 2. *Usually to children.* A face of disappointment or exaggerated misery.
[*parked cars:*] Widespread in Kings, occasional elsewhere except rare in Charlottetown; especially high-school-educated, rural, not senior. [*gym:*] Rare.

They fell out of an ugly tree and hit every branch on the way down.
Someone suffers from facial blemishes.
– 'Referring to zits [pimples] and facial scars or acne problems experienced during teenage years' (university student).
Rare. *Includes young Charlottetown female university student.*

to **look as if their mother beat them with an ugly stick**
to **look as if they took a beating from / got beat (bad) by an ugly stick**
to **look as if they got hit too hard with the ugly stick**
*Also reported
to **look as if one was thrown in the ugly pond**
Someone got hit with the ugly bug.
To appear unattractive and misshapen, as if from an early age. See also THEIR MOTHER GAVE THEM UGLY PILLS FOR BREAKFAST.
Occasional, except rare in Prince and Kings; especially urban. *Includes young Charlottetown female and male university students.*

a face like a bag full of mortal sins / hammers / monkeys
A swollen, lumpy, or irregularly shaped face. Also attested from Newfoundland and Ireland in the form *a face like a plate full of mortal sins*. One university student suggested an unconfirmed meaning: 'guilty [face].' Compare *TTEM*: 'Face like a bagful of spanners Rough and lumpy.'
Rare. *Includes middle-aged Kinkora female teacher, and young Montague student.*

a face so ugly it must hurt / be painful
A pitifully ugly, perhaps twisted, face.
Occasional in Prince and Charlottetown, rare elsewhere; especially high-school-educated. *Includes senior Stanhope man, and senior Coleman woman.*

*****With a face like that, they'd have to sneak up on a drink of water**
Someone has a frightening, ugly face.
Late entry, not surveyed. Reported by

middle-aged grade-school-educated Charlottetown woman.

*so ugly that the doctor slapped their mother
Ill-featured from the very day of birth.
Late entry, not surveyed. Reported by young female university student.

I'm not two-faced or I wouldn't be wearing the one I have.
Ironic; also in third person. Just look at me. Surely you can trust anyone this ugly.
– 'Meaning that the face one has is unattractive. If one had another it would be bound to be better looking' (middle-aged Charlottetown female university student).
– 'I'm being honest with you' (middle-aged grade-school-educated Queens man).
Rare. *Includes senior college-educated Summerside woman, and middle-aged high-school-educated St. Eleanors female medical worker.*

See also HAVE A HEAD LIKE A SEWING MACHINE BUT BE NO SINGER

HAIR

God made only a few perfect people; the rest he gave hair / put hair on.
God only made so many perfect heads; then he covered the rest with hair.
Joking proverb in response to some mockery of baldness. Baldness is obviously a highly desirable condition. (But for a possible reply again, see next entry.)
Occasional, except rare in Kings and Charlottetown; significantly high-school-educated, especially senior. *Includes male university student.*

You can't grow grass on concrete.
Joking proverb. A bald head means a blank mind; quick reply to a more common justification of the bald man's condition than that of the last entry: *Grass doesn't grow on a busy street* 'A bald head means an active mind.' Other variations of the defence to which this proverb is a counter-attack include *Grass grows not upon the highway* (ODEP, 1659–1721) and *You can't grow grass upon the beaten track* (DAP).
Occasional, except rare in Queens; significantly urban. *Includes middle-aged college-educated Charlottetown female social worker, and young female university student.*

like a cat's nest / bird's nest / bee's nest
Messy, rumpled, or matted; comparable to popular *like a rat's nest*. *Last year's robin's nest* for hair is recorded in Perkins, 'More Notes on Maine Dialect,' 125.
– 'Grandmother first used this on me when I walked into the kitchen for breakfast with uncombed hair' (young college-educated Prince man)
– 'Did the rats get into your hair? Your hair is a mess' (senior college-educated Prince woman).
Rare. *Includes senior college-educated Strathgartney female teacher and two young college-educated women from Summerside and Charlottetown.*

like a (bewitched) barley stack
like a bush (in a) barley stack
Spiky, shaggy, rough, uneven. The second informant listed below also gave the meaning 'scatter-brained.'
– 'When someone's hair is messy it looks like a bush barley stack, especially someone whose hair is standing

up or out' (young Charlottetown female university student).
– 'My mom's hair used to be referred to as a "barley stack"' (young Hunter River female university student).
Rare. *Includes senior college-educated Strathgartney female teacher, senior grade-school-educated Summerside female homemaker, and middle-aged Charlottetown man.*

*Playing with the plugs again?
Ironic. Your hair is sticking out frightfully; comparable to more popular *Stick your finger in a socket?*
*Late entry, not surveyed. *Reported by young college-educated Prince man.*

like the Devil in a gale of wind
Loose, ungoverned, uncared for. Probably an echo of a standard proverb with similar wording: *The Devil is busy in a high wind* (ODEP, 1790–1866). *MBP* and *TTEM* record *as busy as the devil in a gale of wind*, and in the form *busier than ...*, this simile is recorded from Maine (Perkins, 'More Notes on Maine Dialect,' 119). Compare *SSPB*: 'looks like the Devil in a gale of wind – to describe someone "so garbed as to look outlandish."'
– 'Older people [say this]' (anon.). Rare.

EYES

so cross-eyed they have to lie on their back to look in the cellar / down a well
Having eyes that converge beyond the normal.
Rare. *Includes senior Summerside female teacher.*

two beautiful blue eyes – one blew east and one blew west
Eyes that diverge outward because affected by walleye; comparable to more common *born on Wednesday / in the middle of the week – and looking both / nine ways for Sunday* (DARE, TTEM). Widespread in Summerside, occasional elsewhere except rare in Queens; significantly urban, especially middle-aged, college-educated. *Includes middle-aged high-school-educated Morell male carpenter.*

*blind in one eye and can't see out of the other
Ironic and often self-mocking. Extremely poor-sighted; parallel to established *deaf in one ear and can't hear out of the other.*
*Late entry, not surveyed. *Reported by senior Kensington woman.*

SKIN

freckles as big as gingersnaps
Large freckles. Gingersnaps are flat, brown cookies. Since they are also spicy and good to eat, this simile is not necessarily derogatory.
– 'To have freckles is to have good looks' (senior high-school-educated Miscouche female teacher).
Occasional except unattested in Kings; significantly senior, high-school and college-educated.

standing by a screen door when a manure spreader went by
... when a horse farted
... when the sun was shining
as if a pot were emptied through a screen door
Destined to have an unfortunately freckled complexion; variants of more general *to get a sun tan through a screen door.*

– 'Did you get a bucket of shit thrown at you through a screen door?' (middle-aged high-school-educated St. Eleanors female teacher).
Occasional in Prince and Queens, rare in Kings and Summerside, unattested in Charlottetown; significantly middle-aged, especially rural.

fly-shit on the face
Vulgar. Freckles.
Not in Survey II. Probably occasional.

The tide's gone out.
Usually to a child. You have not done a good job of washing your face, and it is still dirty around the edges. Also attested from Ireland. Compare *DSUE*: 'tidemark. The dirty mark so many children leave when they wash their neck: joc[ular]: late C.19–20. Hence *I see the tide is high this morning*: domestic c.p. [catchphrase]: C.20.'
Note *TTEM*: 'Tide-mark Dirty mark left on bath, crockery, neck, etc. showing how high the water came.'
Common in Summerside, widespread or occasional elsewhere; significantly urban, especially middle-aged, not college-educated.

an Irish lick and a Scotch rub
an Irish lick and a Scotch promise
A hasty and inadequate washing of the face; extension of more common catchphrases *a lick and a promise* (usually for a hasty house-cleaning) and *a lick and a rub*.
– 'Means half done in a hurry' (senior college-educated Brooklyn female farmer).
Rare. *Includes senior grade-school-educated Queens woman, senior high-school-educated Parkdale female nurse, and Charlottetown man.*

a pound of paint on the jaws of her
Too much makeup on a woman's face.
– 'Or war paint. I hear my grandparents use this a lot' (young Charlottetown female university student).
– 'Whore dust' (anon.).
Rare. *Includes middle-aged Brooklyn man, and young Charlottetown male university student.*

enough rouge to paint a barn door
Usually to or of a woman. Too much rouge.
– 'This saying was used often because we had a neighbour (about 12–14 years of age) who would "coat" herself with makeup' (young college-educated Queens man).
Widespread in Summerside, occasional elsewhere; especially urban, not young.

See also BAKED IN THE SUN

MOUTH AND TEETH

They could eat an apple through a picket fence.
They could eat corn / corn on the cob / straw through a picket fence / through a chicken coop.
They look like a horse eating an apple through a wire fence.
Someone has protruding front teeth. Compare *CCW*: 'Buck teeth? Only man I ever met who could eat grass through a picket fence' (197), and *DARE*: 'be able to eat a pumpkin through a knothole ... [other variants:] She could eat a pumpkin to the hollow through a crack in a board fence ... Could eat an apple through a knothole ... He could bite a punkin through a rail fence ... He could eat corn off a cob through a knothole ... could eat corn-on-the-cob through a

10 Mouth and Teeth

picket fence ... could eat corn through a picket fence.'
– 'Buckteeth, an excessive overbite: "Guildo had the family habit of a set of teeth that could eat an apple through a picket fence"' (Gojmerac, 'Prince Edward Island Expressions').
Rare. *Includes senior Parkdale woman, middle-aged high-school-educated St. Eleanors female nurse, and young Charlottetown female university student.*

a mouth like a codfish
a mouth as big as a codfish
Second variant ironic. A mouth that is contracted or pursed, and hence unappealing. *Mouth like a pickerel* – one of those sayings that 'need no explanation' – is recorded by Perkins, 'Vanishing Expressions of the Maine Coast,' 140.
Widespread in Prince and Kings, occasional in Summerside and Charlottetown, rare in Queens; especially grade-school-educated.

HEIGHT

so tall if they fell down they'd be half way home
Very tall.
Rare. *Confirmed by six informants in two surveys.*

Is it cold up there?
How tall you are! Variant of stock question *How's the weather up there?*; the frequency label below seems illogical, suggesting interference in Survey II from this more common version.
Common in Charlottetown, widespread in Prince, occasional in Kings and Summerside, rare in Queens; especially urban, senior, and young. *Includes senior West Royalty male telephone worker.*

short as a carrot
Short in stature. One informant, a senior college-educated Charlottetown male accountant, supplied the meaning 'bad-tempered.' See also CUT [SOMEONE] OFF LIKE A CARROT.
Rare. *Includes senior college-educated Charlottetown male accountant.*

See also SO HIGH YOU HAVE TO LOOK TWICE TO SEE, STAND THEM IN THE WELL TO CUT THEIR HAIR

SIZE

*wide as the day is long
Large in frame, big-bodied.
**Late entry, not surveyed. Reported by senior high-school-educated Prince woman.*

more rolls than a / the bread bin
more rolls than Bun King
A human body with obviously drooping fat.
– 'An Island saying from the younger generation' (young university student).
Occasional, except rare in Kings; especially grade-school-educated.

well-fed at both ends
Excessively overweight and especially big in the bottom.
– 'My grandparents use this' (young university student).
Rare. *Includes senior Summerside female teacher.*

to go too close / once too often to the trough
*Also reported
They should push away from the trough half an hour earlier.
To have a habit of piggish overeating.
– 'Big and fat – slang' (young university student).

– 'Once too often to the trough – overweight or an eating problem' (middle-aged high-school-educated Charlottetown man).
Widespread in Prince, occasional elsewhere. *Includes college-educated Vernon River female teacher.*

to look like two pigs fighting in a blanket / gunney sack
To have a large rump.
Rare. *Includes middle-aged college-educated Charlottetown female secretary, and middle-aged college-educated female teacher.*

fat as grannie's goose
Attractively plump; parallel to traditional simile *plump as a partridge*. Compare ODEP: 'You find fault with a fat goose,' 1678–1732.
Rare. *Includes Weale collection ['Wilmot Valley, 1983'].*

fat as a bear
Massively overweight; parallel to common derogatory animal similes *fat as a horse / cow / pig / porpoise / seal / whale*. Also attested from Ontario.
Common in Kings and Charlottetown. widespread elsewhere; especially urban. *Includes Weale collection: 'West Prince.'*

*fat as a lump on a stump
Obese, especially in the belly.
*Late entry, not surveyed. Reported by senior grade-school-educated Prince woman.

big as a haystack
big enough to eat (a round ball of) hay
*Also reported
big enough to eat a horse and cart and chase the driver
Very large in body and clearly a big eater; parallel to stock simile *big as (the side of) a barn* and *big as a horse*.

– 'An expression [*eat hay*] for a big, hungry person, like "eat the horse and cart and chase the driver"' (young university student).
[*haystack:*] Common in Prince, widespread elsewhere except occasional in Summerside; significantly senior, especially male. [*hay:*] Rare. *Includes senior college-educated Charlottetown male accountant, and North Lake woman.*

fat as a runny loaf
Overweight but still appealing to some tastes; parallel to traditional simile *fat as butter*.
Rare. *Includes senior grade-school-educated St. Peters female homemaker, senior high-school-educated Arlington male teacher, and middle-aged high-school-educated St. Eleanors female nurse.*

carrying last year's fun
*Also reported
paying for last year's fun
Clearly and thoughtlessly pregnant.
Rare. *Includes young Cardigan man.*

THINNESS

thin as a drink of water
Of persons, lacking substance, probably from excessive dieting; variant of established simile for height *long / tall (as a) drink of water* (NDAS). Also attested from Ireland.
Widespread in Kings, Summerside, and Charlottetown, occasional elsewhere; especially senior, urban. *Includes senior high-school-educated Summerside male farmer, middle-aged grade-school-educated Charlottetown woman, and middle-aged college-educated Charlottetown female secretary.*

big as number nine wire
Ironic. Not big at all, lean, wiry, sinewy. Number nine wire is the thickest gauge used for fences.
Rare. *Includes senior high-school-educated Arlington male teacher, and several university students.*

big / wide as a two-by-four
Ironic and contemptuous. 1. Not big at all, and very straight and rigid in form. 2. Of a woman, small-breasted. Parallel to traditional *big as a broomstick*. This simile is not to be confused with the common schoolyard taunt of 'fatty, two-by-four,' the supposed dimensions of someone very large. Such a confusion probably inflates the frequency label below. Another reported saying, from an anonymous informant, was *head as thick as a two-by-four*, 'stupid.' Compare *NDAS*: 'two-by-four ... Small; insignificant; inferior; ... "We stopped at a two-by-four hotel near the tracks."' A two-inch by four-inch board is the smallest size used in framing houses.
– 'This is very familiar to me as I live on a sawmill. It is said in a *very* sarcastic manner (as two-by-fours are small)' (anon.).
[*two-by-four*:] Common or widespread, except occasional in Charlottetown. *Includes middle-aged high-school-educated Miminegash female homemaker, young college-educated Tyne Valley female clerk, and young Kensington female university student.*

so thin they couldn't be shot behind a broomstick
so thin they couldn't be hit with a shotgun behind a broomstick / behind a crowbar

so thin they could hide behind a broomstick
Affectionate. Thin and straight in the body. Extension of common simile *skinny as a broomstick*.
Rare. *Includes senior high-school-educated Lot 37 woman, and senior Borden male ferry worker.*

so thin you could spit through them
so thin you could shoot a pea through them
so thin the wind could blow right through them
*Also reported
thin as a sieve
Fragile or delicate in build; parallel to conventional exaggeration *so thin you can see right through them*.
– 'Painfully thin' (senior Parkdale woman).
– 'PEI is definitely cold in the winter. Anyone that didn't have the extra "insulation" was "to be so thin the wind would blow right through"' (young college-educated Queens man).
[*spit*:] Common in Prince and Charlottetown, widespread in Queens and Summerside, occasional in Kings; significantly female. [*pea, wind*:] Widespread or occasional in Queens and Charlottetown, occasional or rare elsewhere. [all variants:] especially senior, urban. *Includes* [*spit*:] *senior grade-school-educated New Haven male farmer, middle-aged college-educated Charlottetown female clerk, and young college-educated Tyne Valley female clerk;* [*pea*:] *middle-aged college-educated Charlottetown female social worker;* [*wind*:] *young Charlottetown female university student;* [*sieve*:] *senior grade-school-educated Prince woman.*

so thin they have to walk by twice to make a shadow
so thin they have to stand twice in the same spot to make a shadow
*Also reported
so thin you have to look twice to see them
Affectionate. Extraordinarily but non-specifically thin; variants of more conventional exaggerations *too thin to cast a shadow, so thin they have to stand up twice to make a shadow.* Compare *YA*: 'So thin he had to stand twice in one place to make a shadow,' 127. Also in *CCW*: 'He's so thin he has to stand twice in the same place just to make a good shadow.' Casselman comments, 'Because the getting of food required more energy and time from our pioneer ancestors, a thin person was looked on as a nutritional failure, not a fashionable bean-pole' (196). Compare SO HIGH YOU HAVE TO LOOK TWICE TO SEE.
– 'No shadow even at high noon' (senior grade-school-educated Miscouche female housekeeper).
– 'A pig so thin he has to stand up twice to make a shadow' (middle-aged grade-school-educated Prince man).
Rare. *Includes senior grade-school-educated St. Peters female homemaker, senior Coleman woman, and middle-aged grade-school-educated Charlottetown male taxi-driver.*

so thin if they turn sideways they disappear
so thin if they turn sideways they're invisible
so thin they have to turn sideways to be seen
Affectionate. Extraordinarily slender in profile; also attested from New Brunswick. George Hendricks records *So skinny that, if he turned sideways, he was gone* in 'Texas Folk Similes,' 258. Common in Charlottetown, occasional elsewhere; significantly urban, especially not young. *Includes middle-aged grade-school-educated Charlottetown male taxi-driver, middle-aged college-educated Charlottetown woman, and young Charlottetown female university student.*

so thin a peanut would stick out in their stomach
*Also reported
You could X-ray them with a flashlight.
Of a woman, small-waisted, possibly from excessive dieting; variant of more common exaggeration *so thin if she swallowed an olive she'd look pregnant.* Compare *SD*: 'Thin as the girl who swallowed the pit of an olive and was rushed to a maternity ward.' Rare. *Includes middle-aged high-school-educated St. Eleanors female medical worker, and West Prince anon.*

so thin they have to run around in the shower to get wet
so thin they have to dance in the rain to get wet
so thin they could dodge between the raindrops
Affectionate. Laughably thin.
– 'Mayor Basil Stewart steps on the scale ... "I have to get the weight off before the highway weight restrictions come into effect," jokes the mayor who hopes to drop 109 pounds down to a slim 200 ... "But I don't want to get so thin that I'll have to run around in the shower to get wet"' (Darrach, 'Portly mayor on diet,' 1). Occasional, except rare in Queens. *Includes senior high-school-educated female teacher, and senior Parkdale woman.*

*so thin they have to lean up against the wall to squeal
Of piglets and, by extension, of people, thin to the point of ill health.
*Late entry, not surveyed. *Reported by middle-aged grade-school-educated Prince man.*

so thin they can turn somersaults in their suit
Small everywhere, in torso, arms, and legs.
Rare. *Supplied by a correspondent and confirmed by four informants in two surveys.*

so skinny / thin they'd break if they bent over
Thin-bodied and rigid, lacking suppleness. Also attested from New Brunswick.
Occasional, except unattested in Kings; especially senior, college-educated.

so thin they could be used as a dipstick
Contemptuous. Thin and straight in shape; variant of common similes *thin as a rail / toothpick / match(stick)*.
Rare. *Includes North Lake man, and several university students.*

There's more meat on a hockey stick.
*Also reported
There's more meat on a broom handle / crucifix / golf club.
Someone could do with more bodily flesh; affectionate variant of common similes *thin as a rail / toothpick / match(stick)*. Also in *CCW*: 'Thin? Seen more meat on a hockey stick!' (196). More at SO THIN THEY HAVE TO WALK BY TWICE TO MAKE A SHADOW.
Occasional, except rare in Summerside; reported in Weale collection from Tignish. *Includes young Charlottetown female university student.*

There's more meat on a chicken's forehead.
fat as a hen between the eyebrows
Second variant ironic. Someone has a thin face; comparable to stock simile, *look like a plucked chicken*. Compare *ODEP*: 'As Fat as a hen in the forehead,' 1594–1738; also *MBP*, *DSUE*, and *TTEM*. Compare also *DARE*: 'fat as a match ... Also ... fat as a hen's forehead Thin; small.'
Rare. *Includes senior grade-school-educated New Haven male farmer, senior college-educated Charlottetown male editor, and middle-aged college-educated female farmer.*

There's more meat on a little grey bird.
Imperative, often to a child. You need to eat more; comparable to standard reprimand *You eat like a bird*.
— 'My friend's mother [senior college-educated Charlottetown female homemaker] uses this to describe anyone who is very thin, including her son, because she despairs of ever getting any weight on him' (middle-aged college-educated Charlottetown male lawyer).
Rare. *Includes senior high-school-educated teacher, and middle-aged Charlottetown female university student.*

There's more flesh / meat on a robin's leg.
There's more flesh / meat on a fly's leg.
Someone is extraordinarily thin.
Rare. *Includes senior grade-school-educated Tignish fisherman, and young Charlottetown female university student.*

There's nothing left of [someone] but the bill and coo.
Someone, usually a woman, has lost weight to an extreme point, from diet-

ing to appear sexy; more affectionate than standard simile *eat like a bird*. Also attested from Ireland. Compare *CDEI*: 'bill and coo (S[lang].). Speak lovingly and intimately. An allusion to the sound – billing and cooing – made by doves and pigeons'; also *NDASCE*: 'bill and coo ... to kiss and cuddle.'
Rare. *Includes middle-aged college-educated Mount Stewart librarian.*

All that's left of them is the gear shift.
*Also reported
nothing left but the running gear
1. Someone has grown very weak from an involuntary loss of weight.
2. Someone has suffered a disastrous financial loss.
Rare. *Includes senior grade-school-educated New Haven male farmer, senior grade-school-educated St. Peters female homemaker, senior college-educated Strathgartney female teacher, and middle-aged high-school-educated St. Eleanors female nurse.*

There's more meat on a golf ball.
Someone is exceptionally lean and lacking in flesh. Also attested from Ohio, USA. One informant suggested the unconfirmed meaning 'bald-headed' (senior Parkdale woman).
Rare. *Includes senior grade-school-educated St. Peters female homemaker, senior high-school-educated teacher, senior college-educated Charlottetown male editor, and middle-aged grade-school-educated Charlottetown male taxi-driver.*

There's more meat on a poached egg.
Someone is exceptionally undernourished, poached eggs being often the relatively bland fare of sick persons on a regulated diet.
Rare. *Confirmed by six informants in two surveys.*

There's not enough meat on you to make a sandwich.
Imperative, often to a child. You need to eat more.
Widespread in Prince and Charlottetown, occasional elsewhere; especially senior.

There's more meat on (the Pope's plate on) Good Friday.
Someone is exceptionally lacking healthy flesh.
Rare. *Includes young Charlottetown female university student.*

***so thin you could see the sins on their soul**
Of persons, so fragile as to seem almost transparent.
Late entry, not surveyed. Reported by senior high-school-educated Prince woman.

to look like the skin of a nightmare pulled over a gatepost
To appear dreadfully wasted from mental or physical distress. Also attested from Nova Scotia. Compare LIKE AN APPETITE WITH THE SKIN PULLED OVER.
– 'Eastern Kings' (Weale collection [senior college-educated female teacher]).
Rare.

flat as a June cow-turd
Derogatory. Of a woman, small-breasted. One informant explained 'June' by adding 'Soft runny manure when eating fresh grass' (senior college-educated Cardigan female homemaker).
Not in Survey II. Probably rare. *Includes university student.*

LEGS

bow-legged as a cowboy after a six-day ride
Painfully bow-legged. Compare *DSUE*: '*cowboy* ... A bow-legged man: since ca. 1950.'
Occasional, except rare in Kings and Charlottetown; significantly senior. *Includes young Morell male university student.*

so bow-legged you could roll a barrel between their legs
Exceptionally bow-legged.
Widespread in Summerside, occasional in Prince and Charlottetown, rare in Queens and Kings; significantly senior, urban. *Includes young female university student.*

bow-legged as a grasshopper
bow-legged as a pet pig
Contemptuous. Extraordinarily bow-legged. The pig version may be a corruption of the next entry. Also attested from Moncton, New Brunswick.
– 'Used [*grasshopper*] by my family and friends' (young university student).
[*grasshopper*:] Occasional, except unattested in Kings. [*pig*:] Rare. *Includes young St. Louis male university student.*

no good at catching pigs
Joking but affectionate. Absurdly bow-legged, as if any pig on the loose could run right through the person's legs.
– 'My father says this' (middle-aged college-educated female teacher).
Rare.

CLOTHES

Some place must have burned down.
Ironic. Someone seems to be showing off the amount of money they have to spend, especially on clothes, possibly from a fire-insurance payment for a fire they set themselves.
– 'When I lived in the country (Breadalbane) it seemed quite "accepted" that people burnt their house or car for insurance' (anon.).
Occasional, except unattested in Kings; significantly young, especially urban.

to **look like a new dashboard on an old wagon**
Of new clothing, to look too grand or too youthful for the wearer.
Rare. *Confirmed by five informants in Survey I.*

to **look like a cream of tartar biscuit**
Especially of women, to be beautifully dressed and a bit puffed-up about it.
– 'A fancy lady' (Souris woman).
– 'Dressed to the nines' (anon.).
Rare.

dolled up with a teddy in their hand
*Also reported
dolled up like a teddy bear
Especially of men. Dressed elaborately and ready for a night on the town; *teddy*: 'a long-necked, twelve to sixteen ounce bottle, commonly a beer bottle, usually as used for illicit alcohol.' Compare *TTEM*: '*All dolled up like a barber's cat* (Can[ada]) Resplendently dressed.' One informant volunteered the meaning 'stuffed shirt' (senior grade-school-educated St. Peters female homemaker).
– 'Not appropriately dressed to be carrying a bottle of liquor down the street – overdressed' (anon.).
Rare. *Includes senior Kinkora female nurse.*

dressed like a Beach Grove Johnny
Of men, dressed more formally than the occasion or one's station in life calls for.

– 'Overdressed. Before World War Two, dances were held out at Beach Grove Hotel, the building since torn down and replaced by Beach Grove Home. Those dances were considered classy – hence a well-dressed man might be called "a Beach Grove Johnny"' (senior high-school-educated Lot 37 woman).
Rare.

(all) dressed up like a spare bedroom
*Also reported
all dressed up like a circus horse
Stiffly overdressed and showing off for some special occasion; comparable to traditional *all dressed up like a Christmas tree*. The 'circus horse' variant is probably related to the more common *painted up like a circus horse* ('A woman who uses a lot of makeup' [*DARE: circus*]).
– 'Folk language was full of these apt comparisons. Some of them were ordinary, but the ones which survived the winnowing process of repeated usage were the work of genius, requiring often a real leap of imagination. Consider, for example, ... "all dressed up like a spare bedroom."' (Weale, *Them Times*, 62).
Rare. *Includes senior Borden male ferry worker, and senior West Royalty male telephone worker.*

dressed up like a Protestant priest
Ironic. Not dressed up at all, distinctly underdressed for the occasion. Compare *DARE*: 'dressed up like a preacher ... Well dressed; spruced up.'
Widespread in Summerside, occasional in Prince and Kings, rare in Queens and Charlottetown; especially male. *Includes senior Borden male ferry worker, and middle-aged college-educated Summerside male lawyer.*

dressed like a clothesline in the rain
Ironic and disapproving. Scarcely wearing any clothes at all.
Rare. *Includes three senior grade-school-educated Tignish men: farmer, fisherman, and businessman.*

not enough on to flag a train / a wheelbarrow
1. *Disapproving.* Of women, scantily and provocatively clad. 2. Poorly and inadequately dressed. Woofter records a similar saying: '*not enough clothes on to wad a shotgun* ... a very few clothes. "These children come to school without enough clothes to wad a shotgun"' ('Dialect Words and Phrases from West Virginia,' 361). Compare *DARE*: 'Sayings about a person who seems to you very stupid: "He hasn't enough sense to" ... Flag a freight (train) [Kentucky, Virginia].'
– '"Not enough on to flag a wheelbarrow" – my grandfather's saying' (college-educated West Royalty female nursing administrator).
– '[*Wheelbarrow*] is used by middle-aged and up' (young Charlottetown female university student)
[*train*:] Occasional, except unattested in Charlottetown; especially senior, especially not grade-school-educated. [*wheelbarrow*:] Occasional, except rare in Queens and Charlottetown. *Includes senior grade-school-educated Northam male farmer, senior grade-school-educated Summerside female homemaker, senior high-school-educated Parkdale female nurse, senior Summerside male airbase worker, and young college-educated Bonshaw male waiter.*

VOICE

like a cat with its tail caught in a wringer / in a (screen) door
like a cat with someone standing on its tail
*Also reported
Who's killing the cat?
Of a singing voice, painfully shrill and strident.
– 'Screeching sound – very high pitched. A hurtin' unit!' (young Hunter River female university student).
Widespread in Prince and Queens, occasional elsewhere; especially not young. *Includes senior high-school-educated Glen Valley male farmer, senior Coleman woman, senior North Shore woman, and young Hillsborough Park female university student.*

They couldn't carry a tune if it had handles.
Unable to sing musically; variant of standard saying *not to be able to carry a tune in a bucket / bushel / bushel basket / brown paper bag* (see *DAS, IPI, WPI*).
– 'Not even if it was all wrapped up and tied in a brown paper bag' (young university student).
Occasional. *Includes young Charlottetown university students, male and female.*

If you were singing for a night's lodging, you'd be sleeping outside.
You have a simply terrible singing voice, so don't even try.
Rare. *Includes senior grade-school-educated New Haven male farmer.*

to **have a head like a sewing machine but be no singer**
To sing badly; a pun on the Singer brand of sewing machines. See also I'M NOT AN EIGHT-DAY CLOCK OR A SEWING MACHINE. Also attested from Newfoundland.
Rare. *Includes middle-aged grade-school-educated Charlottetown male taxi-driver.*

HEARING

deaf as a (bag of) hammer(s)
Extremely hard of hearing; parallel to common *deaf as a haddock / shad* and *deaf as a post*. See also DUMB AS A BAG OF HAMMERS.
Widespread in Queens and Kings, occasional elsewhere. *Includes senior grade-school-educated St. Peters female homemaker, senior high-school-educated Covehead female teacher, senior college-educated Bunbury male civil servant, middle-aged Vernon Bridge male teacher, and young Charlottetown female university student.*

Human Age

YOUTH

Young steps are smart.
Young people show attractive energy in the way they walk.
– 'Aunty accompanied me [a young girl] to the front door. She had given me a little fur. It was neat and velvety soft about my neck. "It's a nice morning – not cold," she commented. "And," she added, seemingly more to herself than to me, "Young steps are smart"' (Dixon, *Going Home*, 166).
Rare.

You have to stand them in the well to cut their hair.
The children are growing up fast.
Rare. *Confirmed by three informants in two surveys.*

green as grass and twice as spry
Inexperienced but willing; an extension, possibly sexual, of the stock simile *as green as grass* 'naive, immature.' The extension is a play on themes, since *green* is traditionally associated with youth (and a rural upbringing), *spry* with age, and also with grass. Compare ODEP: 'Green as grass, As,' 1387–1678; ODCIE.
Widespread in Summerside, occasional elsewhere except rare in Kings; significantly older, especially urban.

running / traipsing the roads
out roading
Of (usually) young people, driving aimlessly in a car for entertainment. Also attested from central and western Canada.
– 'This was often used in reference to me before I became a serious university student. I hear it all the time' (young Stanhope female university student).
– 'Used a lot by my mother and her age-group – also the older generation' (young Charlottetown female university student).
– 'Very popular. I hear it a lot in Tignish. But it doesn't have to be just young people that are running the roads and it doesn't always have to be at night' (anon.).
Common; significantly female; especially urban.

Sweet sixteen, sour twenty-one.
Proverb. Watch out: a young woman's mood can alter for the worse in very few years; variant of popular catchphrase *sweet sixteen and never been kissed.*

OLD AGE

old as the fog
three days older than the fog
*Also reported
two days older than the Island
Very aged, and probably a little dense.
– 'Folk language was full of these apt comparisons. Some of them were ordinary, but the ones which survived the winnowing process of repeated usage were the work of genius, requiring often a real leap of imagination. Consider, for example, ... "as old as the fog"' (Weale, *Them Times*, 62).
[*old:*] Occasional except unattested in Summerside. [*older:*] Rare. *Includes senior grade-school-educated St. Peters female homemaker, three senior grade-school-educated Tignish men, and senior Charlottetown female homemaker.*

older than the Stone Age
Very aged and stiff. Another supplied meaning was 'Someone who won't change old ways. He's living in the Stone Age' (university student).
Occasional in Prince, Summerside, and Charlottetown, rare elsewhere; especially senior.

old as the bill of North Cape
Inestimably old-aged; comparable to traditional *old as the hills, a day older than God*. A *bill* is 'a projection of land like a beak' (*W3*). North Cape is the northernmost point of Prince Edward Island. Place names in exaggerated similes of human age are common elsewhere, as recorded in *ODEP*, *BP*, *TEM*, and *DSUE* with British place names like Aldgate, Charing Cross, Cale Hill, Eggerton, Glastonbury Tor, Pandon Gate, and many more.
Rare. *Includes senior Charlottetown female homemaker, middle-aged high-school-educated St. Eleanors female nurse, and a university student.*

a day older than the tides
So old, it seems, as to pre-date the creation of the world. One informant's response was 'older than the second coming of Christ' (West Prince).
Rare. *Includes three senior grade-school-educated Tignish men.*

old as Methuselah's (pet) cat
old as Methuselah's dog / (pet) goat / billy / buck / nanny
old as Methuselah or his cat / dog / [etc.]
old as Methuselah's ghost
Said of persons and pets, extraordinarily long-lived; extensions of the customary simile *old as Methuselah*. As *old as Methuselah's goat* also attested in Newfoundland. Methuselah, a Hebrew patriarch, is said in the Old Testament (Genesis 5:27) to have lived 969 years. Both the name itself and the basic simile *old as Methuselah* are generally proverbial, and amply recorded in standard collections like *ODEP* and *BD*. As for goats, they are 'the hardiest of all animals,' according to *Collier's Encyclopedia* (1984, 11, 171). The last variant, with *ghost*, is probably a play on words with *goat*, or a folk etymology.
Widespread or occasional; significantly senior, especially not grade-school-educated; *goat* versions common in Kings, preferred by rural men.

*I wouldn't like to be hanging since they were [some stated age].
Somebody passed a certain supposed or reported age a long time ago.
Late entry, not surveyed. Reported by senior Charlottetown woman.

*to make it to the grass
To make it through the winter and into the spring.
– 'Winter was a season of grim endurance, and for many old people there was real concern about making it through until spring. They hung on and hung on, especially in March and April, waiting for the reinvigoration of warmer weather. It was the same in the barn. On many farms the cattle would be so weakened by the long winter's confinement, and so malnourished from want of good fodder, that some of them would go down and not be able to get back up on their feet ... [T]he farmers would be greatly relieved when their animals would 'make it to the grass' ... On a sunny morning just before Easter, a priest ... saw an old female parishioner, who had come early to the church for Mass, dancing in the morning light and watching her own shadow on the side of the church. It was spring, the sun was shining, and she was still alive. Her dance was a celebration, the ancient vernal dance of perennial awakening. Once more she had "made it to the grass"' (Weale, *Them Times*, 18).
*Late entry, not surveyed.

See also **Age of Objects**

DEATH

We'll soon be having the cookies on [someone].
Someone is deathly ill, and we'll soon be attending the wake; comparable to common saying *to have the biscuit* 'to die.' A story from Weale's *Them Times* (102) indirectly confirms this entry: 'An old man, frail and dying, was lying in the little room off the kitchen, very near his end. His wife was busy baking, and the aroma of her cooking filled the house. It roused him a bit. "Marion," he called out feebly, "what are you baking? Is it dark fruit cake?" "Yes," she replied, "it is." "Oh!" he said, "my favourite. Could I have a piece when it is finished?" "No dear," she responded curtly, "it's for the wake."'
Rare. *Includes young university student.*

No sweetbreads yet.
Someone is very sick, but in stable condition for the moment.
– 'Meaning the person is not ready to die yet, so wake won't occur soon – Souris, 1983' (Weale collection [middle-aged college-educated eastern Kings woman]).
Rare.

When you die you go to Heaven, Hell, or Cawnpore.
Proverb. Whatever is coming is coming – good, bad, or something in between. See quotation. It is uncertain whether 'Cawnpore' was a standard name for Cavendish Beach. The name may refer to a city in India, now Kanpur, where British troops were massacred in 1857. Compare *BD*: '*Go to Halifax.* A euphemism for "Go to hell." The coinage probably derives from association with the saying

"From Hull, Hell and Halifax, Good Lord, deliver us."'
– 'Cawnpore is the old name for the Cavendish Beach area. My mother went driving there once or more as a girl, when people were just starting to go there (maybe 30's). She had a religious upbringing and going to Cawnpore to her meant she was, if not actually in Hell, at least heading for it quickly (what with all the folks actually trying to enjoy themselves on the Sabbath)' (middle-aged college-educated Charlottetown male lawyer).
Rare. *Includes senior grade-school-educated Prince female homemaker.*

Health

in good twist
1. In good health; physically fit. 2. In good humour; parallel to conventional catchphrase *in good heart*. Also attested from Ireland. The opposite, *in bad twist*, has also been reported (Belfast, PEI).
– 'In good shape, keeping fit' (young grade-school-educated Queens man).
– 'I [a restaurant owner] have a waitress who uses this regularly' (middle-aged college-educated Kings woman). Occasional; especially senior. *Includes two senior college-educated men of Prince and Queens, and senior college-educated Charlottetown woman.*

to be off the walk
To experience poor health.
– 'My sister heard this on the hustings [campaigning for public office]: "so and so is off the walk – something is going round"' (middle-aged college-educated Charlottetown woman).
Rare.

to not see a bit of [some person]
To encounter an acquaintance who looks exceptionally ill. Also attested from Ireland.
– 'She didn't look her usual self' (anon.).

Rare. *Includes senior high-school-educated Darnley female secretary.*

to feel like a shit-house mouse / rat
Vulgar. To feel nauseous.
– '"I felt like a shit-house mouse after I ate the left-overs"' (Gojmerac, 'Prince Edward Island Expressions'). Not in Survey II. Probably occasional.

painful as a hen laying square eggs
Of any action, but especially evacuation of the bowels, painful and awkward.
Occasional in Prince, rare in Queens and Kings.

to thread the needle at ninety yards
They could shit through a straw / a screen door (and never touch / hit a wire).
*Also reported
to shit through the eye of a (darning) needle (at forty / fifty paces).
To have extreme, forceful diarrhea. Compare *DSUE*: 'thread the needle ... (Of the man) to coit with: Anglo-Irish: C.20.'
– 'Meaning a bad case of diarrhea – St. Peters area, 1983' (Weale collection). Occasional or widespread.

24   Health

to go quick and stay long
To have sudden and extensive diarrhea. Compare *DARE*: '*go-quick plant* ... (Perh[aps] from its laxative quality) Rhubarb [Colorado].'
Rare. *Includes senior Montague female homemaker.*

a case of the pollywoggles of the diaphobickalorium
A medical condition I'm not going to tell you about, so there.
— 'There was a verbal device people used which we refer to as "the nonsense response." And it worked like this: if someone asked you something, and you didn't want to tell them, you couldn't come right out and say "Mind your own business" – that would be far too confrontational, far too direct. But what you could do was answer with a nonsense saying, which was really just a slightly more polite way of saying "It's none of your business" ... Suppose you weren't feeling well for one reason or another, and someone asked you how you were or what was wrong, you might reply, "I have a case of the pollywoggles of the diaphobickalorium." You see, nonsense word and nonsense sayings – but the message couldn't be more clear: "Get lost!"' (Weale, 'Them Times' [radio broadcast]).
Rare.

*An onion a day keeps everyone away.
Think of something more original to say; joking reaction to overused proverb *An apple a day keeps the doctor away*.
*Late entry, not surveyed. *Reported by senior college-educated Kings man.*

See also NOT A HUNDRED, DOWN THE LITTLE RED LANE

Character

LAZINESS

lazy as a pet day
Feeling idle, even while knowing that the idleness will have to be paid for later. Though this simile is rare, its root, *pet day*, is well known (*OED*, 1823–1939 [last date L.M. Montgomery, as below]). Note *DPEIE*: '*pet day* ... Common in Egmont, frequent in Cardigan, occasional in Summerside and Malpeque, infrequent in Charlottetown; significantly rural, older, less educated ... "A day of exceptionally fine weather, especially out of season, thought to precede a storm" ... *W3* [*Webster's Third New International Dictionary*] "chiefly Scot" ... *DNE* [*Dictionary of Newfoundland English*] 1933.'
– '"Such a lovely day ... made for us," said Diana. "I'm afraid its a pet day though ... there'll be rain tomorrow."' 'Never mind. We'll drink its beauty today, even if its sunshine is gone tomorrow' (Montgomery, *Anne of Ingleside*, 6).
– 'This is just a pet day; wait to see tomorrow' (anon.).
Rare. *Includes young Charlottetown female university student.*

lazy as a pet pig / fat pig / pet cat
Lazy because feeling, for the moment, self-indulgent, pampered. Also attested from western Canada. Widespread in Charlottetown, Prince, and Kings, occasional elsewhere; especially not young. *Includes three senior North River women, and Wilmot Valley anon.*

lazy as a pet coon / as a hedgehog
Lazy by nature; comparable to standard *lazy as sin*.
– 'Someone who's so lazy they're no good for anything' (young college-educated Charlottetown female student).
– 'Lazy rather than relaxed' (young college-educated Charlottetown female student).
– 'Similar to not worth a pinch of coonshit' (anon.).
Widespread in Prince, occasional elsewhere; especially not young. *Includes a senior grade-school-educated Miscouche woman, and two senior college-educated Charlottetown men.*

lazy as (a) toad(s) at the bottom of a well
Habitually shiftless, taking for granted that all needs will be supplied automatically. This simile is

found elsewhere in the Maritimes, as in Bruce, *Down Home*, 66: 'I attacked a building-supplies store in Halifax because its clerks were doltish and as lazy as toads at the bottom of a well.' Rare.

too lazy to spit
*Also reported
too lazy to breathe
Worn out, enervated. Compare I WOULDN'T WASTE MY SPIT. This proverbial exaggeration is probably associated with the worthlessness of spit in phrases like *not count for spit, not give spit, (not) worth a bucket of warm spit* (as in *NDAS*).
Occasional. *Includes young male university student.*

too lazy to live / to breathe
Lazy to an extreme degree.
Occasional in Prince, Queens, and Kings, rare or unattested in Charlottetown and Summerside; significantly rural. *Includes middle-aged high-school-educated Queens woman, and young female university student.*

too slow to stop quick
Slow but inexorable, like a large ship under way.
Rare. *Includes senior grade-school-educated St. Peters female homemaker.*

***If there's anything slower than stopped, we'll name it after you.**
You are the slowest walker we've ever seen.
*Late entry, not surveyed. *Reported by middle-aged grade-school-educated Prince man.*

only two speeds, slow and stop
only one speed and that's slow
Languid and sloth-like in all movements.
– 'A slow-moving person' (young grade-school-educated Summerside man).
Widespread in Kings, occasional elsewhere. *Includes middle-aged college-educated Kings woman, and young Charlottetown female university student.*

so slow you have to time them on a calendar
Incredibly slow-moving and sluggish.
– 'So slow you've stopped' (middle-aged grade-school-educated Charlottetown woman)
Rare. *Includes young Charlottetown female university student.*

It takes a landmark to see them moving.
*Also reported
They set the buoys by them.
You have to go to extreme lengths to get any work out of them.
Rare. *Confirmed by fourteen informants in two surveys.*

If that dog hadn't stopped to shit, he would've won the race / caught the fox.
*Also reported
... he would have caught the rabbit.
Vulgar proverb. Self-gratification means lost opportunities.
– '"Every time I see that lazy John, I think to myself, if the dog hadn't stopped to shit he would've caught the fox"' (Gojmerac, 'Prince Edward Island Expressions').
Not in Survey II. Probably occasional. *Includes senior grade-school-educated Mt. Stewart male postal worker.*

a cross between a door sill and a door mat
A person who is despicably shiftless in leaving the real work to others.

– 'Someone who is useless or lazy' (senior grade-school-educated Bedeque female homemaker). Rare.

See also I'D STRETCH A MILE BUT I'M TOO LAZY TO WALK BACK, IS YOUR ARM BROKEN?, HANG THEIR COAT ON THE DOG'S NAIL

DISHONESTY

so crooked that (when they die) they could be screwed into the ground
so crooked they could swallow a nail and pass a screw
*Also reported
so crooked they have to screw their socks on in the morning
Deceitful at every possible opportunity; variants of more common comparisons *crooked as a corkscrew* (MBP), *so crooked they could hide behind a corkscrew*, and *too crooked to lie straight in bed* (DCP). Also attested from Tennessee.
– 'Comparison to a screw, meaning a very crooked person' (young college-educated Tyne Valley female clerk).
– 'Someone who is very dishonest' (senior college-educated Charlottetown male editor).
[*ground*:] Widespread in Prince, occasional elsewhere; significantly senior, especially college-educated. [*screw*:] Rare. *Includes senior high-school-educated Covehead female teacher, senior Borden male ferry worker, middle-aged grade-school-educated Charlottetown male taxi driver, and middle-aged college-educated Summerside woman.*

crooked as a crowbar
*Also reported
crooked as a fiddler's elbow
Inclined to sharp manoeuvring, manipulative. Also attested from New Brunswick. One informant's meaning was 'Also used to describe a road or trail' (middle-aged high-school-educated Charlottetown man). The *fiddler's elbow* alternative is probably an extension of the stock simile *busy as a fiddler's elbow*.
– 'I use this myself – someone who would steal from right under your nose' (university student).
Widespread in Queens and Charlottetown, occasional elsewhere; especially male, high-school-educated, not middle-aged. *Includes senior grade-school-educated Charlottetown woman, and young college-educated Queens woman.*

crooked as a (fence) post
crooked as a pole fence
*Also reported
crooked as a stove pipe
Fundamentally unreliable and untrustworthy; variant of conventional *crooked as a rail fence* (as in NDFRRS). Also attested from elsewhere in Canada. Untended fence posts often lean away from the straight perpendicular, while a pole or rail fence erratically zigzags.
– 'A person who cannot be trusted in business dealings. Someone is going to get the best of you in a deal' (young Charlottetown male university student).
– 'Used when someone is cheating or not being straight with you' (young Kensington female university student).
– 'A person is two-faced, would rob one blind of his/her goods. Cannot be trusted (young Hunter River woman).
Common or widespread; significantly not young. *Includes senior grade-school-educated St. Peters female homemaker, senior high-school-educated Summerside male farmer, and senior college-educated Bunbury male civil servant.*

crooked as the Trans-Canada
*Also reported
crooked as the Sherbrooke Road going into Summerside
Devious and unprincipled, particularly in politics. Compare STRAIGHT AS A SLEIGH TRACK ON THE WESTERN ROAD. It is usually the (now defunct) Prince Edward Island railroad that is described as built, for political reasons, with curves into every small community.
– 'Refers to the PEI Trans-Canada highway, picking up every little village' (middle-aged college-educated Queens man).
Rare. *Includes senior grade-school-educated Prince woman, and senior Stanhope man.*

crooked as a rooster
crooked as a barnyard owl
Hard to pin down, wily; comparable to standard animal similes like *crooked as a ram's horn / sow's tail / lamb's tail / dog's hind leg / hen's hind leg*. Compare FOOLISH AS A ROOSTER WITH A SOCK ON ITS HEAD.
Rare. *Includes senior college-educated Charlottetown male accountant, middle-aged high-school-educated West Covehead heavy-equipment operator, middle-aged high-school-educated Queens woman, and middle-aged college-educated Charlottetown woman.*

A snake would break its back getting around them.
so crooked it would break a snake's back getting around them
Someone is well-known for unscrupulous behaviour; comparable to standard snake similes like *crooked as a snake / snake's back / rattlesnake / eel*. One informant supplied *so low he would have to get on a ladder to kiss a snake's belly*.
Rare. *Includes senior college-educated Strathgartney female teacher, and middle-aged grade-school-educated Queens woman.*

two-faced as a double-bitted axe
*Also reported
two-faced as a looking glass
Unfair and duplicitous to a striking extent. A double-bitted axe has two cutting edges facing in opposite directions.
– 'With a friend like you, who needs enemies?' (middle-aged grade-school-educated Charlottetown male taxi-driver).
– 'Talks behind your back' (senior grade-school-educated St. Peters female homemaker).
Common in Kings, widespread in Prince, occasional elsewhere; significantly rural, especially not young.

so two-faced they should wear two hats
Able to profess contradictory positions on different occasions, duplicitous. Compare *ODEP*: 'Two faces (heads) in one hood, To bear (carry, have),' 1425–1888.
Rare. *Includes middle-aged college-educated Arlington male teacher. One informant responded with* so two-faced they can see out of the back of their head.

as many faces as a beech nut
Exceptionally deceitful, worse than double-tongued: a beech nut is three-sided.
– 'Always says what one wants to hear' (Kensington seniors group).
Occasional except rare in Kings.

*They'd never break your heart with a bad answer.
Someone would never deny your request – but would never act on it either.

*Late entry, not surveyed. *Reported by senior college-educated Queens man.*

like frosting on a burnt cake
1. Covering up a deficiency. 2. Repairing a mistake too late. Also attested from Newfoundland.
Occasional except rare in Summerside. *Includes young Charlottetown female university student.*

*like the elephant's bed, a lot of bunk
An untrue and nonsensical thing to say.
*Late entry, not surveyed. *Reported by senior high-school-educated Kings man.*

*honest as the sun
Clearly and helpfully honest.
*Late entry, not surveyed. *Reported by senior Bedeque man.*

See also I'M NOT TWO-FACED OR I WOULDN'T BE WEARING THE ONE I HAVE, I WOULDN'T LIKE TO BE HANGING SINCE THEY WERE [SOME STATED AGE].

CUNNING

deep as the grave
Secretive, having feelings not readily revealed; variant of stock phrases like *black / close / dark / mute / quiet / secret / silent / still as the grave* (as in *SD, BD, EAP, DAPPP*), and like *(not so) deep as a well* (as in *ODEP, MBP*). Also attested from Ireland and recorded in Newfoundland: 'You are as deep as the grave. Your real feelings are not easily judged from your appearance' (English, *Historic Newfoundland*, 38). Occasional except rare in Prince and Kings.

sly / slick as a mouse
Sneaky, covert, stealthy; parallel to standard *sly as a fox*. Compare *SD*: 'Sneaky as a rat in a hotel kitchen.' Widespread in Prince, occasional elsewhere; especially rural, not young or college-educated. *Includes two senior grade-school-educated male farmers of New Haven and Northam, and senior Kinkora female nurse.*

slippery as six fat eels in a barrel of snot
Coarse, uncultivated. Shifty or artful; variant of the standard *as slippery as an eel*. Compare *ODEP*: 'slippery as an eel, As. [1384–1855]'
Not in Survey II. Probably occasional. *Includes senior grade-school-educated Queens woman.*

Eaton's don't tell Simpson's their business.
Simpson's don't tell Eaton's their business.
I'm not going to tell you what I'm doing; possibly a general Canadian variant of well-known New York City saying, *Does Macy's tell Gimbel's?*, 'applied to any competition, especially one involving a surprising and sometimes mysterious victory' (*DCP*). Also attested from Ontario. Eaton's and Simpson's are longtime department-store competitors, first in Toronto then across Canada. Some alternates, of uncertain distribution beyond Prince Edward Island, are *Burger King don't tell MacDonald's ...* and *K-Mart don't tell Towers ...*
– 'Keep certain things to yourself that are not the business of other people' (anon.).
– 'When I would ask my mother what was going on, she would tell me

Simpson's don't tell Eaton's their business' (anon.).
Common in Summerside, widespread elsewhere except occasional in Kings; significantly not young, especially urban, not college-educated.

to have the Devil in them as big as a horse
To be energetically mischievous and tormenting; comparable to standard catchphrases *be the very Devil, play the Devil with, raise the Devil*. In 'Canadian Folk-lore from Ontario,' F.W. Waugh notes 'The Devil is in her as big as a woodchuck (said of a vicious or bad-tempered person) ... A variant is, There's a devil in her the size of a Thanksgiving turkey' (34).
– 'Him and I was very thick. He's an Old Country Irishman, but the devil was into him as big as a horse ... He was a heller' (Hornby, *Belfast People*, 36).
– 'Mischievous – [used by] older people' (anon.).
– 'Means he was a bad person, a practical joker' (anon.).
Occasional in Prince, Kings, and Charlottetown, rare or unattested in Summerside and Queens. *Includes senior Belfast man.*

See also SLICK AS A KITTEN'S WRIST, SLICK AS A BISCUIT, SAY NOTHING AND SAW WOOD.

AVARICE

so greedy they would save the tallow from a mosquito
Miserly to an extreme degree; variant of popular proverbial exaggeration *flay / skin a louse / a flea for its skin / hide and tallow* (ODEP; CCW, 198). An alternate in *SSPB* is 'He's so tight, he'd skin a louse and tan the hide, and save the grease for tallow.'
– 'He's so mean' (senior college-educated Charlottetown male editor).
Rare. *Includes senior grade-school-educated St. Peters female homemaker, and senior Vernon Bridge male farmer.*

so greedy they would steal swill from an orphan pig
Heartlessly and shabbily covetous. The idea of greed leading to ill-treatment of helpless creatures is a common proverbial theme, as in the sayings above and 'You'd take a worm from a blind hen's mouth' (Thompson, *Body, Boots and Britches*, 500).
Rare. *Attested in Weale collection and confirmed by nine informants in two surveys.*

so greedy they would steal the eyes out of your head / your sockets
so greedy they would steal the eyes out of your head and come / go back (at night / the next day) for the holes
... to steal the holes (too)
so greedy they would steal the eyes out of your head and swear to God you looked better without them
Sordid and mercenary on every possible occasion; comparable to established *steal the pennies off a dead man's eyes* (DCP, TTEM). Compare CCW: 'Guy's so cheap he'd pick the pennies off his dead granny's eyes' (198).
– 'A reference I heard in relation to Prime Minister Mulroney recently; also a very shrewd salesperson' (young West Prince male university student).
– 'Couldn't be any greedier' (senior college-educated Charlottetown male editor).
[*steal the eyes ... holes:*] Common or wide-

spread; significantly grade-school-educated, especially middle-aged, rural. [... *and swear to God*:] Occasional except rare in Charlottetown; significantly senior. *Includes middle-aged grade-school-educated Charlottetown male taxi-driver, middle-aged high-school-educated St. Eleanors female homemaker, and middle-aged college-educated Charlottetown female social worker.*

so cheap they wouldn't give you the smell off their last year's shit
too mean to give their shit to the crows
*Also reported
... the smell off their ass
Vulgar. Stingy, cheap, illiberal. Compare *DCP*: 'low Can[adian] ... *wouldn't give you the steam off his shit*,' and *DSUE*: 'too mean to part with (his) shit.'
– 'A very mean person' (young Queens man).
– 'Very tight – usually money-wise' (young university student).
Not in Survey II. Probably occasional.

so mean they would save a fart in a gas bottle
Vulgar. Exceptionally frugal.
– 'Recent' (senior high-school-educated Queens female teacher).
Not in Survey II. Probably occasional.
Includes middle-aged college-educated Queens female nurse.

mean as / meaner than second skimmings
Ungenerous and ill-tempered, curmudgeonly. *Skimmings* are cream removed from the top of fresh milk.
– 'Jane says she will devote her whole life to teaching, and never, never marry, because you are paid a salary for teaching, but a husband won't pay you anything, and growls if you ask for a share in the egg and butter money. I expect Jane speaks from mournful experience, for Mrs. Lynde says that her father is a perfect old crank, and meaner than second skimmings' (Montgomery, *Anne of Green Gables*, 341).
– 'I heard a rumour that he was going to see Lizzie Pye over at Avonlea, and I knew it was time to be stirring, if anything were to be done ... Lizzie Pye wouldn't have done for a stepmother for Althea's boys at all. She was too bad-tempered, and as mean as second skimmings besides' (Montgomery, *Chronicles of Avonlea*, 251).
Rare.

They would squeeze a penny until the water runs out of the Queen's eyes.
They would cut the trees off an Island penny.
*Also reported
They could squeeze a penny to make two.
They would squeeze the topmast off the Bluenose.
'Island penny' *variant archaic*. Someone is extremely grasping, tightfisted, or frugal. The Island 'tree cent,' issued in 1871, featured the Arms of Prince Edward Island: three small oak trees beside a larger one (*DPEIE*). The schooner *Bluenose* appears on the Canadian ten-cent piece. Compare *CCW*: 'Why, he'd squeeze a cent 'til the Queen cried' (198). *TTEM*: 'So mean he would squeeze a quarter till the eagle screamed (Amer[ican]).'
Rare. *The water variant was confirmed by eight informants in two surveys, and the Island penny variant by three. Includes senior grade-school-educated Prince woman.*

tight / close as the paper on the wall / in the parlour
See quotations. Also attested in Weale collection.
– 'Stingy, parsimonious, cheap, mean, ungiving, when referring to money' (anon.).
– 'Referring to a miserly person' (anon.).
Occasional in Prince, Kings, and Summerside, rare in Queens and Charlottetown; significantly senior, not recognized by young informants.

See also TIGHT AS A FIDDLESTRING, ROTTEN AS DIRT

ARROGANCE

brass enough to make a pot and gall enough to fill it
*Also reported
gall enough to start a vinegar factory
A great deal of impertinence or conceit; extension of standard simile *as bold as brass*.
– 'He knows it all and is willing to make sure everyone knows it. Bold and conceited' (university student).
– 'Be liable to do anything' (anon.).
Rare. *Includes senior college-educated Brooklyn female farmer.*

If their brass were gold, they'd be a millionaire.
Someone is extremely saucy, insolent, or brazen. Compare *ODEP*: 'Brass for gold' (Homer).
– 'One such [witty, nineteenth-century] auctioneer was selling cakes one night and it was announced that there was a five-dollar gold piece in one of them. He picked one cake up and said, "I think it is in this one; I guess I'll buy this myself." Mr. Smart in the crowd shouted: "Who'll back your note [money]?" The quick retort was "I suppose you will if you have as much gold as you have brass"' (Pendergast and Pendergast, *Folklore Prince Edward Island*, 18).
– 'If her brass were gold, she'd be a millionaire. Usually her' (anon.).
Occasional in Prince and Summerside, rare elsewhere.

If you broke off where you cracked, you'd be damn short.
Don't get above yourself or put on airs, since you too are human and break wind.
– 'This is a dandy saying of my grandmother. It's a put-down for people getting arrogant. It reduces you to the same "short" level, i.e. we all fart, so don't be getting high and mighty' (middle-aged Georgetown woman).
Rare.

They would shit (too) if they were well fed.
Vulgar. Don't be fooled – that person is no better than the rest of us.
– 'My husband tells me this is a saying used when someone is insufferably arrogant – a know-it-all' (middle-aged Summerside female library technician).
– 'In this case a person bragging a lot of what he has or had done in the past. [I've heard it at the] taxi-stand' (middle-aged grade-school-educated Charlottetown male taxi-driver)
– 'Not as tough as you think you are' (middle-aged high-school-educated Queens male carpenter).
– 'Someone bragging about all they were going to do. This saying would put them in their place.' (senior grade-school-educated Prince female housekeeper).
Not in Survey II. Probably occasional.

Arrogance

a head so high a martingale wouldn't bring it down
A conceited, arrogant, or snobbish manner. A martingale is a harness strap that prevents a horse from rearing, or throwing its head up.
– 'I heard an elderly Alberton man the other day say of someone he regarded as too full of himself: "His head's so high a martingale wouldn't bring it down."' (anon.).
Rare.

to **wear a ten dollar hat on a ten cent head**
To act important while being, in fact, insignificant.
– '"Look at the little fellow [in a plowing match]," shouted a voice in the crowd. "He's hardly above the handles." "Little," muttered Jockie. "Phooey to you! It's not the size. It's what's inside. I'll wager you're wearing a ten dollar hat on a ten cent head, like Grandpa says"' (Stirling, *Jockie*, 179–80).
Rare.

They would drown if they walked in the rain.
Someone is snobbish or conceited, with a 'nose in the air.'
Rare. *Includes young male university student.*

They sure don't think they are the train.
Ironic. Someone has exaggerated ideas about his or her importance.
– 'Describes a haughty or proud female – West Prince' (Weale collection).
Rare. *Confirmed by three informants from Prince.*

to **think they are the people**
To think one is the centre of all attention.
– 'Soon after, Eben brought the family pung [a small box-shaped, one-horse sleigh] and his chubby red mare to the door for Mollie. He had not as yet attained to the dignity of a cutter [a small but more elegant one-horse sleigh] of his own. That was for his elder brother, Robert, who presently came out in his new fur coat and drove dashingly away with bells and glitter. "Thinks he's the people," remarked Eben, with a fraternal grin' (Montgomery, *Further Chronicles of Avonlea*, 253).
Rare.

to **have more nerve than a sore tooth**
To call attention to oneself insistently.
– 'Very bold' (middle-aged college-educated Prince woman).
Occasional; especially high-school-educated. *Includes young university student.*

They think they're [the person's own name]
Someone is so conceited as to think his/her name alone conjures up admiration from all; parallel to common *He thinks he's Lord Mayor of London / cock of the walk / God's gift to women.* Compare QUITE A [SOMEONE'S FIRST NAME].
Occasional in Prince, Kings, and Summerside, rare elsewhere; especially female. *Includes senior high-school-educated Covehead female teacher, and middle-aged Charlottetown man.*

King Shit from Turd Island
*Also reported
... **Turd Mountain**
They think they're King Shit, but they're only Fart, the Messenger
Vulgar. Ridiculously self-important; a Prince Edward Island extension of the conventional *King Shit*.
Not in Survey II. Probably occasional. *Includes senior high-school-educated Queens female teacher.*

You may be a good man where you come from, but you're not where you come from.
Don't give yourself airs around here – we have our own standards.
Rare. *Confirmed by eight informants in two surveys.*

*My brother slept with a man who came from Antigonish!
Stop boasting; you're just not that special. Comparable to more usual *What a long tail our cat has!*
Late entry, not surveyed. Reported by middle-aged college-educated Prince man.

enough crust to start a bakery
Obtuse insensitivity to the feelings of others, insolence.
Rare. *Confirmed by thirteen informants in two surveys.*

*more gall than a snake
A sense of confidence based on trickery.
Late entry, not surveyed. Reported by young college-educated Prince woman.

bold as a pet pig
Very assured and impudent.
– 'You know, around the world, folk language is filled with expressions which refer to animals; they're a rich source. "As bold," for instance, "as a pet pig." I like that one. It refers probably to a little pig that's been bottle-fed and gets to the place where he thinks he owns the farm' (Weale, 'Them Times' [radio broadcast]).
– 'Folk language was full of these apt comparisons. Some of them were ordinary, but the ones which survived the winnowing process of repeated usage were the work of genius, requiring often a real leap of imagination. Consider, for example, ... "as bold as a pet pig"' (Weale, *Them Times*, 62).
– 'Very inquisitive as well as bold' (anon.).
Widespread in Prince and Kings, occasional in Summerside and Charlottetown, rare in Queens; especially not young.

OBSTINACY

stubborn as Solomon's mule
Extremely hard to control; parallel to stock simile *stubborn as a pig on ice*. Also attested from Ireland. Montgomery's other simile in the citation, *stupid as an owlet*, is not in this dictionary, since it is relatively widespread (see *DAPPP*, 272).
– '"Don't be unjust to Mark, Aunt Rachel. He has been very good and kind." "He's as stupid as an owlet and as stubborn as Solomon's mule," I said, for I *would* say it. "He's just a common fellow"' (Montgomery, *Further Chronicles of Avonlea*, 269–70).
Occasional. *Includes young Charlottetown female university student.*

stubborn as a calf at a new gate
Resisting change, suspicious of newness. Also attested from Alabama.
– 'You know, around the world folk language is filled with expressions which refer to animals; they're a rich

source ... "As stubborn as a calf at a new gate." I like that one [on PEI] – the kind of curiosity that cattle have for things is caught up, I think, in that saying' (Weale, 'Them Times' [radio broadcast]).
Rare.

bold as a ram / country bull in a gap
Self-assured to an obnoxious degree.
– 'Don't argue with him, he's boss' (anon.).
Rare.

You can't keep a good dog off your leg.
Proverb. You can't control someone who is that persistent; joking variant of standard *You can't keep a good man down.*
– 'Can't hold a good man back. "After working with all of these ambitious young men, I see that you can't keep a good dog off your leg"' (Gojmerac, 'Prince Edward Island Expressions').
Rare.

like shit stuck to the bottom of your shoe(s) / to the wall
Vulgar. Immoveable, inseparable.
– 'To stick fast to a substance, a person, an opinion. "They're always together – just like shit stuck to the wall"' (Gojmerac, 'Prince Edward Island Expressions').
Not in Survey II. Probably occasional.
Includes middle-age college-educated Queens male teacher, and young Charlottetown female university student.

INNOCENCE

They have straw in their hair.
They still have the cowshit on their boots.
They still have the balsam on them.
Second variant vulgar. Someone has just arrived in town from the country, and shows it; comparable to slang word *hayseed* 'a rustic,' and to popular saying *(still) wet behind the ears* (*DAS*). The balsam fir, which is common in rural Prince Edward Island, yields a sticky resin. Compare *OED*: '*to have straws in one's hair* ... to be insane, eccentric, or distracted.'
– 'Country bumpkin' (middle-aged grade-school-educated Charlottetown male taxi-driver).
– 'Still countrified' (senior Parkdale woman).
[straw, balsam:] Rare. *Includes middle-aged college-educated Queens male teacher, and young Charlottetown female university student.*
[cowshit:] Not in Survey II. Probably widespread.

still shitting yellow
Vulgar. Immature, juvenile. Also attested in Weale Collection ('Souris 1983').
– 'Still wet behind the ears' (anon.).
Not in Survey II. Probably widespread. *Includes young college-educated Charlottetown female university student.*

The only time they were off the Island was when they were up a tree.
Someone is completely untravelled, provincial, homebound. Compare UP A TREE.
– '[George] Brown [a Father of Confederation] ... was correct in his observation that there were, and still are,

those living here who have never been off the Island. One woman from Murray River, describing a mutual acquaintance, told me that "the only time he was off the Island was when he was up a tree," and I detected in her tone of voice the same insinuated reproach' (Weale, *Them Times*, 5).
Occasional except rare in Charlottetown; significantly senior. *Includes senior Summerside male airbase worker.*

happy as if they were wise
Foolishly complacent; comparable to standard proverb *Ignorance is bliss.* Compare PPS: '*Happy.* Better happy than wise.'
– 'To be as happy as if he were in his right mind' (anon.).
– 'You'd almost think he was wise' (anon.).
Occasional except rare in Charlottetown; especially male.

They wouldn't say 'barnyard' in case there was shit in it.
Vulgar. Someone is ridiculously fastidious in speech. Compare *CCW*: 'He wouldn't say shit if his mouth was full of it' (93).
Not in Survey II. Probably occasional.

See also GREEN AS GRASS AND TWICE AS SPRY.

ECCENTRICITY

queer / crazy / odd as the crows
Habitually strange or unexplainable, beyond human ken. Also attested from British Columbia and Newfoundland. Crows and jays are often said to be among the most intelligent of birds, which may account for their being regarded as out of the ordinary. Compare *SD*: 'Queer as a jaybird.'
– 'My mother says this a lot. She used to live in Miminegash but is now in Tignish' (anon.).
– 'Older people mostly use this' (young Charlottetown female university student).
– 'I hear and use this a lot' (young Stanhope female university student).
Common; especially senior, not grade-school-educated.

crazy / stupid as Tom Clarke's (old) dog
... Tom Dort's ...
... Tom Creed's ...
... Tom Dooley's ...
... Tom Duke's ...
... Tom Pepper's ...
... Tom's ...
... dog, and he died howling / barking at the moon
... dog, who would put his rear in the brook for a drink

queer as Tom Peck's bulldog
Given to unpredictable, wild behaviour. Compare *SSPB*: '*crazy as Luke's dog* – a proverbial metaphor used on Cape Sable Island. It is usually completed with "and he died barking at the moon"'; and *PPS*: '*Tom Tyler.* As crazy as Tom Tyler's old bitch.' Also in *CCW*: 'He's stunned as Tom's dog – put his arse in the water to get a drink' (197).
– 'A person would be described as "crazy as Tom Clarke's dog." Now I heard that one about the Brae. I heard in Murray Harbour, though, it was adapted: it was "as crazy as Tom Dort's dog." And in Sturgeon it was "as crazy as Tom Creed's dog." A common saying with a common origin, doubtless, but had been adapted in these three different communities, and all Tom's dogs' (Weale, 'Them Times' [radio broadcast]).

– 'Tom Dooley's dog is supposed to have sat in a snowbank barking at the moon. Naturally he got part of his anatomy frozen' (St. Georges female teacher).
Widespread in Prince, occasional elsewhere except unattested in Charlottetown. *Includes senior grade-school-educated Prince female homemaker, senior high-school-educated Summerside male farmer, and middle-aged grade-school-educated Prince man.*

crazy / busy as a cut cat
running around like a cut cat
going around worse than a cut cat
Behaving in a frantic and distracted manner. *Cut* here means either 'drunk' or 'castrated.' Also attested from central and western Canada. Lewis Poteet's *Talking Country* (51) has *lazy as a cut dog*: 'simile deriving from the loss of urge to fight or wander which results from the castration of a male dog. – Lawrence Colony [in Quebec's Eastern Townships]'
– 'There's a whole series of those [sayings about mental eccentricity] to describe a person whose mental state is being brought into question ... I'm just giving you some of them: "as crazy as a cut cat"' (Weale, 'Them Times' [radio broadcast]).
– 'Uneasy, restless' (senior grade-school-educated Miscouche female housekeeper).
– 'Irresponsible' (anon.).
Widespread in Prince, Queens, and Kings, occasional in Summerside and Charlottetown; significantly not young, especially rural, male. *Includes senior high-school-educated Lot 37 woman, senior college-educated Bunbury male civil servant, and young college-educated Charlottetown woman. Also attested from central and western Canada.*

a strange cup of tea
Any person or thing curious or odd; variant of standard *not my cup of tea*. Also attested from New Brunswick and Ireland.
Widespread in Prince and Charlottetown, occasional in Queens and Summerside, rare in Kings; especially college-educated.

not left long enough in the oven
Habitually odd in a crude, underbred way; comparable to popular catchphrase *to have a bun in the oven* 'to be pregnant' (*DSUE*).
– 'Half-baked' (West Prince).
Rare. *Includes senior college-educated Strathgartney female teacher.*

not operating on all batteries
Not behaving in a fully conventional or expected manner; variant of stock catchphrases *not running on all (four) cylinders, not running on a full tank, not playing with a full deck.* Compare NOT MUCH FEED IN THE FEED BOX.
– 'Something missing when thinking' (middle-aged college-educated Prince woman).
Occasional in Prince, Queens, and Charlottetown, rare elsewhere.

*****They're a case without a lid.**
Someone is peculiar or unusual, possibly in a pathological way; extension of common *to be a real case*.
Late entry, not surveyed. Reported by senior college-educated woman.

to **have a few pegs / slats / black keys missing**
*Also reported
a few links / sticks missing
three sticks short of a load
To be generally eccentric, though amiable and unthreatening; comparable to popular catchphrases *a screw miss-*

ing, a few marbles missing, not to have all their marbles, not to have both oars in the water. See also HAVE A FEW BALES SHORT OF A LOAD, TWELVE BISCUITS SHY OF A DOZEN. Also attested from New Brunswick. Compare *NDAS*: 'have some (or a few) buttons (or marbles) missing ... To be insane; be eccentric'; and *DAS*: 'button(s) missing, have a (few) ... "Colloq[uial]. Also common in Eng[land]."'
– 'Whenever someone was considered "dense," this saying was often used. Another saying is "The lights are on but nobody's home"' (young college-educated Queens man).
[*pegs:*] Widespread in Prince, Queens, and Charlottetown; occasional elsewhere. [*slats:*] Occasional in Kings, Summerside, and Charlottetown, rare elsewhere; significantly urban. [*keys:*] Rare. *Includes senior Summerside female teacher, and middle-aged Vernon Bridge male teacher.*

to **have more black keys than white**
To act in a backward or contrary manner, painful to the observer. The standard piano has far more white keys than black.
– 'A similar expression I've heard is "two bricks short of a load," or "not playing with a full deck"' (young university student).
Rare. *Includes three senior grade-school-educated Tignish men.*

There's no light(s) (on) upstairs / in the upper storey / attic.
Someone habitually fails to pay attention; variant of common sayings *The lights are on but nobody's home* and *something wrong in the upper storey*. See also HAVE A NICE APARTMENT BUT THERE'S NO ONE HOME, HAVE SPACE FOR RENT. Compare *NDAS*: 'upper story ... late 1700's The brain; the mind: "definite shortcomings in the upper story."'
– 'Used by parents and self. Not necessarily stupid but dizzy' (young university student).
Occasional except rare in Kings; significantly college-educated, especially senior. *Includes senior high-school-educated Charlottetown man, senior college-educated Prince woman, and middle-aged college-educated Charlottetown man.*

There's one room in the attic / upstairs not plastered / not finished.
There's the ceiling of one room not finished.
There's a loose board in the attic.
There's static in the attic.
Someone commonly behaves in a brainless but harmless way; comparable to stock catchphrases *bats in their belfry, rats in their attic*. See also THERE'S NO LIGHT UPSTAIRS, HAVE A NICE APARTMENT BUT THERE'S NO ONE HOME, HAVE SPACE FOR RENT, and HAVE A FEW PEGS MISSING.
– 'Every village has got at least one fella with one room in his attic not plastered' (Boyles, 'Living in Harmony,' 74).
– 'You might say of someone that "he has one room upstairs not plastered." And a lot of these have reference to an earlier time, because I remember as a child there were many people had parts of their upstairs that weren't finished' (Weale, 'Them Times' [radio broadcast]).
– 'Not a clear reception' (senior grade-school-educated Tignish male farmer).
[*room:*] Occasional. [*static:*] Occasional except unattested in Kings; significantly senior. [*board:*] Rare. *Includes senior high-school-educated Arlington male teacher,*

senior Parkdale woman, and middle-aged grade-school-educated Charlottetown male taxi-driver.

The hamster gets off the wheel sometimes.
Someone occasionally behaves erratically or unreasonably.

Rare. *Confirmed by four informants in Survey II, including young female university student.*

See also **Intelligence**

Intelligence

dumb as a bag / sack of (claw) hammers
dumber than ...
crazy as ...
dense as ...
stupid as ...
clumsy as ...
to have as much sense as ...
to have as much sense as a bag of nails
*Also reported
graceful as a sack of hammers
dumb as a left-handed hammer
dense as a sack of wet mice
Stupid and awkward. See also DEAF AS A HAMMER. The frequency label combines results on several of the variants. Also, in the form *crazy as a bag of nails*, attested from Newfoundland and Ontario; Curtis, *Slow Men Working in Trees* (New Brunswick), records: '*bag of hammers* What many Frederictonians compare their sanity to.' Compare also *DSUE*: '*bag of nails, a* A state of confusion: Aus[tralian]: C20'; and *SSPB*: '*stupid as a bag of hammers* – simile from near Halifax.'
– 'I think this saying and its variations are of very recent vintage, e.g. around 1980. I had never heard them before then but they became "in vogue" in our government office about then (as we criticized our superiors, ha)' (middle-aged college-educated Queens woman).
– 'Pisquid area' (young male university student).
– 'Folk language was full of these apt comparisons. Some of them were ordinary, but the ones which survived the winnowing process of repeated usage were the work of genius, requiring often a real leap of imagination. Consider, for example, ... "as clumsy as a bag of hammers"' (Weale, *Them Times*, 62).
– 'There's a whole series of those to describe a person whose mental state is being brought into question, you know: ... "As crazy as a bag of hammers"' (Weale, 'Them Times' [radio broadcast]).
Common in Charlottetown, widespread elsewhere; significantly urban, male. *Includes senior grade-school-educated Covehead male farmer, senior high-school-educated Lot 37 woman, two middle-aged grade-school-educated and high-school-educated Charlottetown men, and young female university student.*

Intelligence 41

dumb as a frog on a log
Slow-thinking, stolid; possibly related to standard *like a bump on a log*, 'idly, uselessly' (*NDAS*).
Occasional except rare in Queens and Kings. *Includes young college-educated Queens man.*

dead as a codfish
Unthinking, unresponsive; possibly a variant of customary simile *dead as a herring*, in association with *like a dead fish* for a limp handshake. Sayings of this kind usually refer to physical death: *dead as a herring / mackerel / smelt / pelcher* (as in *OED, ODEP, MBP, DARE, DSUE,* and *DAPPP*, 1820–1880).
– 'Boring' (anon.).
Rare. *Includes senior Vernon Bridge male farmer, senior high-school-educated Covehead female teacher, and young Charlottetown female university student.*

empty as last year's bird's nest
Of a mind, currently blank, lacking ideas. Compare DRY AS THE INSIDE OF A WOODPECKER'S BOARDING HOUSE. Compare also *SSPB*: 'dry as last year's robin's nest – Shelburne simile'; and *SD*: 'Dry as last year's crow's nest.'
– 'Empty head' (senior college-educated Brooklyn female farmer).
– 'Lack of intelligence' (senior college-educated Montague male artist).
Occasional except rare in Queens.

***stupid as a boiled worm**
Blindly, fixedly brainless.
*Late entry, not surveyed. *Reported by senior grade-school-educated Covehead male farmer.*

stupid / crazy as a marsh hen
Habitually flighty or deranged; possibly a variant of conventional *crazy as a March hare*. Compare *DSUE*: 'mad as a March hare'; also *SD*. Compare also *MBP*: 'mad as a wet hen.'
– 'Yes, you're plain dumb' (senior Parkdale woman).
– 'My husband heard this expression when he was going to school' (senior grade-school-educated St. Peters female homemaker).
Rare. *Includes St. Georges female teacher.*

stupid as a cat who can't climb a tree
Unexpectedly foolish.
Rare. *Confirmed by twelve informants in two surveys.*

stupid / silly / crazy as a billy goat
*Also reported
stupid as a hedgehog
Unreasonable or unteachable.
– 'As stupid as can be' (senior college-educated Charlottetown male editor).
Widespread or occasional except rare in Summerside; significantly senior, especially rural. *Includes two senior grade-school-educated female homemakers of Summerside and St. Peters.*

to **not have the brains God gave a goat**
*Also reported
... the brains God gave a louse
... the brains God gave little apples
Congenitally weak-brained; variant of proverbial phrase *You don't have / You ain't got the brains God gave a goose* (*DCP*). Compare *TTEM*: 'Hasn't the brain God gave a cinnamon bun (Calif[ornia]).'
– 'Stupid, absent-minded' (university student).
Occasional; significantly senior; especially not college-educated. *Includes senior college-educated Charlottetown woman, and young high-school-educated Queens man.*

sharp as a bowling ball / as a marble / as a ball bearing
*Also reported
stupid / stunned as a doorknob
Ironic. Thick from ear to ear, possessing no brains at all; reversal of common *sharp as a tack*. The frequency label combines informant reactions to the three versions surveyed independently.
– 'Not sharp at all' (senior college-educated Montague male artist).
– 'Used by parents and self' (young university student).
– 'This saying is similar to "a few pegs missing"' (young college-educated Queens man).
Widespread in Charlottetown, occasional or rare elsewhere; especially urban. *Includes senior Stanhope man, and middle-aged college-educated Queens woman.*

bright as a two-watt (light) bulb
Ironic. Thoughtless, inattentive, dull.
– 'Said when you are talking about someone who is stupid or does a stupid thing' (young Kensington female university student).
– 'Real dull and real dumb' (senior college-educated Charlottetown male editor).
Common or widespread except occasional in Queens; significantly urban, especially middle-aged, high-school-educated. *Includes senior high-school-educated Covehead female teacher, and senior high-school-educated Summerside female seamstress.*

to **have a head like a (thumb)tack**
To act foolishly at all times; comparable to established slang word *pinhead* (*OED*: 'a person of little intelligence, a fool). Compare *ODEP*: 'You have a Head and so has a pin (nail),' 1709–1823. *Rare. Confirmed by fourteen informants in two surveys.*

a good head for bouncing bricks off
An extraordinarily obtuse, thick-headed person. See also next entry.
– 'Refers to a stupid person' (middle-aged college-educated Bunbury male teacher).
Occasional except unattested in Kings; significantly urban, especially not grade-school-educated.

a good head if you like cabbage
A foolish and ridiculous person; response to *He/she is a good head*, playing on popular slang *cabbagehead* 'a stupid person' (see *NDASCE*). See also previous entry. Also attested from Newfoundland, along with *a good head if you like turnips* and *A good egg if you like them scrambled*. Compare *PPS*: 'Head ... Two heads are better than one, even if one is a cabbage head.'
– 'Solid' (senior grade-school-educated St. Peters female homemaker).
– 'Not a nice person' (young Charlottetown female university student).
Widespread in Prince and Summerside, occasional elsewhere; especially rural, male; especially not young, grade-school-educated. *Includes senior grade-school-educated Summerside female homemaker.*

to **have a brain made of Swiss cheese / of sawdust**
To be absent-minded; comparable to more common simile *brain like a sieve*. [*cheese*:] Widespread in Charlottetown, occasional in Summerside, rare elsewhere; significantly urban. [*sawdust*:] Rare. *Includes middle-aged college-educated Charlottetown female social worker, and young female university student.*

Intelligence 43

to **have a few bales / bags / nuts short of a load**
... a few cents short of a dollar
... a few cookies short of a dozen
... two biscuits short of a dozen
... seven pickles short of a full jar
*Also reported
a few apples short of a picnic
one ant short of a picnic
Their driveway doesn't quite meet the road.
To be a slow thinker; minor variants of typical catchphrases *one brick / a few bricks / three bricks short of a load / of a wall, a few cards short of a deck / pickles short of a barrel, two / three / a few sandwiches short of a picnic, half a bubble off plumb, not running on a full tank, The elevator doesn't go all the way to the top.* See also HAVE A FEW PEGS MISSING. Note also 'He's three short a dozen. A bit stupid' in Curtis, *Slow Men Working in Trees,* and 'He's a few ounces short of a pound' in Halpert, *Folklore Sampler from the Maritimes,* 137. Compare *DSUE*: 'shillings in the pound; e.g. *eighteen* or, say, *twelve and six,* to indicate slight mental dullness or mild insanity; "He's only twelve and six in the pound": NZ: from ca. 1925.'
– 'Slow to catch the meaning of a phrase or thought, or just simply slow' (young Hunter River female university student).
– 'Some brains short' (senior college-educated Charlottetown male editor).
– 'Heard this [*cents*] from lots of people, all ages (young university student).
– 'This [*nuts*] is used by most of the people I know' (young university student).
Common or widespread, except *cents, nuts* occasional in Queens and Kings, and significantly urban; *seven pickles* generally rare. *Includes variously senior grade-school-educated Miscouche female housekeeper, senior grade-school-educated St. Peters female homemaker, senior Borden male ferry-worker, middle-aged college-educated Summerside male lawyer, and young Cornwall male university student.*

twelve biscuits / eggs shy of a dozen
twelve inches shy of a foot
Totally and hopelessly imbecilic; extensions of typical catchphrase *a brick / a few bricks / three bricks short of / shy of a (full) load / of a wall,* and others in previous entry. See also HAVE A FEW PEGS MISSING.
Occasional; especially senior. Includes two senior Charlottetown men, high-school-educated and college-educated.

not much feed in the feed box
*Also reported
not many eggs in the basket
Not many brains. Compare NOT OPERATING ON ALL BATTERIES.
Rare. Includes senior grade-school-educated Northam male farmer, and young university student.

not a hundred
Short for not one hundred percent. 1. Mildly stupid. 2. Slightly ill; variant of established *not batting a thousand.*
– 'The lights are on but nobody's home' (anon.).
Occasional; especially urban. Includes senior college-educated Queens woman.

to **have a nice apartment but there's no one home**
to **have a lovely staircase but no upstairs**
*Also reported
The upstairs apartment is vacant.
To have the kind of good looks that hide a vacant mind. See also THERE'S NO LIGHT UPSTAIRS. Poteet's *Talking*

Country: Eastern Townships, 75, records *'upstairs* – in "he's got no upstairs," a way of saying that someone is mentally deficient or slow. In more general use is the more cumbersome "he's got nothing upstairs." – Sawyerville [Quebec].'
Rare. *Includes senior high-school-educated Summerside male farmer, senior high-school-educated Parkdale female nurse, and senior Stanhope man.*

to have space for rent
to have a vacancy in one's forehead
*Also reported
rooms to let in the upper storey
To be absent-minded or feeble-minded; see also THERE'S NO LIGHT UPSTAIRS and THERE'S ONE ROOM IN THE ATTIC NOT PLASTERED. Halpert's *Folklore Sampler from the Maritimes*, 137, records 'Nobody Home. Rooms to let,' attributed to Amherst, Nova Scotia. Compare *TTEM*: '*He has apartments to let* Is feeble-minded (because he has vacancies upstairs).'
– 'Gaps in thinking' (middle-aged college-educated Prince woman).
[*space*:] Occasional except rare in Prince and Kings; especially young, urban.
[*vacancy*:] Rare.

so stupid they'd miss the floor if they fell out of bed
Inept, always doing the wrong thing.
Rare. *Includes young male university student.*

stupid as pissing the bed awake
Vulgar. Unable to see the obvious.
– 'In this present age of surface descriptions and literal, one-dimensional conversation, these sayings [apt comparisons], and hundreds of others like them, are reminders of the evocative oral commerce of that disappeared folk culture. They recall a time when metaphor was the key to wisdom, and imagination more important than mere information. And anyone who can't see that is "as stupid as pissin' the bed awake"' (Weale, *Them Times*, 62).
Not in Survey II. Probably occasional.

There must be two of them because one couldn't be that stupid.
They must have had a twin because one person couldn't be that stupid.
Someone is so weak-minded as to appear to have only half a brain.
Occasional; especially middle-aged.
Includes senior grade-school-educated New Haven male farmer.

They've got two clues – one's lost and the other's looking for it.
If they had two clues, they'd be out looking for one another.
If they had two clues, they'd make a click.
There's two clicks in a clue, and they haven't even got a click.
Responses to proverbial assertions *They haven't got a clue* and *They haven't got two clues to rub together*. Someone is even stupider than you think. Halpert's *Folklore Sampler from the Maritimes*, 120, attests the first variant from Wolfville, Nova Scotia. *NDAS*: '*click* ... An insight, esp a sudden one; flash of comprehension.' See also IF BRAINS WERE RUBBER ...
– 'Not very intelligent' (middle-aged college-educated Prince woman).
– 'From Mount Stewart area' (young male university student).
Occasional, except *click* variants rare.
Includes middle-aged college-educated Summerside woman.

Intelligence

If clues were shoes, they'd be barefoot.
Someone understands nothing; parallel to standard proverbial assertion, *They haven't got a clue*. Halpert's *Folklore Sampler from the Maritimes*, 120, attests this saying from Wolfville, Nova Scotia.
– 'One of Grandma's favourites – I hear it all the time' (young university student).
Widespread in Summerside and Charlottetown, occasional in Queens and Kings, rare in Prince. *Includes senior high-school-educated Arlington male teacher, and middle-aged grade-school-educated Charlottetown woman.*

to not have an inkling and that's only a tenth of a clue
Someone understands nothing; extension of standard proverbial assertion, *They haven't got a clue*. *Inkling*, 'vague idea,' is a play on words, as if the second syllable, *-ling*, were the suffix meaning 'little' or 'petty' (as in *duckling*, *princeling*); the true origin of *inkling* is not clear (*OED*).
– 'Used very often during the elementary grade' (young Queens man).
Occasional except rare in Queens and Kings. *Includes senior Prince woman.*

If brains were rubber, they wouldn't have enough to stretch around the hair on a flea's leg.
If it rained brains, they wouldn't even get wet.
If brains were water, they would die of thirst.
If they had a brain / had a clue, it would be lonesome.
If they had a brain it would rattle.
If they had two brains they would rattle.
Someone is ridiculously and totally simple-minded. Related to more common proverbial exaggerations like *less brains than God gave a goose*, *Where were you when God passed out brains?*, *If brains were dynamite, they couldn't blow off their hat / blow their nose*, and *If they had a brain / had a clue, they'd be dangerous* (*DCP*). *CCW* quotes an informant of North Rustico, PEI: 'If brains were leather, you wouldn't have enough to make spats for a louse' (196), which was received too late for larger treatment in the present dictionary. See also THEY'VE GOT TWO CLUES – ONE'S LOST AND THE OTHER'S LOOKING FOR IT. *Rattle* is especially rural, *bird* especially urban.
'He's a bird-brain' (anon.).
[*lonesome*:] Common except widespread in Charlottetown. [*rattle*:] Widespread or occasional. [*bird*:] Occasional or rare. [*rubber, rained*:] Rare. *Includes, variously, senior grade-school-educated St. Peters female homemaker, senior Borden male ferry-worker, senior Summerside male airbase worker, senior Kinkora female nurse, senior Parkdale woman, young Donagh male university student, and young Montague female university student.*

They know as much about [something] as my arsehole (knows about soap-blowing / knows about snipe shooting).
Vulgar. Someone is totally ignorant of the subject at hand.
Not in Survey II. Probably occasional.

They couldn't box strawberries / apples.
*Also reported
They couldn't even skin an eel / a rabbit.
1. Someone is incapable of performing even the simplest task. 2. Someone would make a very bad boxer.

Compare *DCP*: *'couldn't knock the skin off a rice pudding* ... [compare] the contempt for a poor boxer in the punning Brit. disparagement *box? Him, box? He couldn't box bloody kippers!'*
– 'He couldn't fight his way up Fitzroy Street [in Charlottetown] on a windy day' (young university student).

– 'An old fashioned saying often with some other object [instead of strawberries, as in questionnaire]' (anon.) Rare. *Includes young Charlottetown female university student.*

See also **Eccentricity**

Certainty

ASSURANCE

That's a God's fact.
Potentially offensive. That's for certain; parallel to traditional *God's truth*. *That's a God's honest fact* has been attested from Newfoundland.
– 'When stressing a statement' (middle-aged West Prince male journalist).
– 'To make sure of your speech' (middle-aged Stanhope man).
– 'The truth – always used' (senior college-educated Canoe Cove teacher).
Common or widespread. *Includes middle-aged college-educated Charlottetown librarian, and young Charlottetown female university student.*

I'd bet a sweet cent.
I'm certain. Extension of standard verb *to bet,* 'to declare.' Also attested from Ontario.
– 'Expression from Mt. Stewart area, as in "I bet a sweet cent he's not going to come"' (middle-aged college-educated Charlottetown librarian).
Rare.

You can bank a fire.
You can count on it. Probably a combination of standard informal verb *to bank on,* 'to rely on,' and phrase *to bank (up) a fire,* 'to cover a fire in order to have coals later.' Also attested from Ireland.
– 'Sometimes when you are at sea it is right calm. Then you feel little cold drafts – getting cooler all the time. You can bank a fire that there is a big Nor'wester on its way' (Walsh, 'Trapsmashers,' 3).
Rare. *Includes young Charlottetown female university student.*

*That'll put different water on the beans.
That changes my mind for me. (In the context given by the informant, a customer in a store reacted to being told of an unexpected tax on the purchase of a birthday card.)
*Late entry, not surveyed. *Reported by senior Charlottetown female clerk.*

The smoke goes up the chimney just the same.
Proverb. Whatever else happens, fundamental things will continue in the way they always do; parallel to common *The sun will still shine, It will be*

48 Assurance

there after you. Compare *ODEP*: 'Many Chimneys, little smoke 1583–1616.' Widespread in Prince and Summerside, occasional elsewhere; significantly senior, especially not college-educated. *Includes senior grade-school-educated New Haven male farmer.*

There's a difference between scratching your arse and tearing it (all to pieces / all to hell with a wire brush)
Vulgar proverb. Exercise caution in all things.
– 'My father says that when someone is building a great big pig barn or something, and getting in over their head' (anon.).
– 'I've heard mostly "and tearing it all to pieces" – in Prince County and sometimes PEI generally' (anon.).
Includes young Charlottetown female university student. Not in Survey II. Probably widespread.

You only get one shot at a shell-bird / shell-duck.
Proverb. You can fool a shrewd person only once; comparable to standard *Opportunity knocks but once.* Cited in *DAP* from this evidence in manuscript form. Also known in Newfoundland, according to English, 'Historic Newfoundland,' 38, and Porter, 'Some Newfoundland Phrases,' 297. Compare *DNE*: 'shell-bird ... Merganser [a fish-eating, diving duck], esp lesser red-breasted merganser; shell-duck.'
– 'As a teenager, we would say this as a play term' (young college-educated Queens man).
Rare. *Includes senior grade-school-educated Prince woman.*

I wouldn't take a farm to do that.
I wouldn't do that under any circumstances, not even for a bribe; variant of common *I wouldn't do that for any money.*
– 'This usually means in our community you couldn't make me do that at any price' (anon.).
– 'Also a dare' (anon.).
Occasional; significantly senior and unattested by young; especially female, high-school and college-educated.

The bottom has fallen out of the basket / bucket.
Disaster has struck; extension of standard *The bottom falls (or drops) out of,* 'There is a collapse of' (*OED*, 1637–1957). Compare *MBP*: [quoting John Heywood, *A dialogue conteining the number in effect of all the proverbes in the Englishe tongue,* 1546] 'He brought the bottome of the bag cleane out.'
– 'Probably from the basket used for harvesting potatoes' (senior high-school-educated Charlottetown businessman).
Widespread in Prince, Summerside, and Charlottetown, occasional elsewhere; especially urban, male, not middle-aged. *Includes young Charlottetown female university student.*

not charming likely
Ironic. Not likely at all; impossible; probably a euphemism for common *not bloody likely.*
– 'No way!' (young Tignish female university student).
– 'Are you kidding?' (senior Summerside female teacher).
– 'Meaning the answer is definitely no' (middle-aged college-educated Tyne Valley woman).
Common in Prince and Summerside, occasional in Queens, rare in Charlotte-

town, unattested in Kings. *Includes senior grade-school-educated St. Peters female homemaker.*

They wouldn't be [some adjective], now would they?
Ironic. Someone is very much [the quality of the chosen adjective (for example *rich*, *pretty*, *greedy*)]. A Newfoundland variation is *I know they're not ...*
– 'This ironic construction is very frequent, among the youths at least, of Georgetown' (young college-educated Murray Harbour librarian).
– 'This is very popular in Tignish. It isn't really something we would say all the time, but instead of *rich* [the given adjective on the questionnaire] we would replace it with many other words depending on the situation' (anon.).
– 'Means he or she is [some adjective] – Georgetown' (Weale collection).
Rare. *Includes middle-aged college-educated Waterside woman, and young Charlottetown female university student.*

It wasn't the neighbours that needed it.
Ironic. At last, something clearly necessary has been done.
– 'This is exactly what I said when my mother finally broke down and got her new glasses, which she badly needed' (middle-aged college-educated St. Peters female social worker).
Occasional.

*I never saw the sky over them before.
That person is totally unknown to me.
Late entry, not surveyed. Reported by senior high-school-educated Charlottetown woman.

Be near nothing.
Usually ironic. 1. It's fine; I think highly of it. 2. It's useless, not worth my time. Compare DPEIE: 'Tongue-in-cheek words like *chocolates*, *fudge*, and *weak* ... are used in the western end of the province, especially around Tignish, to mean roughly the opposite of what they seem to mean. The practice extends to words not in this dictionary ..., like *handsome*, *hateful*, *intelligent*, *like* (verb), *sad*, *stupid*, and *ugly*' (174). Compare also GET SALVE.
– '"Do you like ice cream?" "Be near nothing"' (anon.).
– 'A lot of people from Tignish say this ... We just say "Be near nothing." It's very popular, especially amongst the teenagers. It doesn't always mean what you have [i.e., the meaning on the given questionnaire: "actually the opposite: to be worth something"]. There are a lot of ways to use it. An example is: "Be near nothing going there." Which means I'm not going there' (anon.).
Rare.

See also A CHEV'S A CHEV AND A FORD'S A FORD, I'D CHASE A CROW A MILE FOR [SOMETHING]

FUTILITY

You might as well expect the tide to wait while you paint the sand.
Proverb. You have set yourself a task that is doubly impossible; probably a variant of standard *Time and tide wait for no man.*
Rare. *Includes senior grade-school-educated New Haven male farmer, and middle-aged college-educated male teacher.*

You might as well try to keep the tide out with a pitchfork.
You might as well try to bail the river with a pitchfork.
Proverb. You have set yourself an impossible task.
— 'Useless' (senior college-educated Charlottetown male editor).
Rare. *Includes senior grade-school-educated Prince woman.*

You might as well try to keep Niagara Falls back with a fork / teaspoon.
You might as well try to climb Mount Everest.
Proverb. That is an utterly hopeless proposition.
Occasional except rare in Queens and Kings; significantly senior, especially urban. The variants were surveyed separately; the frequency label above combines their results. *Includes senior Summerside female teacher, and middle-aged female university student.*

You might as well spit on a fire in a barn full of straw.
Proverb. It is hopeless to try and stop some disaster in progress.
Rare. *Includes young male university student.*

*You might as well try to climb to the top of the barn.
Proverb. That's one of the most ridiculous ideas I've ever heard.
*Late entry, not surveyed. Reported by senior grade-school-educated Prince woman.

I wish I was born richer and not so good-looking.
Joking. I could have made something of myself if only I hadn't been given so many disabilities.
Widespread in Summerside, occasional elsewhere; significantly grade-school-educated.

*There's nowhere that'll go in a day.
That car has totally broken down.
*Late entry, not surveyed. Reported by middle-aged college-educated Victoria man.

See also YOU MIGHT AS WELL TAKE WATER FROM THE PUMP, LIKE FROSTING ON A BURNT CAKE.

WORTH

not worth the mustard / salt on a ham sandwich
not worth the butter on a biscuit / on their bread
not worth the knife they butter their bread with
Of a person, utterly worthless; compare *salt for one's porridge*, a traditional expression of insignificance (*BD*).
— '[A context would be] two fellows fighting, one telling the other fellow, "You're not worth ..."' (middle-aged grade-school-educated Charlottetown male taxi-driver).
[*sandwich*:] Occasional except rare in Charlottetown, unattested in Kings; significantly senior. [other variants:] Rare. *Includes senior grade-school-educated New Haven male farmer, senior grade-school-educated Tignish male businessperson, middle-aged high-school-educated Miminegash female homemaker, and young university student.*

not worth a patch for your pants
not worth a patch on a good man's arse
Of a problem, insignificant, not worth worrying about.
— 'Men who aren't worth marrying' (senior high-school-educated Covehead female teacher).
Rare.

not worth the sweat off a dead man's arse / balls
Vulgar. Of a person or thing, worthless, not worth paying for.
– 'Referring to the money paid for something' (anon.).
Not in Surveys I or II; no frequency label possible.

useless as a bucket under a bull
Of actions, totally useless.
Occasional except rare in Summerside and unattested in Kings; especially not college-educated. *Includes senior grade-school-educated Summerside female homemaker, senior college-educated Charlottetown male editor, and middle-aged high-school-educated Miminegash female homemaker.*

useless as a screen door on a submarine
useless as a whipstand on an automobile
*Also reported
useful as a snowball in the Bay of Fundy
Of objects, useless to the point of being a hindrance. Compare *ASD*: 'useful as flywire door on a submarine.'
– 'A useless tool' (middle-aged high-school-educated St. Eleanors female nurse).
– 'I heard this [*whipstand*] from a middle-aged woman who said her mother used it all the time' (middle-aged high-school-educated Queens male insurance adjuster).
– 'This [*screen door*] is very recent' (senior high-school-educated Covehead female teacher).
[*submarine*:] Widespread in Summerside, occasional in Prince, rare in Queens and Kings, and unattested in Charlottetown.
[*automobile*:] Rare. *Includes senior Stanhope man, and young Stanhope female university student.*

useless as a deuce in a jackpot
Of persons, unhelpful, not pulling one's weight.
– 'Lazy; wouldn't know what work was' (university student).
– 'Not much good' (senior grade-school-educated St. Peters female homemaker).
Rare.

*****useful as a second pocket on a Sunday shirt**
Ironic. Not useful at all; quite superfluous.
Late entry, not surveyed. Reported by middle-aged grade-school-educated Queens woman.

They need [something] as badly as a toad needs a tail
Someone would be hindered by what he or she most wants; variant of more common *need [something] as a toad needs side pockets*. For other variants see *MBP* and previous entry.
Rare. *Includes senior Borden male ferry-worker.*

They need [something] as badly as they need a second nose.
They need [something] as badly as a goat needs a beard.
Ironic. Someone already has quite enough of what he or she desires; variant of more common *need [something] as badly as a cat needs two tails, need [something] like a / another hole in the head*. '"Need as" similes with opposite meanings lend themselves to endless variations' (*SD*). Haber's 'Canine Terms,' 85, cites 'As little use for a thing as a dog has for two tails.' For other variants, see next entry. Compare *DCP*: 'I need that like a cow does two tails'; and *SD*: 'The exact wording of this [*dog needs two tails*], as

with anything handed down through common usage, varies with each user; for example, a popular variation of the same theme is "He don't need it any more than a dog needs two tails."'
– 'Used by parents and self. Don't need object' (university student).
[*nose:*] Occasional except unattested in Kings. [*beard:*] Rare. *Includes [nose] middle-aged college-educated Prince woman, young college-educated Queens woman, and male university student; [beard] senior grade-school-educated Miscouche female housekeeper.*

*more [something] than Carter has liver pills
More (something, for example *gall* or *money*) than anyone should have. 'Carter's Little Pills' is the trade name of a laxative produced by Carter-Wallace, Inc., New York City. Note also *NDFRRS*: '"more something than Carter had oats" a very great deal of the thing named [examples are "money" and "postcards"].'
**Late entry, not surveyed. Reported by two middle-aged high-school-educated women of Prince and Queens.*

You might as well take water from the pump / the tap.
You might as well take a drink of water.
You might as well go to the liquor store.
Your proposed solution to the problem is no solution at all.
– 'Reference to medicine that did no good' (Weale collection, Souris 1983 [middle-aged college-educated woman]).
Occasional.

to **not amount to a row of postholes**
Not to add up to anything substantial; variant of stock catchphrase *not amount to a row / hill of beans*. Compare *NDAS*: '*a load of VW radiators (or postholes or wind)* ... An empty truck; no cargo whatever.'
Occasional; significantly senior, especially college-educated, rural. *Includes young Charlottetown female university student.*

useless as a piss-hole / pee-hole in the snow / in a snowbank / in last year's snowbank
*Also reported
... in a blanket
Vulgar. Serving no purpose whatever; parallel to common saying *eyes like two piss-holes in the snow*, 'sunken, yellow eyes' (*DSUE*).
– '"Piss-hole" is much more common [than other variants]' (middle-aged college-educated Queens male teacher).
Not in Survey II. Probably widespread. *Includes senior college-educated Canoe Cove male teacher, middle-aged college-educated Georgetown woman, and young Charlottetown female university student.*

*I'd rather watch paint dry.
The activity you propose is totally boring.
**Late entry, not surveyed. Reported by Vernon River man.*

See also BE NEAR NOTHING.

UNCERTAINTY

to **have pitches and sloughs ahead**
Also spelled *slews, sloos, slues*. To be facing an uncertain future; parallel to common catchphrase *to have its ups and downs*. In *DPEIE pitches* and

Uncertainty

sloughs are defined as hollows in snow-covered roads that cause vehicles, such as a horse-drawn sleigh, to lurch forwards and sideways respectively. This catchphrase was formerly used literally, as in Bagnall's 'When I Was Very Young,' 1: 'They [drivers of sleighs] had to contend with "pitches" and "slews" and gullies of slush which delighted the children but which must have been nigh to unbearable to both adults and horses.'
– 'There are many pitches and sloughs before you – heard at a wedding speech' (young college-educated Kings woman).
Rare. *Includes young Charlottetown female university student.*

when cows vote / sing
Probably never; variant of conventional *when pigs fly*.
Rare. *Includes middle-aged high-school-educated Charlottetown man.*

when I thrash the turnips
Probably never, since turnips are not 'thrashed.'
– 'I'll pay you when I thrash the turnips' (high-school-educated woman).
Rare. *Includes university student.*

You have to plant or cut sets.
Proverb. There's no time to waste and you have to choose, so make a decision; parallel to more common *Fish or cut bait.* A *(potato) set* is a small potato tuber, or a portion of one, used for planting.
– 'You have to do one thing or another to live – reference to potato farming' (senior college-educated male teacher).
Occasional except rare in Charlottetown; especially senior.

not know whether to shit or wind one's watch
Vulgar. Indecisive; variation of the more common *not know whether to shit or go blind* and *Shit or get off the pot.*
– 'Souris' (anon.).
Not in Survey II. Probably widespread.
Includes young Charlottetown female university student.

You can't sweep the floor and wipe your ass at the same time.
Vulgar proverb. You can't do two things at once; parallel to the popular put down *[Someone] can't chew gum and walk at the same time*, which describes someone inept rather than an attempt to do two things at once. Compare I CAN'T DANCE AND HOLD THE BABY TOO.
Not in Survey II. Probably occasional.

if nothing splits / cracks worse than a shingle
If nothing goes wrong, God willing; a catchphrase that makes any accompanying promise very tentative, since wooden shingles are, by definition, split.
– 'Wilmot Valley, 1983' (Weale collection).
Rare. *Includes middle-aged Vernon Bridge male teacher.*

If you can't get a board, take a slab (and if you can't get a slab, take an old tin can).
Proverb. Be satisfied with what is possible; parallel to standard *Half a loaf is better than none.* One informant suggested that train conductors on Prince Edward Island would use this saying whimsically: 'All aboard! And if you cannot get a board, take a slab' (anon.).
– 'If you cannot get what you really

want, you should settle for something less – Morell (1983)' (Weale collection).
Widespread in Kings, occasional elsewhere; significantly senior, especially male.

If you see a new moon through glass, it is trouble while it lasts.
Proverb. Bad luck is coming. Compare HANG A POWDER HORN ON THE TIP OF THE MOON and THE MOON IS HOLDING WATER. Also attested from Ireland.
– 'After decades of scientific teaching in our schools and universities, many of us remain inveterately, enduringly, incurably superstitious ... Nor do I believe that it's bad luck to place three lighted lamps on a table, to look at the new moon for the first time through glass, or to count the number of buggies or sleighs in a funeral procession' (Weale, *Them Times*, 34–5.
– 'Souris (1983)' (Weale collection).
Rare.

See also I CAN'T DANCE AND HOLD THE BABY TOO.

Foolishness and Mistakes

to **talk when they should have listened**
to **jig when they should have jagged**
to **bob when they should have weaved**
Ironic. Of persons, to have a minor injury, such as a bruised forehead, that was probably caused by a foolish action like walking into a door; variant of more general slang *zig when they should have zagged*. The possibility of a merely literal interpretation by informants in Survey II may lie behind the odd distribution suggested by the frequency label for *talk*. The frequency label is also less credible for the *bob* variant, thanks to its literal application in boxing.
– 'Someone who took a beating' (young male university student).
– 'Say to someone who looks like they've been hurt' (senior Summerside female teacher).
– 'Made a mistake – chose the wrong thing' (anon.).
– 'Used by my family members when together on holidays' (young female university student).
– 'This [*bob*] is boxing lingo and I have heard it applied to other situations' (middle-aged Queens woman).
[*talk*:] Common in Kings and Summerside, widespread in Prince and Charlottetown, occasional in Queens; especially urban. [*jig, bob*:] Widespread in Summerside and Charlottetown, occasional elsewhere; significantly urban; [*bob*:] especially male, not grade-school-educated.

to **not know if they're pitching or catching**
To be confused, mixed up; comparable to popular catchphrase *not know if they are coming or going*.
– 'Recent' (senior high-school-educated Covehead female teacher).
Occasional in Queens, Kings, and Summerside, rare in Prince, unattested in Charlottetown. Also attested from Saskatchewan.

so foolish it would trip a goat
Of an action or idea, ineffectual.
– 'Tignish' (anon.).
– 'You know, around the world folk language is filled with expressions which refer to animals; they're a rich source ... [Like] this one: "so foolish it would trip a goat." I mean, some of these I have no idea – you know there's genius in them but you're not quite sure why' (Weale, 'Them Times' [radio broadcast]).
Rare.

foolish as a rooster with a sock on its head
Of persons, behaving in an absurd, embarrassing manner. See also CROOKED AS A ROOSTER.
Rare. *Confirmed by nineteen informants in two surveys.*

to make as much sense as a three-legged frog / a sucking turkey
*Also reported
... as much sense as a dead cow
To suggest an idea that is utterly unworkable.
Rare. *Includes North Lake man, and young male university student.*

as much as a bargain
As much as a person can achieve, a near thing.
– '"I haven't been turned out," grinned Mary, as she stepped in and shut her door. "I came up to Carter Flagg's two days ago and I've been stormstayed there ever since. But old Abbie Flagg got on my nerves at last, and tonight I just made up my mind to come up here. I thought I could wade this far but I can tell you it was as much as a bargain. Once I thought I was stuck for keeps. Ain't it an awful night?"' (Montgomery, *Rilla of Ingleside*, 207).
Widespread in Prince, occasional elsewhere except rare in Queens; especially not middle-aged.

*****Cut your fingernails on Sunday and the Devil will be after you all week.**
Once you break one rule, it is easy to break others, so do not yield to temptation. Compare DON'T BUY ANYTHING ON MONDAY OR YOU'LL BE SPENDING ALL WEEK.
– 'Years ago, before secularization and psychoanalysis, the Devil was no mere abstraction. He was a real presence in the midst of life, as real and omnipresent as God himself, and if God was to be praised, it was no less your duty to spurn the Devil. If you gave him an entrance, any small opening of idleness or spiritual inattentiveness, any tiny crack of willed misbehaviour, he would be sure to slip in and triumphantly claim your soul. "The Devil finds work for idle hands," was one way of expressing the danger. "Cut your fingernails on Sunday and the Devil will be after you all week" was another' (Weale, *Them Times*, 36).
*Not surveyed.

See also YOU ONLY GET ONE SHOT AT A SHELL-BIRD, ALL OVER THE POND

Mood

HAPPINESS

If I was any better I'd be bigger / twins / dangerous.
If I was any better I couldn't stand it.
If I was any happier there would be two of me.
*Also reported
If I was any happier I wouldn't be working.
If I was any better I'd be sick.
I'm so delighted that I can scarcely contain myself.
– 'To be as happy as one can be' (senior college-educated Charlottetown male editor).
– 'I usually hear [*couldn't stand it*] from Islanders aged 20–40 who are having fun doing something' (university student).
Occasional; significantly senior, male. *Includes senior grade-school-educated St. Peters female homemaker, senior college-educated Strathgartney female teacher, and middle-aged grade-school-educated Charlottetown male taxi-driver.*

happy as a dead duck
happy as two dead ducks
Very happy. No irony is intended, apparently.
– 'Referring [*ducks*] to me and my husband being happy' (anon.).
Common in Kings, widespread elsewhere except occasional in Charlottetown; significantly not young, especially rural. *Includes senior grade-school-educated New Haven male farmer, and young Charlottetown female university student.*

lucky as a pet crow
Especially lucky.
Occasional except rare in Queens and unattested in Charlottetown. *Includes middle-aged college-educated Summerside male lawyer.*

to **dance around like a fish in a bucket**
To twirl around for sheer joy.
– '"When the [telegraph] cable was laid [across the Northumberland Strait], Gisborne [the engineer] was sure mighty glad. He danced around like a fish in a bucket." Danced like a fish in a bucket! He talked on reminiscently but I heard no more. My mind had settled on the fish in the bucket and refused to budge' (Champion, *Over on the Island*, 13).
Occasional in Prince and Charlottetown, rare in Queens and Summerside, unattested in Kings.

Hoot and holler and wave your donut!
Go ahead, celebrate: you deserve it! Also attested from Fredericton, New Brunswick.
– 'I've heard this when someone had just won something' (young college-educated Queens man).
Rare.

to be up in high C
To be very excited. The catchphrase *up to high doh* 'greatly excited,' is known both in Ireland (personal correspondence) and in Scotland (as listed in Aitken, 'Extinction of Scotland,' 106).
– 'My own dear friend I am very glad to be once more able to say I got a letter from you and of course it was very welcome indeed as all your letters are. It came Saturday night along with seven others – eight in all so you may guess I was up in high C about it' (Montgomery, *Letters to Penzie MacNeill*, 54).
Rare.

to cut a notch in the beam
To take special note of some memorable experience. Also attested from Newfoundland. Compare *DNE*: '*notch the beam*: to express surprise or amazement about something.'
– 'Cut a notch in the beam if you did something that was smart, for to always remember' (senior grade-school-educated Prince woman).
Rare. *Includes middle-aged college-educated Prince woman.*

See also HAPPY AS IF THEY WERE WISE, KING OF THE TROUGH.

MISERY

a long streak of misery
A person with many worries. Compare *DPEIE*: '*misery* ... often plural in phrase "to have the miseries."' In widespread dialect use. Also attested from Ireland.
Common in Kings and Charlottetown, widespread elsewhere; significantly not young, especially college-educated, female. *Includes young St. Louis male university student.*

a face as long as the Western Road
An absurdly solemn or woebegone expression. See also STRAIGHT AS A SLEIGH TRACK ON THE WESTERN ROAD. The 'Western Road' of Prince Edward Island (Highway 2 from Summerside to Tignish) has sections that are extremely long and straight by Island norms.
Occasional except rare in Queens and Charlottetown; significantly senior, high-school-educated. *Includes senior high-school-educated Summerside male farmer.*

to have their mouth turned upside down
To show a face of gloom or melancholy; probably related to conventional catchphrase *down in the mouth*. Rare. *Confirmed by seven informants in two surveys, including young university student.*

See also A FACE LIKE SOMEONE WHO WON THE 100 YARD DASH IN A 90 YARD GYM.

ANXIETY

nervous as a long-haired cat beside an open hearth
Very apprehensive of imminent disaster; variant of conventional *nervous as*

a (long-tailed) cat in a room full of rocking chairs (as in *CCW*, 197). See also BUSIER THAN A COW CALVING, BUSIER THAN A CAT IN A ROUND ROOM TRYING TO FIND A CORNER TO DO HIS BUSINESS. Rare. *Includes senior grade-school-educated Tignish male fisherman.*

*nervous as a hemophiliac in a razor-blade factory
Very nervous in front of an audience.
*Late entry, not surveyed. Reported by young Charlottetown university student.

sitting like a cat in a sandbox
Adopting a tense, constrained posture, like that of a cat using a litterbox. See also BUSIER THAN A COW CALVING, BUSIER THAN A CAT IN A ROUND ROOM TRYING TO FIND A CORNER TO DO HIS BUSINESS.
– 'An uncle from Stanhope uses this a lot. He uses it also for someone who looks like they are sitting around doing nothing' (university student).
Rare. *Includes senior Coleman woman.*

to be worked up like a dog's dinner
To be agitated and confused; probably a play on *dog's breakfast*, 'some outcome that is mixed up or lacking in organization.' Compare *DSUE*: '*dog's breakfast*. A mess: low Glasgow.'
– 'Excited' (young Charlottetown female university student).
Rare. *Includes middle-aged Charlottetown female homemaker.*

You could have bought me for two cents (half spent).
Boy, was I embarrassed. Compare *SDCP*: '*two cents' worth* one's opinion or advice, for what it's worth, especially in *to put in one's two cents' worth*. The phrase is also loosely applied to any idle remark or unsought comment.'

– 'Abe Gormley ... holding a letter that's had at least half a bottle of perfume dumped on it, and looking like you could have bought him for two cents half-spent, made me more than a trifle suspicious' (Boyles, 'Living in Harmony,' 110).
Common or widespread except occasional in Charlottetown; significantly senior, especially not college-educated.

to make easy
To calm down, be quiet, start behaving; often in imperative, as to a child. This catchphrase was not surveyed; the entry is taken from *DPEIE*.
Infrequent except rare in Queens and Charlottetown.

You need a cold cloth.
You need to calm down; parallel to common *Take a cold shower*.
– 'You sound crazy or touched' (Weale collection).
– 'Take a pill' (anon.).
Widespread in Prince, occasional in Kings and Charlottetown, rare elsewhere.

Calm your hormones.
Don't get your hormones all excited.
Just relax, will you? Parallel to common *Take a valium, Don't get your shorts in a knot*.
– 'Used when a person gets excited about something. Relax. Many young people use it more frequently than do, say, our parents' (young Hunter River female university student).
– 'Used frequently in High School. I first encountered it there' (young Stanhope female university student).
– 'Relax; do not get too sexually aroused' (young college-educated Cornwall male youth worker).
Widespread except occasional in Queens; significantly young, female. *Includes middle-aged Vernon Bridge male teacher.*

60 Anxiety

Don't get your water (all) hot.
Calm down. Euphemistic variant of general *Don't get your piss all hot* and others still more vulgar. The frequency label may be inflated by the popularity of these more general alternates (for which see *SDUE* and *DCP*).
– 'Simmer down – used by my mother in Pisquid' (young university student).
– 'Don't come before your water boils' (West Prince).
Common in Summerside, widespread in Kings and Prince, occasional elsewhere; especially senior.

to **make buttons / button holes**
to **make button holes and sew them on**
to **make paper dolls**
To wait with great impatience, to fidget. Compare *NDAS*: 'cut out dolls (or paper dolls) ... To be insane; behave dementedly,' and *DCD*: 'making dolls' eyes ... evasively pert answer to a query as to what one does for a living.'
– 'My daughter set out to drive to a wedding and she was fifteen minutes late. Then she had to stop for a road construction gang. As you can imagine, she sat there making buttons!' (senior high-school-educated Charlottetown woman).
[*buttons:*] Occasional except rare in Charlottetown; significantly senior. [*button holes:*] Rare. *Includes senior college-educated Strathgartney female teacher, middle-aged high-school-educated St. Eleanors female medical worker, and young Summerside female housekeeper.* [*paper dolls:*] Rare. *Includes senior college-educated Montague male artist, and young male university student.*

to **dig / sell postholes**
To become impatient with waiting. Occasional in Prince, Queens, and Kings, rare elsewhere. *Includes senior grade-school-educated Prince woman, and senior Summerside female teacher.*

See also CRAZY AS A CUT CAT, SWEAT LIKE A HEN HAULING WOOD, BUSY AS A FART IN A MITT

SHOCK

Wouldn't that boil / burn / fester your britches!
Wouldn't that burn your brother's bacon!
*Also reported
Wouldn't that cook your buns!
That makes me really angry; related to widespread exaggeration *Wouldn't that rot / wet your socks / shock your socks off?* (as in *ADS*). Another somewhat old-fashioned proverbial exaggeration of this form is widespread both on Prince Edward Island and elsewhere: *Wouldn't that jar / sour / cramp your mother's / grandmother's preserves / pickles / applesauce?* (see *DCP*: 'A Can. c.p. [catchphrase], expressing surprise and current c. 1910'). Compare *DKS*: *'wouldn't it rip your ration book / rock you / root you / rotate you / rot your socks / make you spit / make you spit chips?* extensions of above exclamation [*wouldn't it!* exclamation of disgust or exasperation], sometimes including being startled or unsettled ... NZA [New Zealand Australia].'
– 'Can you believe it?' (middle-aged college-educated Charlottetown female social worker).
[*britches:*] Widespread except occasional in Charlottetown; especially not young.
[*bacon:*] Rare. *Includes [britches] senior*

high-school-educated Charlottetown female secretary, and senior college-educated Charlottetown male accountant; [bacon] senior grade-school-educated Northam male farmer.

Wouldn't that frost your eyeballs / your eardrums!
*Also reported
Wouldn't that frost your fanny / your ass / your socks / your preserves / the backside of a cow!
Wouldn't that fluff your feathers!
That is really shocking. More at previous entry. Compare *DARE*: *'frost ... Also with off*: To discomfit or irritate (someone) ... "Wouldn't that frost you?"'
– 'Heard from my grandmother' (university student).
Widespread or occasional; [*eyeballs*:] significantly older; [*eardrums*:] especially high-school-educated. *Includes senior grade-school-educated St. Peters female homemaker, senior college-educated Cardigan female homemaker, senior Stanhope man.*

*Wouldn't that blow the hen right off her nest!
That is extremely shocking.
Late entry, not surveyed. Reported by middle-aged grade-school-educated Prince man.

Wouldn't that bring grandmother back from the dead!
Wouldn't that make the old people go queer!
Something new and unconventional is shocking; parallel to standard *make [someone] turn over in the grave*. Compare *OED*: *'This beats my grandmother*; said of something that excites astonishment'; and *DCD*: *'enough to make my gran turn in her urn* is applied to acts and attitudes that would have shocked grandma: since c. 1960.'

– 'First heard it [*old people*] from a member of a job-entry group with which I was working in Summerside' (middle-aged college-educated Summerside female librarian).
[*grandmother*:] Widespread in Prince and Charlottetown, occasional elsewhere; significantly senior, especially female. [*old people*:] Rare. *Includes senior high-school-educated Covehead female teacher.*

Wouldn't that make an old dog piss on her pups!
Wouldn't that give the dog's arse heartburn!
Vulgar. Something new and unconventional is shocking and unnerving.
– 'Excite or surprise. "That scare you gave me would make an old dog piss on her pups"' (Gojmerac, 'Prince Edward Island Expressions').
Not in Survey II. Probably occasional.

You could have floored me with a pitchfork!
Ironic. I was really surprised; deliberate reversal of common *You could have knocked me over with a feather*.
– 'Johnny says, "I got somethin' to tell ya." Well, I figured it must be this new car or a broad he managed to get a date with. Instead he takes me right by surprise and says, "Goin' back home – quittin' today" ... You could have floored me with a pitchfork! Back home. Well, I mean, what was so good about back home? No money there. He was crazy to even think about it' (Donna Gallant, 'What's a Fella Gonna Do?' 90).
– 'Embarrassed or stunned – not really common' (anon.).
Widespread in Kings, occasional elsewhere except rare in Charlottetown; significantly male, especially rural.

IRRITATION

short in the grain
Short-tempered.
– 'Short fuse, quick on the draw' (senior Borden male ferry-worker).
– 'Touchy' (senior college-educated Cardigan female homemaker).
– 'Lacking patience, cranky. A teacher in high school used to say this' (young university student).
Common in Kings, widespread in Queens, occasional elsewhere; significantly young, especially rural, female.

*to take a twister
To be out of humour, disturbed by an unexpected event.
Late entry, not surveyed. Reported by senior college-educated Kings man.

to **get their neck / pantyhose / shorts in a knot**
To get into a mood of sulkiness or constrained irritation; comparable to popular *nose out of joint*. Also attested from Ireland.
– 'For me this has a Tyne Valley connection' (senior college-educated Charlottetown teacher).
Occasional in Prince, Kings, and Charlottetown, rare in Queens and Summerside. *Includes young high-school-educated Summerside man, and young college-educated Charlottetown woman.*

to **have an itchy prick**
Coarse and vulgar. To be fretful, irritated.
– 'Angered beyond reason. "Our old principal sure has an itchy prick today"' (Gojmerac, 'Prince Edward Island Expressions').
Not in Survey II. Probably occasional.

I can't dance and hold the baby too.
I can't dance with a baby in my arms.
Surely it's obvious I can't take on another job: my hands are full; possibly related to common slang *to be left holding the baby*. Compare I'M NOT AN EIGHT-DAY CLOCK OR A SEWING MACHINE and YOU CAN'T SWEEP THE FLOOR and WIPE YOUR ASS AT THE SAME TIME. Compare also *ODEP*: 'You will neither Dance nor hold the candle. 1721 ... That is, you will neither do, nor let do.'
– 'Older saying – heard from my father' (young university student).
Occasional in Prince, Summerside, and Charlottetown; rare elsewhere; significantly urban, especially senior. *Includes senior grade-school-educated Prince woman, middle-aged male Parks Canada worker, and young college-educated Queens man.*

Clean the dirt / hay / straw / potatoes out of your ears.
Are you growing potatoes in your ears?
*Also reported
Clean the bananas out of your ears.
Pay attention, for goodness' sake.
– 'Told to a person who has missed part of a conversation' (anon.).
– 'I have heard "Clean the shit out of your ears" directed at country kids in urban schools' (young college-educated Charlottetown male lawyer).
– [*potatoes*:] 'Pay attention! (New Glasgow)' (Weale collection).
Occasional except rare in Charlottetown. *Includes young female university student.*

to **take the cluck(ing) (out) of(f) [someone]**
To quiet (an irritating person) down; comparable to standard *take the wind out of their sails*.

– 'In the same way that clucking hens were cured of their disposition by putting them under a box or barrel for a few days, mothers would sometimes say in exasperation to their annoying children, "I'll take the clucking out of you, if I get my hands on you"' (middle-aged college-educated Mount Stewart male librarian).
– 'But that Pat McGee – he kept poor Minnie pregnant in the summer and barefoot in the winter. Eight children in fourteen years! ... Harold said he'd turn me on Pat and that'd take the cluckin' off him' (Hennessey, 'Trial of Minnie McGee,' 1983, 17).
– 'I heard a woman who had a hysterectomy say, "They took the cluck out of me this time"' (anon.).
Common in Kings, occasional elsewhere; significantly senior, especially college-educated.

*They're a twenty-nine.
Someone is in an ominously poor humour. Compare *SSPB*: '*twenty-nine* – "She's a TWENTY-NINE this morning" means "she's growly" ... or "she's in a bad mood." The term makes a metaphor of "29," a very low reading on a falling barometer, a prediction of stormy weather. – Pubnico.'
*Late entry, not surveyed. *Reported by middle-aged college-educated Kings man.*

Their mother gave them ugly pills for breakfast.
Someone, usually a child or youngster, has been surly all day. See also LOOK AS IF THEIR MOTHER BEAT THEM WITH AN UGLY STICK. Compare *DSUE*: '*ugly pills.* "Anyone who manifests a surly disposition is apt to be accused of having taken ugly pills" ... Can[adian].: since late 1950s [contributed by John Douglas Leechman, Canadian anthropologist and author].'
Occasional except rare in Queens; especially urban. *Includes young female university student.*

*They should have taken their anti-grouch pill.
Someone got up this morning in poor humour.
*Late entry, not surveyed. *Reported by middle-aged college-educated Kings woman.*

ANGER and CONTEMPT

right tight in the face
Rigid with anger. *Right* as an intensifier is close to standard usage on Prince Edward Island (see *DPEIE*, 174–5).
Rare. *Includes young Charlottetown female university student, and a Victoria resident (anon.).*

to **hate my eyes for looking at [someone]**
To regard someone as so despicable that any connection of mine with him or her is demeaning. Also attested in Newfoundland: '"I hates my eyes for looking at you" is how a Newfoundlander said it to my brother' (senior college-educated Queens woman).
Rare. *Includes young college-educated Charlottetown woman.*

I'd stab [someone] but I'd be sorry for the knife.
That person aggravates me almost beyond endurance.
– 'I'd stab him but he's not worth the time or energy' (university student).
Rare. *Includes senior high-school-educated St. Catherines female homemaker, and six university students.*

I'd hit [someone] but they say manure splatters.
Someone is contemptible, but dangerously so; parallel to standard proverbs *to be tarred with the same brush* and *He that touches pitch shall be defiled* (ODEP).
Occasional except rare in Prince. *Includes male university student.*

I wouldn't waste my spit (on [someone]).
Someone is beneath contempt; comparable to common *I wouldn't waste my breath*. Compare TOO LAZY TO SPIT.
– 'This saying was often used. Also, a similar saying is "I wouldn't waste my energy on her"' (young college-educated Queens man).
– 'Used by parents and self. The other person one may be talking of isn't worth it. I wouldn't waste my breath' (university student).
– 'Would not give him the sweat off my brow!' (university student).
Widespread in Prince, occasional elsewhere; especially young. *Includes middle-aged high-school-educated Charlottetown woman.*

They'd hear more than my prayers.
I'm extremely angry, so it's a good thing that person isn't here right now. *To say more than one's prayers*, 'to tell a lie' is attested from Ireland.
– 'Used when someone is giving a bawling out – "they'll be hearing more than prayers"' (senior high-school-educated Queens woman).
Rare.

Down comes your goose house (and fifty feet of the barn).
Down comes your dog house.
Archaic. You cross me and just see what happens to you: disaster will follow. Compare Jay Taylor in 'Snake County Talk': '*down goes his cob-house* ... Failure to realize one's plans. "If I don't have a good crap [crop] this year, w'y down goes my cob-house"' (206). (A cob-house is 'a house built by children out of corn-cobs, hence applied fig[uratively] to any insecure or unsubstantial scheme' [OED]).
– 'To (figuratively) bring someone down abruptly' (anon.).
– 'If you don't do what's right you'll get into real trouble' (senior college-educated Strathgartney female teacher).
– 'Parent to child in anticipation of child's wrong doing' (anon.). 'I'll get you for that' (senior Summerside female teacher).
– '"Down comes your goose house" was quite familiar' (senior college-educated Covehead female teacher).
Rare. *Includes two senior grade-school-educated Summerside female housewives, and middle-aged high-school-educated St. Eleanors female nurse.*

EXCLAMATIONS

by the living John Bull! / cripple!
Euphemism, but strong oath. In the name of the living God! Comparable to more widespread *by the living Lord Harry!* More at next entry. Compare DNE: '*by the living man*: by the living God.'
– 'Cuss words of long ago' (senior high-school-educated Lot 37 woman).
– 'When we covered English in the elementary grade, this saying [*John Bull*] was used' (young college-educated Queens woman).
Rare. *Includes senior grade-school-educated Summerside female homemaker.*

by the (holy) (Lord) liftins!
*Also reported
by the liftin Jehoshaphat / George!
Euphemism, mild oath. In the name of the living God! Parallel to conventional *by gosh / golly / gum* and to *Jumping Jehosaphat!* (as in *NDFRRS*). Also attested from New Brunswick and Ireland. Note *DSUE*: 'by occurs in many oaths, strong or (e.g., *by golly*) mild, blasphemous or ludicrous or innocuously senseless. Although many of these are neither s[lang] nor coll[oquial] some of the funny or witty ones are coll[oquial]. or s[lang]: e.g. *By the jumping Moses, by the living jingo, by my bootlaces.*'
– 'Heard this frequently in the Murray Harbour area' (young college-educated Murray Harbour male librarian).
– 'Variations of this from my grandfather on my mother's side' (young college-educated Prince man).
Widespread in Prince, Queens, and Kings, occasional in Charlottetown, unattested in Summerside; significantly rural, especially young, not grade-school-educated.

by the end of the stick!
I'll be damned! Possibly an extension of the common catchphrase *the short / dirty end of the stick* 'the worst of some encounter' (*NDAS*). More at previous entry. A forthcoming volume of *DARE* suggests another possible meaning for *stick* here: 'a portion of alcohol,' with citations from Massachusetts and New York State (letter to the editors).
Rare. *Includes three grade-school-educated Tignish men, and young university student.*

Holy wick!
Holy cow! Gee whiz! *Wick* is British slang for 'penis' (*DSUE*).
Rare. *Includes senior Stanhope man.*

Well, pinch my cheeks and call me cute!
I've never heard such a thing!
Rare. *Confirmed by fifteen informants in two surveys, including young male university student.*

Social Life

SOLITUDE

lonesome as a gull on a rock
*Also reported
lonesome as a pole cat
Quite forlorn. Also known in Newfoundland according to English, 'Historic Newfoundland,' 39. Compare *SD*: 'Leaving me alone like a shag [cormorant] on a rock,' and *DKS*: '*like a shag on a rock* alone, abandoned, forlorn. NZA [New Zealand Australia]'; also *ASD*, *TTEM*.
— 'You know, around the world folk language is filled with expressions which refer to animals; they're a rich source ... "As lonesome as gull on a rock": that has a nice Maritime flavour to it' (Weale, 'Them Times' [radio broadcast]).
Rare.

all soul alone
Totally alone and feeling it intensely; comparable to popular and lighter *all by one's lonesome*. Compare SSPB: '*mother soul alone* an intensive way of saying "alone." From the German *mutterseelenallein* "all alone" ... Lunenburg'; and *DARE*: 'all (of) one's lone,' 1890–1917.
— 'If everyone else had gone away and left me alone, usually delivered in a mournful voice' (senior college-educated Queens woman).
Widespread in Kings, occasional or rare elsewhere; especially senior.

black spark alone
Isolated and lonely. More at previous entry.
— 'I've heard old men in Tignish say of an old widow, "She is living black spark alone" i.e. isolated' (anon. senior).
Rare.

to **get around like the button on the outhouse door**
Ironic. Not to get around at all, to be confined to the limited circle of home. See also A TONGUE LIKE A BUTTON ON A BACK BARN DOOR. For *button*, see *DPEIE*: 'This is used to hold a door shut. You take a piece of wood and drive a nail through the middle of it and when the door closes you put the thing down. This is a small piece of wood that rotates on the nail and falls into place.' Attested in New Brunswick: '"I have been around, but so has the button on the backhouse door" ... Probably said in ironical self-depreciation' (Halpert, *Folklore Sampler*

from the Maritimes, 126).
Rare. *Includes senior grade-school-educated Northam female homemaker, and senior Parkdale woman.*

to **live so far in the back woods they have to come out to hunt**
To live somewhere incredibly remote. Compare *YA*: 'They lived so deep in the woods they kept possums for yard dogs and a groundhog to tote the mail,' 127.
Occasional; significantly male, especially senior.

COMPANY

A warm smoke is better than a cold fog.
Proverb. Inside is better than outside, whatever the company. Recorded in *DAP* from this evidence in manuscript. Also known in Newfoundland, according to Porter, 'Some Newfoundland Phrases,' 294.
– 'Souris (1983)' (Weale collection).
Rare.

to **put the bow to the fiddle**
To have a party.
Occasional, significantly senior.

to **lay leather to the hardwood**
to **lay cowhide to the hemlock**
Archaic. To dance, especially to stepdance. Compare *DARE*: '*cowhide* ... A shoe or boot made of cowhide ... "Irish-soaled cowhides on a pine flooring" [citations chiefly from New England].'
– 'Dancing with leather boots on a hardwood floor' (senior Kinkora female nurse).
– 'Grandparents use this' (young university student).
Rare. *Includes St. Georges female teacher.*

(But) the night owl has the fun.
Proverb. Response to standard *The early bird gets the worm.* The party isn't over yet, so you can't go to bed. Another response supplied was *But who wants to eat worms?* (anon.).
Rare. *Includes senior grade-school-educated St. Peters female homemaker, middle-aged high-school-educated St. Eleanors female medical worker, and young Kingston female university student.*

It's not late until it's twelve and then it's getting early.
It's not late until it's twelve / two and then it's too late.
It can't be time to leave the party – in fact, it is never time to leave the party; comparable to established saying *The night is young.*
– 'Said by wide-awake and hospitable host who wants tired guests to stay longer' (middle-aged college-educated Charlottetown male civil servant).
Widespread in Kings, occasional elsewhere except rare in Queens; especially senior. *Includes senior grade-school-educated Queens woman.*

not asked if you had a mouth on you
Not offered something to eat or drink when visiting. Also attested from Ireland. Compare *DNE*: '*have a mouth on one*: to be hungry or thirsty.'
Rare.

to **beat the feet**
To walk away, depart. Compare *DNE*: '*beat the paths / streets / roads*: to be out at night.'
– 'I've heard this one down around Souris' (anon.).
Occasional; especially urban, male.
Includes young Charlottetown female university student.

68   Company

*He's like a tom-cat, coming home from a different direction every morning.
He's a philanderer.
*Late entry, not surveyed. *Reported by senior Tyne Valley woman.*

See also IT'S TIME TO FIND THE GAPS.

BAD MANNERS

to hang their coat on the dog's nail
Especially in the form 'Don't hang your coat on the dog's nail.' To throw one's coat down carelessly or rudely.
– 'My aunt used to say this when we (as children) used to go to her house' (young college-educated Charlottetown man).
Rare. *Includes senior college-educated Charlottetown male accountant.*

Were you born on a raft?
Were you born in a barrack?
Were you born in the woods with no door on?
Were you born in a boat?
Were you born in a sawmill?
Were you brought up in a barrack / boat / sawmill?
*Also reported
Were you born in a henhouse?
... in a hole?
... in an igloo?
... under a bridge?
Especially used as a reprimand to a child, on a cold or windy day. Close the door, won't you? All are variants (in order of frequency) of the more popular *Were you born in a barn / in a tent / in a field (with the gate open)?* (as in *DARE, DCP, DKS*), and *to be brought up in the woods* (*EAP*). All five *born* variants here were surveyed separately. Note that a *barrack* is 'a square structure of four long posts and a roof that is raised or lowered to cover straw, hay, or grain' (*DPEIE*). The meaning of 'deaf' for *born in a sawmill* (as in the dictionaries cited at the end of this paragraph) was not recognized by our informants. *Born in the bush*, 'silly or gullible,' is recorded in Alsopp, 'Some Parallels to Swift's *Polite Conversation*,' 36. [The 'parallel,' in Jonathan Swift's *A Complete Collection of Genteel and Ingenious Conversation*, 1738, 55, is 'What, do you think I was born in a Wood to be scar'd by an Owl?'] Compare *ODEP*: 'Born in a mill, He was 1598–1678 ... "deaf"'; also *DSUE*, and *TTEM*: 'Shouts loudly (as would be necessary to overcome the noisy clacking etc.).'
– 'Said to one who comes in a house and does not shut the door' (middle-aged high-school-educated St. Eleanors female medical worker).
– 'Came in the house and did not shut the door' (senior grade-school-educated New Haven male farmer).
[*raft*:] Common except occasional in Prince and Summerside; especially not young. [*barrack* and *woods*:] Occasional; significantly senior, especially not grade-school-educated. [*boat* and *sawmill*:] Rare. *Includes senior high-school-educated Summerside male farmer, senior high-school-educated Darnley female secretary, senior college-educated Charlottetown male accountant, senior college-educated Cardigan female homemaker, senior Coleman woman, middle-aged high-school-educated West Covehead male heavy-equipment operator, and middle-aged college-educated Charlottetown female social worker.*

Is your arm broken?
What is it you have, a broken arm?
Why can't do this little thing yourself? An unconfirmed meaning supplied by a young grade-school-

educated Queens man is 'not working,' i.e., unemployed.
- 'Someone asks you to do something and this is reinforcing it (hasn't written home)' (senior Summerside female teacher).
- 'Reply to someone asking for someone to pass an item' (senior grade-school-educated Tignish male fisherman).
- 'Meant in a sarcastic way: why haven't I heard from you?' (senior Parkdale [Charlottetown] woman).
Common in Queens, Summerside, and Charlottetown, widespread elsewhere; especially urban, especially not senior or high-school-educated. *Includes two senior Summerside female homemakers, middle-aged Kinkora female teacher, middle-aged high-school-educated St. Eleanors female nurse, and Charlottetown male taxi-driver.*

Do you supply towels with your showers?
Thanks, but I had a shower today.
Your sneeze, or spitting while talking, was unpleasantly extensive. Also attested from New Brunswick. Compare *DCP*: 'Say it, don't spray it ... Aus[tralian].'
- 'We always said this in our teens' (middle-aged college-educated Kings woman).
Widespread in Charlottetown, occasional in Queens and Kings, rare in Prince and Summerside. *Includes young Charlottetown female university student.*

Did you get any on you?
Ironic (mock concern). Your burp, sneeze, or spitting was uncouth. Occasional; significantly young, especially grade-school-educated. *Includes senior Stanhope man.*

better out than an eye
*Also reported
better out than a farmer's eye
Somewhat coarse. Never mind – there are worse offences than breaking wind or burping. Compare *MBP*: 'Better eye out than alwaie [always] ake [ache]' (1546–1670). Compare also *CCW*: 'Down east they say, *It's better to belch it than squelch it. And suffer the pain.* A writer in Burnaby, BC, offers this after someone burps out loud – *Bring it up again and we'll vote on it*' (92).
- 'By way of an apology' (middle-aged college-educated Queens male teacher).
Not in Survey II. Probably occasional. *Includes middle-aged college-educated Charlottetown male teacher.*

to cut [someone] off like a carrot
To interrupt another speaker very abruptly, as growing carrot tops are sometimes cut off prematurely. See also SHORT AS A CARROT.
- 'Silas was a man who would surprise you with his comparisons ... [H]e was telling me how one person had rudely interrupted another in conversation. "He cut him off like a carrot," was the way he put it. I mean, you could learn to talk from a man like that. I don't know if Silas coined any of these himself. Probably not. More likely they were passed down to him from the old people: verbal heirlooms, to be used, and then passed on to the next generation like a fancy vase or a fine tool' (Weale, *Them Times*, 61–2).
Rare. *Includes North Lake woman.*

ignorant as a brush fence
*Also reported
ignorant as dirt
Lacking social graces, awkward, clumsy. See also HOMELY AS A BRUSH FENCE. Note *DPEIE*: 'ignorant ... Rude, ill-mannered.'
Rare. *Includes senior college-educated Canoe Cove male teacher, and middle-aged college-educated Loyalist male teacher.*

to **give [someone] flowers while they're still alive**
To show timely appreciation; comparable to standard *give credit where it's due*. Also attested from New Brunswick. The possibility of a literal interpretation by survey informants may have inflated the frequency label below.
– 'To show kindness or consideration to the living rather than eulogize the dead' (senior college-educated Charlottetown woman).
– 'Why wait until they are dead to send flowers?' (senior high-school-educated Prince woman).
Widespread in Prince, occasional elsewhere; significantly senior. *Includes middle-aged grade-school-educated Kings woman, and middle-aged college-educated Prince woman.*

Talking

SILENCE

Say nothing and saw wood.
Keep out of this, mind your own business. Also attested in Maine: 'A person who told too intimately his or her affairs was said to "turn himself wrong side out," in contrast with a "close-mouthed person." "Say nothing and saw wood" was an injunction' (Perkins, 'More Notes on Maine Dialect,' 120). Compare *TTEM*: '*Saw wood* (Amer[ican]) Attend to your own affairs; continue working as normal.'
– 'A woman in the Co-op [grocery store] checkout hears the next customer behind her use by mistake the same shareholder's number she just used, her own – which means she would get the dividend on his huge bag of groceries. Hearing this story, a friend of mine [senior high-school-educated Charlottetown woman] said, "That's a case of say nothing and saw wood" – keep your mouth shut and you'll be glad you did' (senior high-school-educated Charlottetown woman).
– 'Keep out of argument' (middle-aged Brookfield male carpenter).
Widespread in Summerside, occasional elsewhere; especially high-school-educated.

Shoot geese.
Please get on with the matter at hand. One informant identified this saying literally with goose hunting, giving the meaning 'Keep quiet or you'll scare away the geese we're here to shoot' (anon.).
Occasional in Prince, Summerside, and Charlottetown, rare elsewhere.

Somebody is dead in Rustico.
Ironic. Keep quiet – I'll give you a reason later. Supplied as a New Glasgow family saying, but confirmed by six other independent informants.
Rare.

to **not sell the catch / their cabbage twice**
To choose not to repeat oneself; variant of more common *chew / boil one's cabbage twice* (*DARE*). The greater frequency of the *cabbage* is probably due to overlap with this more common proverbial phrase; hence it is listed second here. Compare *IP*: 'It's no use boiling your cabbage twice.'
– 'A reply for when asked to repeat something and one doesn't wish to do

so' (senior high-school-educated Lot 37 woman).
– 'Don't say the same thing over and over again' (senior college-educated Charlottetown male editor).
– 'Secret; no gossiping' (university student)
[*catch:*] Rare. [*cabbage:*] Occasional; significantly senior, especially college-educated. *Includes three senior grade-school-educated Tignish men, and three young university students.*

It must have been a lie – I swallowed it.
I forget what I was going to say, but it couldn't have been important.
– 'Whenever you couldn't remember something' (senior high-school-educated Prince woman).
– 'When you're made to feel guilty by an elder' (young college-educated Queens man).
Widespread in Prince and Summerside, occasional elsewhere; especially not middle-aged. *Includes senior college-educated Kings man, young grade-school-educated Charlottetown woman, and young college-educated Summerside woman.*

to pick the talk out of [someone]
To persuade (a shy person) to speak. Rare. *Includes senior college-educated Souris woman.*

CHATTER

to kick the cat
To chat, gossip, talk in neighbourly fashion. Also attested in Ireland.
– 'Telling stories, chatting, pleasant conversation' (anon.).
– 'Shoot the shit' (young college-educated Charlottetown female pharmacist).
Widespread in Prince, occasional elsewhere. *Includes young Charlottetown male university student.*

to talk so much that their tongue gets sunburned
To talk too much. Supplied by a senior in the early research for *DPEIE*, and confirmed by fifteen informants in two surveys for the present work. Rare.

a mouth (going) five miles faster than their face
A habit of talking fast; comparable to stock exaggeration *tongue hinged in the middle and talking with both ends* (DCP).
– 'You're talking so much that no one can get a chance to say anything' (young West Prince male university student).
Rare.

a tongue (going) like a button on a back barn door
A habit of talking all the time and to little purpose. See also GET AROUND LIKE THE BUTTON ON THE OUTHOUSE DOOR. Note *DPEIE*: '"This [*button*] is used to hold a door shut. You take a piece of wood and drive a nail through the middle of it and when the door closes you put the thing down. This is a small piece of wood that rotates on the nail and falls into place" [oral informant].'
– 'Talking fast and saying much' (middle-aged high-school-educated Charlottetown female homemaker).
– 'If you tied your tongue in the middle it would wag at both ends' [a conventional saying] (anon.).
Rare.

a tongue / mouth like a threshing machine / hay cutter / winding blade / sewing machine
A habit of speaking constant malice; parallel to popular *motor-mouth*. Compare *ODEP*: *'Your Tongue runs nineteen to the dozen'* 1785–1854, and *'Her Tongue runs on pattens (wheels),'* ca. 1450–1670; also *DSUE*.
– 'Talks about others behind their back – gossip' (young Hillsborough Park female university student).
– 'She has a sharp tongue (cutting)' (senior high-school-educated Summerside male farmer).
Occasional; especially not young. Includes senior St. Georges female teacher, senior college-educated Charlottetown male editor, and senior North Shore (Queens) woman.

more tongue than a Mountie's boot
a tongue like a Mountie's boot
A rough, harsh way of talking; a pun on *tongue* with probable reference to the high, riding-style boot worn as part of the dress uniform by officers of the Royal Canadian Mounted Police. Also attested from other regions of Canada.
Occasional except rare in Kings; significantly male, especially urban. Includes middle-aged high-school-educated Charlottetown male, and young Charlottetown female university student.

*a mouth like the back of a dump truck
A habit of talking vulgarity.
**Late entry, not surveyed. Reported by middle-aged college-educated Victoria man.*

to talk the ear off an elephant / a monkey / a stalk of corn
Usually preceded by 'would' or 'could.'
To talk incessantly and loudly.
– 'I've been told in various jobs that I have this communicative quality' (young college-educated Queens man).
– 'Talk you crazy' (senior college-educated Prince man).
Common in Charlottetown, widespread or occasional elsewhere. *Corn* variant only occasional. *Includes senior grade-school-educated Prince female homemaker, and middle-aged Charlottetown female university student.*

See also TALK A HOLE IN AN IRON POT.

SMOOTH TALK

a tongue as oily as a churnful of butter
A facility for smooth and deceptive language. Also attested in Ireland. This simile was supplied by a *DPEIE* informant and subsequently confirmed by four informants in two surveys for the present work.
Rare.

They could sell fleas to a dog / to a donkey.
They could sell a heating pad / coals to the Devil.
They could sell oil / sand to the Arabs.
They could sell snow to an Eskimo.
They could sell toothpicks to a wooden Indian.
Potentially offensive to groups named.
Someone is extremely persuasive; parallel to conventional *sell iceboxes / ice cubes to Eskimos, bring coals to Newcastle*.
– 'Good salesman' (senior college-educated Charlottetown male editor).
[*fleas:*] Occasional in Kings, Queens, and Charlottetown, rare in Prince and Summerside. [*others:*] Rare. *Includes senior*

grade-school-educated New Haven male farmer, and senior high-school-educated Covehead female teacher.

They could charm the heart (out) of a grindstone / a wheelbarrow.
They could charm the heart of a grindstone and make a wheelbarrow dance.
Someone is a convincing talker, whatever the opposition; parallel to traditional *charm the Devil, charm the birds out of the trees*. Also attested from Victoria Beach, Nova Scotia, by Helen Creighton ('Folklore of Victoria Beach,' 134). Compare *DSUE*: '*enough to charm the heart of a broomstick.*'
– 'Very good with words and uses speech to get whatever (s)he wants – manipulate' (middle-aged college-educated Prince woman).
– 'A shrewd character' (young college-educated Queens man).
Rare. *Includes senior college-educated Darnley female secretary, and college-educated Vernon River female teacher.*

ARGUMENTS

A Chev's a Chev and a Ford's a Ford
1. Don't make false comparisons. 2. *Proverb.* You get what you pay for. See also THEY COULDN'T AFFORD TO CALL A FORD A FORD. Some survey informants may have taken this saying literally.
– 'Apples are apples; oranges are oranges (used in mathematical contexts)' (young college-educated Cornwall male youthworker).
– 'I have three cars and a Ford; from a auto dealer (Chev) – like Chev's are real cars and a Ford is a Ford' (young West Prince male university student).
– 'That's what you pay for' (senior college-educated Charlottetown male editor).

Widespread in Prince, occasional elsewhere; especially rural.

off their eggs and on to the straw / potatoes / onions
Straying from the point, wide of the mark; extension of established catchphrase *off one's eggs* (as in *DSUE*). The *potatoes / onions* variants suggest a connection with the stock catchphrase *off one's nut / onion* (as in *NDAS, TTEM*).
– 'Some expressions of disagreement with something said: ... (a hen sitting on a setting of eggs might leave the eggs and sit somewhere else – therefore she would be all wrong so far as doing what she was supposed to be doing' (senior high-school-educated Queens woman).
– 'He is off his eggs a little (little stupid)' (senior grade-school-educated New Haven male farmer).
– 'Off one's eggs and on to potatoes (crazy)' (two senior grade-school-educated Summerside female homemakers).
Rare. *Includes senior grade-school-educated Prince woman, and middle-aged high-school-educated Miminegash female homemaker.*

You have your brake lights ahead of your high beams.
Your argument is illogical, getting ahead of itself; comparable to standard *cart before the horse*.
Rare. *Includes senior grade-school-educated Tignish male farmer, fisherman, and businessman.*

a tongue that would blister a stone
An insistently hurtful way of arguing. Compare *ODEP*: '*Tongue breaks bone, and herself has none,*' ca. 1225–1659 [from Proverbs 25.15: 'A soft tongue breaketh the bone'].

– 'Anne once reproached the Captain for his baiting of Miss Cornelia. "Oh, I do love to set her going, Mistress Blythe," chuckled the unrepentant sinner. "It's the greatest amusement I have in life. That tongue of hers would blister a stone. And you and that young dog of a doctor enj'y listening to her as much as I do"' (Montgomery, *Anne's House of Dreams*, 164). Rare.

to **talk / wear a hole in an iron pot / a lead pot / a tin pot**
to **talk the lid / handle off an iron pot** / [etc.]
to **talk the bottom / arse out of an iron pot** / [etc.]
Usually preceded by 'would' or 'could.' To win arguments by incessant talking; variants of common sayings in form *talk the X* (leg, hind leg, bark, etc.) *off a Y* (dog, donkey, bird, etc.). See also TALK THE EAR OFF AN ELEPHANT. Compare SO HUNGRY I COULD EAT THE BOTTOM OUT OF AN IRON POT. Compare also *EP*: 'Talk ... [Lancaster] ... He'd talk the leg off a brass pon [pan].' Other common alternates are found in *EP, DKS,* and *MBP*.
– '[Interviewer:] "These are marvellous, so wonderfully descriptive, and they lend such humour in their lives, don't they, eh?" [Weale:] "The language was colourful and lively, yes ... I have [one] just for you actually ..." "He could talk a hole in an iron pot"' (Weale, 'Them Times' [radio broadcast]).
– 'My mother-in-law [middle-aged, high-school-educated, western Queens] said of a contentious or argumentative person, "She'd wear a hole in an iron pot"' (young college-educated Kings man).
Common in Kings, widespread in Queens, occasional elsewhere; significantly senior. *Includes young Charlottetown female university student.*

See also A TONGUE LIKE A THRESHING MACHINE.

NONSENSE GREETINGS

How's your belly button?
How's your belly for beans / biscuits?
How's your feet and ears?
How's your old straw hat?
How's your old straw hat – or would you rather have your brown felt?
How are things with you anyway? Parallel to popular *How's your belly where the pig / bear bit you?, How's your belly for spots?* (*DCP*), and other such intentionally provocative or sexually suggestive greetings. *Felt is a noun/verb pun.*
– 'Similar to Acadian expression: *Comment ça flippe?* "How's it going?"' (young St. Louis male university student).
– 'We mostly said this [*belly button*] to small children, preschool or younger, as a means of teasing them' (young college-educated Queens woman).
– 'Used it [*belly button*] in our teens' (middle-aged college-educated Kings woman).
– '[Replying to *How's your old straw hat?*] Pretty well felt' (middle-aged grade-school-educated Tignish man).
– '[*feet and ears*:] Wilmot Valley (1983)' (Weale collection).
Widespread or occasional, except *belly button, feet and ears, old straw hat* common in Prince, Kings, Summerside respectively, and *belly for beans, feet and ears* rare in Queens, Charlottetown respectively. *Includes senior college-educated Charlottetown woman, middle-aged college-educated*

76   Nonsense Greetings

St. Peters male teacher, Rollo Bay woman, and North Lake woman.

What's growing on you?
I can see something's wrong – what's the matter? Not to be confused with standard verb phrase *to grow on [someone]*, 'to be become increasingly pleasing.'
– 'This saying comes from down east (Souris)' (young college-educated Queens man).
– 'I've heard this from my younger brother and his friends' (middle-aged Charlottetown female university student).
Widespread in Charlottetown, occasional elsewhere except rare in Kings; especially young, urban, male.

NONSENSE REPLIES

How are you?

king of the trough
*Also reported
head toad in the puddle
Very well indeed, thank you, and feeling in control; variant of standard catchphrase *king of the hill*. Compare *OED*: 'on the pig's back ... in a fortunate position; on top of the world; riding high.'
– 'Means – to be top dog' (middle-aged high-school-educated St. Eleanor's female nurse).
– 'Taking all the water' (senior grade-school-educated St. Peters female homemaker).
Rare. Includes young Charlottetown female university student.

I've been better but it cost more.
I could be better but it would cost a lot more.
Joking evasion. Something's wrong but I'm not going to tell you; extension of standard reply *I could be better*.
Widespread in Summerside and Charlottetown; significantly senior, urban, especially male. *Includes senior high-school-educated Glen Valley male farmer, and young university student.*

See also IF I WAS ANY BETTER I'D BE BIGGER, A CASE OF THE POLLYWOGGLES OF THE DIAPHOBICKALORIUM

Where are you going?

I'm going to Souris / to Tignish / to the Magdalen Islands / to Newfoundland for a load of postholes.
I'm going ... for a truck / wagon load of postholes.
I'm going to Souris for a load of jelly beans / fish.
... to Tignish for a load of rotten fish / smelts.
... to the Coleman tea.
... to Dundee.
... north for a load of Eskimos.
I'm going to the breakwater to fork off the fog (with a pitchfork).
... to the moon to get some green cheese.
... to sell some plaid shirts / some postholes.
... to sell / catch some rabbit tracks.
I'm going up Jumbo's hole to see the moon rising.
I'm going fishing – do you want to build the boat?
*Also reported
I'm going to Jerusalem for a load of Bibles.
... to China – want to come?
... to the fog locker for a can of green paint.
... to get a bucket of steam.
... to get a two-by-four stretcher.

... to get Friday's fish at Saturday's market.
I'm going downstairs behind the fish barrels.
Joking evasion. I'm not telling you, it's none of your business; comparable to widespread catchphrases *Going to see a man about a horse*, and *Going crazy – care to join me? / – ever been there? / – want to come? / – which way did you take?* Souris, the departure point for the Magdalen Islands ferry, and Tignish are major towns at opposite ends of Prince Edward Island; Dundee is a well-known farming community in the centre of Kings. The distribution of the variants that includes these place names is clearly affected by this geography. '*Hauling post holes ... Driving an empty truck*' is cited by Frazier in 'Truck Drivers' Language,' 92. Compare *NDAS*: '*a load of VW radiators (or postholes or wind) ... An empty truck; no cargo whatever*'; also *TTEM*.
– '[Interviewer:] It strikes me that another question that a person might not wish to answer at all is that most delving question, "Where are you going?" [Weale:] Yes, well, there are many ways of getting around that one. [A friend] told me that when he was growing up in St. Georges, he once asked that question to his father and got this answer: "I'm going to the Magdalen Islands for a load of postholes." Or a similar Souris expression, in that area, was: "I'm going to the breakwater to fork off the fog." Or if you lived up in the western part of the Island you might be told: "I'm going to Tignish for a load of rotten fish," or "I'm going to the Coleman tea." I myself recall being told: "I'm going fishing – do you want to build the boat?" or again, "I'm going crazy – do you want to come?" ... Someone might also tell you that they were "going up Jumbo's hole to see the moon rising," or that they were "going to sell some rabbit tracks,"' (Weale, 'Them Times' [radio broadcast]).
– '[*Dundee* is] used in Souris W. by someone who didn't want to say where he was going or was going nowhere in particular' (Weale collection).
[*Souris ... postholes* and *Dundee:*] Occasional in Queens, Kings, and Charlottetown, rare in Prince and Summerside. [*Tignish ... fish:*] Widespread in Prince, occasional elsewhere, except rare in Charlottetown. [*moon:*] Widespread in Charlottetown, occasional elsewhere; significantly female, especially urban. [other variants:] Rare. *Includes variously senior grade-school-educated New Haven male farmer, senior high-school-educated Miscouche female teacher, middle-aged grade-school-educated Charlottetown male taxi-driver, middle-aged grade-school-educated Charlottetown woman.*

Where have you been?

up a tree
up to the top of the barn
up on the roof sorting airmail (with the crows)
upstairs in the cellar picking chickens out of feathers
Joking evasion. I'm not telling you, it's none of your business. Compare THE ONLY TIME THEY WERE OFF THE ISLAND WAS WHEN THEY WERE UP A TREE. Compare also *NDAS*: '*up a tree ...* In a predicament; faced with a dilemma; helpless'; also *TTEM*.
– '[Interviewer:] Could you give us some examples from traditional Island speech [of "the nonsense response"]? [Weale:] Well, let's

suppose some curious neighbour or family member ... asked you where someone was, you might say ... "She's upstairs in the cellar picking chickens out of feathers," and one I heard from Charlottetown, "She's up on the roof sorting airmail with the crows" ... [Interviewer:] Let's suppose that I was to ask you, "Hey, David, where have you been?" [Weale:] "Up a tree." Or perhaps "up to the top of the barn"' (Weale, 'Them Times' [radio broadcast]).
– 'Used to hear [*roof*], and I use the first part, but not "with the crows" (middle-aged college-educated Kings woman).
[*tree:*] Widespread or occasional. [other variants:] Rare. *Includes* [*tree:*] *senior grade-school-educated Bedeque female homemaker;* [*barn:*] *senior Coleman woman;* [*roof:*] *three grade-school-educated Tignish men, and senior high-school-educated Summerside man.*

out behind the barn
Joking evasion. I'm not telling you, it's none of your business. The frequency label may be inflated by the popularity of the standard senses of this catchphrase, including 'up to no good,' or more precisely 'up to no good sexually,' and 'slow-witted.'
– 'Reply to a question one does not wish to answer: "Where were you?"' (senior college-educated Summerside man).
– 'Nowhere to be found' (senior college-educated Kings man).
– 'Can mean I don't know where he is, or simply a humorous non-answer' (senior college-educated Charlottetown man).
Widespread or occasional. *Includes senior college-educated Prince woman, and young St. Louis male university student.*

What are you doing?

making a baloney sandwich
baking a cake
learning to knit
the same thing I did last year (and piling it up)
I was thinking I might move the barn / the chicken house / the moon.
*Also reported
I was just about to walk the goldfish.
Joking evasion. I'm not telling you just now, it's none of your business; *the same thing I did last year* is parallel to a common joking response to the question 'What time is it?': *Same as it was this time yesterday (only a day late) / this time last year.* Thompson's *Body, Boots and Britches* [folklore of New York State], 500, records similar evasions: 'Peeling pertaters with a buzz-saw,' and 'making a handle to a hen's nest.'
– 'Let's suppose that some curious neighbour or family member asked you what you were doing or what you planned to do. You might say, "I was thinking I might move the barn," or "The same thing I did last year and piling it up"' (Weale, 'Them Times' [radio broadcast]).
– 'Telling a story [*baloney*] that is an untruth' (middle-aged college-educated Prince woman).
– 'Used [*same*] if a person does not really want to reveal what he/she was actually doing' (senior college-educated Charlottetown woman).
[*same:*] Widespread in Prince and Charlottetown, occasional elsewhere; especially young. [*baloney:*] Occasional in Prince and Charlottetown, rare elsewhere. [other variants:] Rare. *Includes senior high-school-educated Prince woman, senior Stanhope man, young high-school-educated Queens woman, and young college-educated Murray Harbour male librarian.*

What is it?

a doodle-daddle for a goose's / duck's / horses's saddle
a doodle-daddle for a goose's / [etc.] / bridle / waddle
a nooden-nadden for a goose's necktie
an oodle-addle / a hoody-addle / a hoodle-haddle / a hoodle-laddle / a loodle-laddle / a wiggle-waggle / a flim-flam for a goose's necktie
a nooden-nadden / oddle-addle / [etc.] / for catching eels / flies
a silver new nothing with a whistle on it
a silver new nothing to wind up the sun
a silver new nothing to hang on the end of your nose
a silver know-nothing ...

Joking evasions, usually to a child, of such questions as 'What is it?' 'What will you bring me?' and 'What are you making?' I'm not telling you just now, it's none of your business. Note standard colloquialisms *doodad*, 'any small object with an unknown name,' and *flim-flam*, 'nonsense.' Some of these variants were surveyed separately, which has probably produced misleading results; the frequency of such catch-phrases as a group is probably high. Sub-parts of the *doodle-daddle* type are largely interchangeable. For a thorough study of nonsense evasions of this kind, including further alternatives, see Smith, 'Whim-Whams for a Goose's Bridle,' 32–49. Compare *DKS*: '*wigwam for a goose's bridle* evasive and/or dismissive answer to question about what one is doing; variant of "whim-wham to bridle a goose," a "whim-wham" being any fanciful object; eg "What's that you're making?" "Oh, just a wigwam for a goose's bridle." NZA [New Zealand Australia],' and *DCP*: '*making a trundle for a goose's eye* or *a whim-wham for a goose's bridle*'; also '*weaving leather aprons* ... The insistence on *goose* may fairly be assumed to imply that the enquirer *is* a goose (a silly person) to be asking such a question.' Compare also *DNE*: '*loodle-laddle* ... also *doodle-daddle, oodle-addle* ... A contraption; esp a deliberately humorous or evasive name given to an object in order to puzzle a child.'
– 'Also a lot of these [nonsense responses] were especially useful, of course, for excessively curious children ... I mean, personally I don't think a child can be excessively curious, but supposing you just wanted to discourage the curiosity or escape the ensuing conversation. I mean, suppose you're working in the shop, and the child comes up and says, "What are you making?" Well, this was the answer they might receive: "a doodle-daddle for a goose's saddle" or "a doodle-daddle for a goose's bridle," or again, "a silver new nothing to wind up the sun," or a variation, "a silver new nothing with a whistle on it"' (Weale, 'Them Times' [radio broadcast]).
– '"I'm going to buy a loodle-laddle for a goose's bridle." Said by someone rummaging at a sale' (young St. Louis male university student).
– '"Flim-flam for a goose's necktie." Expression used by my grandparents to reply to child's persistent questions, "What's this?"' (anon.).
Rare (in any one form). *Includes senior grade-school-educated Prince woman, and middle-aged college-educated Georgetown businesswoman.*

Where is it?

down cellar behind the axe / the fish barrels / the fish bowl
down cellar beside the furnace behind the axe / [etc.]
in the pigs' barrel behind the piano
Joking evasion. I'm not telling you, it's none of your business; parallel to more traditional *up in Annie's room (behind the clock / wallpaper (DCP).* The first *cellar ... axe* variant is also attested from British Columbia and New Brunswick (Curtis, *Look What the Cat Drug In!*). Compare *DARE*: '[*down cellar*] Used in joc[ular] evasive expressions; ... People come in and say, "Well, where's your wife?" or "Where's your husband?" "Oh, they're down cellar tyin' the dog loose." But when they didn't have a dog a-tall [New York State].'
– '[I]f someone asked you something, and you didn't want to tell them, you couldn't come right out and say, "Mind your own business" – that would be far too confrontational, far too direct. But what you could do was answer with a nonsense saying, which was really just a slightly more polite way of saying [it] ... [I]f someone asked you where something was, you might retort "It's in the pigs" barrel behind the piano,' or "It's down cellar behind the axe"' (Weale, 'Them Times' [radio broadcast]).
– 'From Mt. Stewart area [*cellar*]' (young university student).
– 'Grandfather used this [*cellar*] when he couldn't find something' (anon.).
[*cellar*:] Widespread in Kings, occasional elsewhere except rare in Charlottetown; significantly not young, especially college-educated. [*piano*:] Rare. *Includes senior high-school-educated Parkdale female nurse, senior college-educated Charlottetown male accountant, senior college-educated Summerside woman, and New Annan female homemaker.*

It's not up your arse or you'd feel it.
Joking evasion. I'm not telling you, it's none of your business.
Not in Survey II; probably occasional.

How many were there?

thousands (and thousands) from Tyne Valley alone
Ironic. There certainly weren't very many, whatever people say. The population of Tyne Valley is listed in the 1991 census as 215.
– 'Because I was born in Tyne Valley, the illustration and the phrase [in Pratt, 'Proverbial Islander'] "Thousands from Tyne Valley alone" caught my eye ... It may be, as you suggest, that it is now a jocular comment on the size of a crowd. I suggest, however, that it was originally a cynical comment on the accuracy of reporting by the Canadian Press and CBC. A forest fire, in 1961 or 1962, burned across the Island in a belt several miles wide and destroyed a number of farms. One night the CBC national news carried the report that "two thousand persons have been evacuated from Tyne Valley alone." There was, in fact, an evacuation: a man and his wife, whose home was endangered. The population of Tyne Valley, cats and dogs included, is probably less than 500"' (correspondent).
– 'This is used at points distant from Tyne Valley. It's used in jocular speech when one wishes to exaggerate a report of a crowd, as in "There was quite a crowd, thousands and thousands from Tyne Valley alone"'

(middle-aged college-educated Charlottetown male lawyer).
– 'Common once. Now seen only in Island literature' (anon.).
Rare. *Includes senior high-school-educated Stanley Bridge female homemaker, senior female university student, and senior college-educated Charlottetown female professor.*

Where are you taking me?

I'm taking you nowhere and treating you like a dog when we get there.
I'll give you nothing, take you nowhere, and treat you mean when we get there.
Joking evasion, perhaps to a child. I'm not telling you yet, it's a surprise.
– 'A family in Kinkora uses this' (anon.).
Widespread in Charlottetown, occasional elsewhere except rare in Kings. *Includes senior grade-school-educated Prince woman, and middle-aged college-educated Prince woman.*

How long is it?

twice as long as from the centre to either end
Joking evasion of the questions 'How long is it?' and 'How long will it take?' I'm not telling you just now, it's none of your business. Also attested from Alberta.
– 'And if they asked you how long you would be, you might say, "Twice as long as from the centre to either end"' (Weale, 'Them Times' [radio broadcast]).
Rare. *Includes senior Summerside male airbase worker.*

What's to eat?

bees' knees and fried onions
roast ghost on toast
*Also reported
three mosquitoes fried in butter
Joking evasions of the questions 'What have we got to eat?' and 'What did you have to eat?' I'm not telling you, it's none of your business; parallel to more common *elephant's kidneys on toast*. Various dictionaries (e.g., *DSUE*) confirm more general uses of *the bees' knees* as 'something perfect,' and of *bee's knee* as 'something insignificant.'
– 'There was a verbal device people used which we refer to as "the nonsense response." And it worked like this: if someone asked you something, and you didn't want to tell them, you couldn't come right out and say "Mind your own business" – that would be far too confrontational, far too direct. But what you could do was answer with a nonsense saying, which was really just a slightly more polite way of saying "It's none of your business" … If I had been somewhere for a meal and you asked me what was served, I might just tell you "Roast ghost on toast" – end of conversation' (Weale, 'Them Times' [radio broadcast]).
Rare. *Includes middle-aged college-educated Summerside woman, and middle-aged Charlottetown female university student.*

Want something to eat?

No thanks, I've just had a banana.
Joking. Not just now, thank you. Probably related to more established catchphrase, *Have a banana!*, and to former music-hall songs 'I had a banana / With Lady Diana,' and 'Yes,

we have no bananas' (as in *DCP* and *DSUE*).
Widespread in Summerside, occasional elsewhere except rare in Kings; significantly urban, especially male. *Includes senior grade-school-educated Prince woman.*

NONSENSE FAREWELLS

Don't let your antifreeze.
Don't let your antifreeze boil over.
**Also reported
Don't let your meatloaf.
So long, and take care of yourself.
– 'I've heard it in my teens' (middle-aged college-educated Kings woman). Occasional, except unattested in Queens and Charlottetown; especially high-school-educated. *Includes young high-school-educated Prince man, and young female university student.*

May the rats never leave your flour barrel with a tear in their eye.
Farewell, and I hope you prosper. See also THE FLOUR IN THE BARREL WOULD TAKE A MOUSE TO ITS KNEES. Compare *TTEM*: '*It is a sair time when the mouse looks out o' the meal barrel wi' a tear in his eye* (Sc[ottish])'; and *DARE*: '*flour barrel full, keep the ...* To provide for one's family.'

– 'A blessing ... which meant you would never go hungry' (Weale, 'Them Times' [radio broadcast]).
Rare. *Includes young university student.*

Fair weather to you and snow to your heels.
Goodbye and good luck. Also known in Newfoundland (Porter, 'Some Newfoundland Phrases,' 295).
– 'Good luck on your journey – Egmont Bay, 1983' (Weale collection).
Rare.

I've got to go and snare a rabbit.
I have other business that I'm not telling you about; the business might be getting something to eat. This entry was supplied originally by Anna Gojmerac, 'Prince Edward Island Expressions.'
Widespread in Prince, occasional in Kings, Summerside, and Charlottetown, rare in Queens; especially young, urban.

See also AN ONION A DAY KEEPS EVERYONE AWAY, THEY'VE GOT TWO CLUES – ONE'S LOST, THE OTHER'S LOOKING FOR IT, EATONS DON'T TELL SIMPSONS THEIR BUSINESS.

Food

HUNGER

to put another [something] in for the stranger
To make ample food, as if for more eaters than are present.
– '[A woman] from Murray Harbour said this was a common saying around the kitchen – it meant "Put plenty in the pot"' (Weale collection). Rare.

hungry as a bunch of starving Russians
Of a group of children, very hungry.
Rare. *Confirmed by seven informants in two surveys, including young female university student.*

so hungry I could eat leftover leftovers
Very hungry.
Rare. *Confirmed by twelve informants in two surveys, including young male university student.*

so hungry I could eat the plate / the table
Very hungry.
[*plate*:] Widespread in Prince and Charlottetown, occasional in Queens and Summerside, rare in Kings; especially urban, not senior. [*table*:] Occasional in Queens and Charlottetown, rare elsewhere; especially female. *Includes young female university student.*

so hungry I could eat the bottom out of an iron pot
so hungry I could eat an old book / cobwebs / my spats
Very hungry. Compare TALK A HOLE IN AN IRON POT. The *old book* and *cobwebs* variants are also attested from Moncton, New Brunswick. A *spat* is a cloth or leather covering for a man's upper shoe and ankle.
[*iron pot*:] Widespread in Kings and Charlottetown, occasional elsewhere; significantly senior. [*others*:] Rare. *Includes senior high-school-educated Arlington male teacher.*

so hungry I could eat the east end of a horse / skunk going west
Very hungry; parallel to popular *so hungry I could eat the south end of a northbound horse / billy goat, so hungry I could eat a horse / bear / whale.* Compare A FACE LIKE THE EAST END OF A TRAIN GOING WEST. Attested from Vancouver: 'hungry enough to eat the south end of a north-bound polar bear.' Compare also *ODEP*: 'He is so Hungry

84 Hunger

he could eat a horse behind the saddle,' 1641–78.
Rare. *Includes senior high-school-educated Parkdale man, senior high-school-educated St. Catherines female homemaker, two senior high-school-educated female teachers of Summerside and Covehead, and young Queens female university student.*

so hungry my belly is flapping
Very hungry; other such sayings in more general use include *so hungry my stomach is sticking to (playing tag with) my backbone / is eating itself, so hungry my stomach thinks my throat is cut,* and *I'm so empty I can feel my backbone touching my belly button* (DCP).
Rare. *Includes three senior grade-school-educated Tignish men (farmer, fisherman, businessman).*

You'll never put air under that.
1. You've taken far more food on your plate than you can possibly eat; comparable to standard *Your eyes are bigger than your stomach.* 2. You'll never be able to lift that [heavy weight]. A 1979 survey for *DPEIE* found sixteen informants, all rural, who knew this proverbial challenge in meaning 1. It is probably associated with buffet meals at parties. One informant in a later survey responded, 'never make an accusation stick' (young Charlottetown female university student).
Rare. *Includes young Montague female university student for meaning 1; senior college-educated Canoe Cove teacher, and young Queens man for meaning 2.*

like an appetite with the skin pulled over
Habitually and obsessively hungry.
See also LOOK LIKE THE SKIN OF A NIGHTMARE PULLED OVER A GATEPOST.

– 'My son is sixteen, and he's just like an appetite with the skin pulled over him' (Gojmerac, 'Prince Edward Island Expressions').
Rare. *Includes young female university student.*

EATING

boiled / cooked with axehandles
Of food, excessively hot.
– 'Axehandles [because made] of hardwood burn hotter than softwood' (middle-aged Georgetown woman).
– '[As if] fire was made with axehandles' (senior Kensington man).
Rare.

baked in the sun
1. Of food, overcooked, burnt. 2. Of persons, sunburnt. Also attested from Ireland. Gojmerac's 'Prince Edward Island Expressions' comments that this saying 'refers to cooked food which has not sufficiently browned,' a meaning not supported by informants for this collection.
– 'I've heard older people (50–60 years up) say this [sense 2] quite often in summer' (anon.).
Common. *Includes three young Charlottetown female university students.*

dry / thirsty as a burnt potato
dry / thirsty as a burnt boot
*Also reported
dry as a Mountie's boot
dry as a strap
1. Of food, overcooked and dried out; variant of standard *dry as an old boot.* 2. Of persons, very thirsty. Also attested from Ontario. Compare *SD*: '(Her voice was) dry as burned paper.'
– 'Something is tough and has no

taste. Probably has a rubbery texture too (young Hunter River female university student).
– 'Similar to "tough as shoe leather" ... cooked cut of meat' (anon.).
[*potato*:] Widespread in Prince, occasional elsewhere; significantly senior, especially rural. [*boot*:] Occasional except rare in Summerside; especially senior. *Includes two senior grade-school-educated male farmers of Margate and Vernon Bridge, senior college-educated Charlottetown male civil servant, senior college-educated Charlottetown male editor, and young Charlottetown female university student.*

*You couldn't cut it with the knife itself.
That meat was extraordinarily tough.
*Late entry, not surveyed. *Reported by senior college-educated Charlottetown woman.*

tough as leather judgment
Of meat, especially steak, not easily chewed; extension of traditional simile *tough as leather* (ODEP).
– 'Likely goes back to the strap or cat-of-nine-tails when those things were used to whip or punish people' (anon.).
Widespread in Queens and Kings, occasional in Summerside and Charlottetown, rare in Prince; significantly senior, female.

*This may be a young animal, but it led a tough life.
This meat is surprisingly tough.
*Late entry, not surveyed. *Reported by middle-aged college-educated Kings man.*

They must have run that cow to death.
They must have used that cow as a horse.
*Also reported
a lot of miles on that old cow.
This beef is terribly tough.
[*death*:] Occasional; significantly senior, college-educated, especially female. [*horse*:] Rare. *Includes three senior grade-school-educated Tignish men (farmer, fisherman, businessman), middle-aged college-educated Arlington male teacher, and young Charlottetown female university student.*

a cow so old it must have had a vote
a cow so old the rings were falling off its horns
*Also reported
a cow so old it died of old age / of natural causes
a cow so old she had to be lifted when she lay down
A cow used for beef that turns out to be tough. See also OLD ENOUGH TO VOTE, and sections 'Old Age' and 'Age of Objects.' See *DPEIE* for the related phrase *on the lift*, which goes beyond the catchment area for the present dictionary.
– 'My father, a farmer, used this saying often' (young college-educated Queens man).
[*vote*:] Occasional except rare in Queens; especially not middle-aged. *Includes senior grade-school-educated Prince woman, middle-aged high-school-educated Charlottetown man, and university student.*

It must have been older than the first settlers.
It must have been one of the first settlers.
This beef or chicken is extremely tough. A senior grade-school-educated Prince woman widened the meaning of this saying to include persons, comparing it to OLDER THAN THE STONE AGE. See also sections 'Old Age' and 'Age.'
Rare. *Includes senior Summerside female teacher, and young university student.*

to chase a crow a mile for [something].
Also found in negative. To judge something [usually food] to be really excellent. Also attested from Ireland.
– '"I wouldn't chase a crow a mile for it": you don't like something very much – usually something to eat' (senior Parkdale woman).
– 'Some day you'll chase a crow for that (waste)' (anon.).
Occasional. *Includes middle-aged Murray River female librarian, and young college-educated western Queens woman.*

to eat so fast you can see a biscuit going down.
To eat hoggishly, without sufficient chewing.
– 'Eating faster than I can dish it out' (university student).
– 'Gobble it like a dog' (middle-aged college-educated Charlottetown woman).
Rare. *Includes senior Summerside female teacher.*

down the little red lane
Especially to children. Of food or medicine, down the throat; parallel to standard *down the hatch*. Also attested from Ireland and Michigan.
– 'Asking a child to eat his food or take his medicine' (middle-aged college-educated Vernon Bridge male teacher).
Rare.

Open the barn door and down the hatch.
*Also reported
Over the lips and over the gums, look out stomach, here it comes.
Especially to children. Here comes some good medicine for you; extension of standard *down the hatch*.

– 'Being that I lived on a farm, this saying was often used' (young college-educated Queens man).
Widespread in Prince and Queens, occasional in Kings and Charlottetown, rare in Summerside; significantly rural, especially not grade-school and college-educated. *Includes senior Summerside female teacher.*

*This tastes like more.
This food is delicious, thank you.
Late entry, not surveyed. Reported by middle-aged college-educated Charlottetown female librarian.

hole, heart, and soul
Thoroughly; a pun on *whole/hole* and a vulgar extension of established catch-phrase *heart and soul*. Also attested from Newfoundland.
– 'hole, heart and soul ... entirely, completely. "He ate the trout hole, heart and soul"' (Gojmerac, 'Prince Edward Island Expressions').
– 'To put all you've got into any task' (anon.).
Occasional, except rare in Summerside.

*to eat as much as two men and a dog
To gulp down food voraciously and in huge quantities.
– 'I worked across in New Brunswick and Nova Scotia in the lumber woods putting up camps there ... This fella said to me, "I'm going to quit today, Harry" ... And then ... another fella ... said he'd go too. He says to me, "Do you know, my heart; it's acting up today." There was nothing wrong with his damn heart, no more than there was with mine. And he'd eat as much as two men and a dog' (Hornby, *Belfast People*, 38).
Late entry, not surveyed.

Eating 87

stuffed to the guppers
Swollen from having just eaten too much; possibly a nonsense variant of popular catchphrase *stuffed to the gills*, with a play on *guppy*, 'small fish.' The editors have not found a meaning for *guppers* as such.
– '*Stuffed to the guppers* – the effect from having over-eaten. "After that beer and pizza party, I was stuffed to the guppers"' (Gojmerac, 'Prince Edward Island Expressions').
Rare.

*That will hold me till you get a rope.
Thank you, I have eaten extremely well, in fact more than I should have, and my sides are bursting.
*Late entry, not surveyed. *Reported by young Charlottetown woman.*

See also SO THIN IT ONLY HAS ONE SIDE.

Drink

THIRST

so thirsty I could drink a biscuit
Very thirsty, especially for alcohol. Compare *ODEP*: 'Dry as a biscuit,' 1599–1620.
Rare. *Includes senior college-educated Strathgartney female teacher.*

dry as a drunk on the wagon for a month
Craving alcohol.
Rare. *Includes three senior grade-school-educated Tignish men: farmer, fisherman, businessman.*

dry as a wooden leg / an old wooden bucket / a wooden bridge in Africa
dry as a cork leg
*Also reported
dry as a wooden spoon
1. Of persons, very thirsty, especially for alcohol. 2. Of a bottle, quite empty; parallel to standard *dry as a (wooden) chip* and *dry as a bone*. The most popular simile of this kind, *dry as a wooden god*, is also used in New Zealand, with variants *wooden idol / statue / Indian (in the middle of the Sahara)* (DKS).
[*bucket:*] Occasional except rare in Queens; significantly senior, especially grade-school-educated. [*bridge:*] Rare. *Includes senior grade-school-educated Margate male farmer, senior grade-school-educated Cardigan female homemaker, young grade-school-educated Queens man, and young Charlottetown female university student.*

dry as the inside of a woodpecker's boarding house
1. Of persons, very thirsty, especially for alcohol. 2. Of the weather, lacking moisture. Compare EMPTY AS LAST YEAR'S BIRD'S NEST. Compare also *SSPB*: 'dry as last year's robin's nest'; and *SD*: 'Dry as last year's crow's nest.'
– 'Dry party' (anon.).
Rare. *Includes middle-aged grade-school-educated Charlottetown male taxi-driver.*

dry as a cow's ass / crow's crotch at fly-time
Vulgar. Very thirsty, especially for alcohol; variant of familiar *tight as a bull's hole / arse in fly-time*.
Not in Survey II. Probably widespread. *Includes senior high-school-educated Arlington male teacher, middle-aged grade-school-educated Charlottetown male taxi-driver, and middle-aged high-school-educated Kings male carpenter.*

I'm so dry I feel like a raisin / a prune.
*Also reported
dry as a mouthful of choke cherries
I need a drink badly.
Rare. *Includes middle-aged college-educated Kings man.*

I'm so dry I'm spitting sparks / dust
I'm very thirsty. See also DRY AS A DUST STORM.
– 'Craving liquids; hung over' (university student).
Widespread in Charlottetown, occasional in Summerside and Prince, unattested in Queens and Kings; significantly urban, especially middle-aged. *Includes senior grade-school-educated Covehead Road male farmer, senior West Royalty male telephone operator, middle-aged college-educated Charlottetown male engineer, and young Cornwall male university student.*

I'm so dry I can't / couldn't spit
Especially with a hangover. I'm very thirsty. Compare *PPS*: 'Spit ... So dry he'd have to prime himself to spit.'
Widespread in Prince, Summerside, and Charlottetown, occasional in Queens and Kings; especially urban, university students.

I'm so dry I'm cracking / squeaking.
I'm very thirsty.
Common in Prince, widespread in Kings and Summerside, occasional in Queens and Charlottetown; significantly high-school-educated, not young. *Includes senior grade-school-educated New Haven male farmer, and middle-aged college-educated Charlottetown female social worker.*

See also DRY AS A DUST STORM, DRY AS A BURNT POTATO.

DRUNKENNESS

so fond of liquor they would drink it out of a dirty straw
so fond of liquor they would drink it out of a sheep('s) / cow('s) track / out of a wagon track
*Also reported
... out of a(n) (old) sock / rubber boot / chamber pot
Someone has a drinking problem. Another suggestion was 'so fond of liquor they would suck it through a shitty sock,' a variant of *He'd drink the stuff if he had to strain it through a shitty cloth* (attributed by *DCP* to Canada, 1920).
[*straw*:] Occasional in Prince, Queens, and Kings, rare in Summerside and Charlottetown; especially rural. [*track*:] Rare. *Includes (for various forms) senior grade-school-educated Miscouche female housekeeper, senior Kinkora female nurse, senior Parkdale woman, middle-aged high-school-educated Miminegash female homemaker, and middle-aged college-educated Charlottetown male teacher.*

so drunk they couldn't hit the ground with their hat
so drunk they couldn't hit the ground if they fell on it
so drunk they'd spit and miss the ground
Very drunk.
Rare. *Includes senior Borden male ferry-worker, middle-aged high-school-educated St. Eleanors nurse, and middle-aged college-educated Charlottetown woman.*

drunk as a boot
*Also reported
dizzy as a coot
Very drunk. Hanford records '*drunk as a coot ... Alabama*' in 'Metaphor and Simile in American Folk Speech.' 161.

— 'I've heard this a lot in southeastern Prince Edward Island' (young college-educated Murray Harbour male librarian).
— 'Used a lot by every generation' (young Charlottetown female university student).
Common in Kings and Charlottetown, widespread in Prince and Queens, occasional in Summerside; especially young, male.

drunk as arse
*Also reported
drunk as fart
Coarse and vulgar. Very drunk.
— 'Even though this is rather gross, I've often heard "to be drunk as arse"' (young Queens female university student).
Includes middle-aged grade-school-educated Charlottetown male taxi-driver, and middle-aged college-educated Queens male teacher.
Not in Survey II. Probably widespread.

drunk as seven barrels of shit
*Also reported
drunk as two / three / four barrels of shit
drunker than two barrels of shit
Coarse and vulgar. Very drunk. Also attested from New York State, by an Island informant who worked there 'on a farm in 1950.'
— 'Stinking drunk' (anon.).
Includes Weale collection ('Kinkora'), and senior college-educated Queens male teacher.
Not in Survey II. Probably widespread.

full as a banana
As drunk as a person can be; variant of widespread simile *full as an egg*. The traditional simile *full as a tick* is used on Prince Edward Island for both food and alcohol. Compare *DARE*: '*full* Drunk (chiefly Scots dial; cf EDD [*English Dialect Dictionary*]).'
— 'Used in one of the traditional folk songs at the Island folk festival' (Weale collection).
Rare.

full as a teddy bear
As drunk as a person can be; parallel to traditional *full as a tick* [see previous entry]. Also attested from Ohio and Michigan. Compare *DPEIE*: '*teddy* ... A long-necked, twelve to sixteen ounce bottle, commonly a beer bottle, usually as used for illicit alcohol.'
Widespread in Queens, occasional elsewhere; significantly senior. *Includes three senior grade-school-educated Tignish men (farmer, fisherman, businessman), senior college-educated Charlottetown male editor, and young college-educated Charlottetown female pharmacist's assistant.*

all over the pond
1. Drunk. 2. Confused, disorganized, or disoriented.
Rare. *Includes middle-aged college-educated Summerside male teacher, young college-educated Murray Harbour male librarian, and young Charlottetown female university student.*

(to have) **too many gingersnaps last night**
Ironic. To be hung over.
Rare. *Includes middle-aged college-educated Bunbury male teacher.*

See also TIGHT AS A FIDDLESTRING.

Bedtime and Rising

I'd stretch a mile but I'm too lazy to walk back.
I'd walk a mile if I didn't have to walk back.
Very tired; almost too tired to go to bed. The two variants were mistakenly surveyed separately.
[*stretch:*] Widespread except occasional in Kings; significantly senior, high-school-educated, female. [*walk back:*] Widespread in Summerside, occasional elsewhere; significantly senior, especially high-school-educated, urban. *Includes senior grade-school-educated St. Peters female homemaker, and middle-aged high-school-educated West Covehead male heavy-equipment operator.*

to be all in but the buttons / shoelaces
To be completely worn out. Compare *NDASCE*: *'all in ... exhausted.'*
– 'Done in' (senior grade-school-educated St. Peters female homemaker).
– 'Degrees of tiredness might be expressed as "all in but the buttons"' (senior high-school-educated Lot 37 woman).
Widespread in Kings, occasional elsewhere; significantly senior, especially female. *Includes senior grade-school-educated Northam male farmer, senior grade-school-educated Miscouche female housekeeper, senior high-school-educated Margate male farmer, and middle-aged high-school-educated St. Eleanors female medical worker.*

to be knocking nails
To have a head nodding from sleepiness.
– 'Lazing in chair and head nodding – New Glasgow' (Weale collection).
Rare.

It's time to find the gaps.
It's late and time to go home.
– 'This is an expression indicating time to leave now: "time to find the gaps" – as in [while going directly across the fields, rather than by the road] the line trees so common between neighbouring farms in days gone by' (senior high-school-educated Lot 37 woman).
Rare. *Includes senior high-school-educated female teacher.*

Get off the flour barrel and scale the wall.
Especially to children. Get up to bed now.
– '*Off the flour barrel and scale the wall* ... To go to bed. "You'd better get off the flour barrel and scale the wall because it's past your bedtime"'

(Gojmerac, 'Prince Edward Island Expressions').
Rare.

It's time to climb / buckle up / hit the (little / big) (old) wooden hill.
Especially to children. To climb the stairs in order to go to bed; variants of common British catchphrase *climb the wooden hill* (as in *DSUE*, and in Dunkling, *Guinness Book of Curious Phrases*, 15). There is a play called *The Wooden Hill* about L.M. Montgomery and her family, by Don Hannah; a *Globe and Mail* story on this play reads in part: 'His title ... refers to this unhappy household's insomnia. "When I was a kid," he explains, "when it was bedtime my father used to always say it was time to climb the wooden hill, it's time to go upstairs. It's an East Coast expression, a lovely expression about going to bed ... The whole play is about going to bed; this was a family that never slept. The parents roamed the house and kept the children awake"' ('Climbing the hill,' A18).
– 'My mother said "You better hit the wooden hill" to me all the time at bedtime when I was a child. My family still uses the term' (young college-educated Dunblane female government worker).
– 'Buckle up the big wooden hill – Go upstairs to bed. "Tell the babysitter that the kids have to buckle up the big wooden hill at 8:30 p.m."' (Gojmerac, 'Prince Edward Island Expressions').
Rare. *Includes senior Coleman woman, middle-aged high-school-educated Charlottetown man, and middle-aged Vernon Bridge male teacher.*

to **count the steps**
To go to bed.
Rare. *Includes middle-aged college-educated Emyvale male teacher.*

to **hit the flea pen / flea bag**
To go to bed; comparable to popular *to hit the hay / the feathers / the sack*.
Rare. *Includes senior grade-school-educated St. Peters female homemaker, middle-aged high-school-educated St. Eleanors female nurse, and young West Prince male university student.*

to **hit the fart sack**
Vulgar. To go to bed; extension of popular *to hit the sack*. Also attested from Alberta 'from my father' (young Charlottetown female university student).
Not in Survey II. Probably common. *Includes middle-aged grade-school-educated Charlottetown male taxi-driver.*

to **get to blanket harbour**
to **go to bunky harbour**
*Also reported
to **hit the blankets**
to **hit the crate**
Especially with children. To go to bed; comparable to popular *to hit the hay / the feathers / the sack*.
– 'I've mainly heard this used only in my home village of Souris, PEI' (university student).
[*blanket harbour:*] Occasional in Kings, Summerside, and Charlottetown, rare in Prince and Queens. [*bunky:*] Rare. *Includes senior St. Georges female teacher, and middle-aged high-school-educated Charlottetown man.*

Go to bed with the hens and get up with the roosters.
Proverb. For a healthy life, go to bed

early and get up early; variant of traditional *Early to bed and early to rise, makes a man healthy, wealthy, and wise* (*CODP* 1496–1984). The frequency label may be inflated by the popularity of this rhyme. Compare *ODEP*: 'Go to Bed with the lamb, and rise with the lark' (1555–1833).
Common or widespread; significantly senior, female. *Includes middle-aged college-educated Charlottetown female social worker.*

to be **up at crow piss (time)**
*Also reported
up at the crack of crow piss
To be up very early in the morning. Also in *DPEIE*.
– 'Very early' (college-educated Queens female nursing administrator).
– 'My father was always up at crow piss' (anon.).
Not surveyed. *Includes North Lake man, young high-school-educated Queens woman, and young female university student.*

Work

HARD WORK

*The day after tomorrow will be the middle of the week and no work done yet.
It's Monday, the Sabbath is over, and we've got to get to work.
– 'The idea of leisure time, now a common and perfectly acceptable concept, was virtually unknown in that farming society [before the Second World War] ... Hazel Robinson from North Tryon shared with me a saying from that part of the Island which captures perfectly the compulsion to work. On a Monday morning it apparently was not uncommon to hear someone say, "The day after tomorrow will be the middle of the week and no work done yet"' (Weale, *Them Times*, 80).
*Not surveyed.

to kill (a) bear(s)
to go for bears
To get a lot done. Sometimes in negative, hence rueful. Leslie Dunkling's *Guinness Book of Curious Phrases* notes 'I've been *killing adders* (busy) all morning,' from Pembrokeshire, England. Similarly, *rat-killing* is 'a Texas term for busy work or what one is doing,' according to Hendrickson, *Whistlin' Dixie*, 192.
– 'Doing hell and all. Great and wonderful things. Getting a lot done' (middle-aged college-educated Hampton male teacher).
– 'More common [is] "I didn't kill a bear" – I didn't accomplish much' (anon.).
Rare.

to sweat like a hen hauling wood
To perspire heavily from physical labour or from nervousness. Waugh records *Sweats like a hen drawing rails* in 'Canadian Folk-lore from Ontario,' 1918, 36.
– 'We had the poor waitress sweating like a hen hauling wood because of our large order' (Gojmerac, 'Prince Edward Island Expressions').
Rare.

We'll soon see the rabbit.
Keep at it and the work will soon be done. The Weale collection notes this saying as heard in 'Wilmot Valley, 1983.' One informant responded with 'A woman is about to give birth' (anon.). John Fowles vividly describes an incident such as Weale describes below in the first chapter of his novel

Daniel Martin (Toronto: Collins, 1977), though he does not use this saying.
– 'If you were talking about something that was going to happen soon, you'd say, "We'll soon see the rabbit." And this referred to when someone would be cutting the grain, or cutting the hay, and starting at the outside of the field. And as they went around with the cutter, and if there were a rabbit in the field, the rabbit would continue to go to the centre until, at the very end, of course, there'd be nowhere else to go, and the rabbit would have to make a dash for it. So the saying, "We'll soon see the rabbit" meant we'll soon be finished the job.' (Weale, 'Them Times' [radio broadcast]).
Rare.

to thresh another rally
to thresh a little rally
To do another spurt of the usual work. 'At roughly ninety-minute intervals, work was halted to allow the horses to rest. For no reason that I was ever able to discover, the ninety-minute work period was called a "rally"' (Devereux, *Looking Backward*, 10). This quotation as well as those below are from *DPEIE* under 'rally "a spell of work; any spurt of activity."' The regional and social label in *DPEIE* for 'rally' is 'frequent in Cardigan, occasional in Malpeque, rare elsewhere; significantly rural, male; unattested under thirty.'
– 'I guess we'll thresh a little rally' (middle-aged Summerside woman).
– 'Rally is also used when chopping wood: "One little rally and we'll be all done"' (middle-aged Montague female homemaker).
– 'Rally could be used for any work that you do in cycles or with playing cards' (middle-aged Brudenell female homemaker).
Rare.

if they harrow what I plowed
*Also reported
You couldn't harrow the headlands of what I've plowed.
If someone could work as hard as I have at this (but that's impossible).
– 'When you've done all I've done, if you harrow what I plow, I'll take my hat off to you' (anon.).
– 'Earned what they owned because they worked hard' (senior high-school-educated Covehead female teacher).
– 'You couldn't harrow the headlands of the area I plow (no comparison)' (young college-educated Queens man).
Widespread in Prince, occasional elsewhere except rare in Charlottetown; significantly senior, rural, male; especially not grade-school-educated. *Includes senior college-educated Charlottetown male editor, and senior college-educated Summerside woman.*

BUSYNESS

busier than a toad eating lightning
*Also reported
busier than a toad eating grubs
Working very quickly.
– 'My grandmother used this saying' (young Queens man).
Rare. *Includes senior grade-school-educated St. Peters female homemaker.*

busier than a cow calving
busier than a cat having kittens
Completely absorbed with work or a project in the making; probably related to more common *busier than a hen laying, busier than a cow's tail in fly-*

time, and *busier than a cat covering its business*. See also NERVOUS AS A LONG-HAIRED CAT BESIDE AN OPEN HEARTH and SITTING LIKE A CAT IN A SANDBOX. The *cat* variant is also attested from New Brunswick.
– 'Very busy. A cow calving is one of the very busiest things' (senior college-educated Charlottetown male editor).
– 'Used many times for "busy"' (senior high-school-educated Summerside male farmer).
– 'Grandfather and friends in Alberton use this [cat] saying' (young university student).
[*cow*:] Widespread in Prince and Kings, occasional in Queens and Summerside, rare in Charlottetown; significantly senior, rural, male. [*cat*:] Widespread except occasional in Charlottetown; significantly not young.

busier than a cat in a round room trying to find a corner to do his business
*Also reported
busy as a squint-eyed cat trying to catch all the mice it sees.
Frantic with work that cannot possibly be completed; extension of common *busier than a cat covering its business*. See also NERVOUS AS A LONG-HAIRED CAT BESIDE AN OPEN HEARTH and SITTING LIKE A CAT IN A SANDBOX. A comparable well-known standard saying is *busy as a one-armed paper-hanger / bill-poster / bootlegger*, with its extensions like *in a gale* and *with crabs / hives / the itch*, and variations like *busier than a one-legged man in an ass-kicking contest* (*DCP, TTEM*). Maritimes writer Silver Donald Cameron reports 'busy as a dog in a field full of stumps' ('Nova Scotia,' 26). Compare also *DCP*: '*busy as a dog building a nest in high grass* ... Also *busy as a jockey's whip on a long-shot coming down the stretch*.'
Rare. *Includes senior grade-school-educated Prince woman.*

busy as a rooster in a three-storey barn
busy as a rat in a shed with three lofts
Overworked and preoccupied.
– 'A very busy person doesn't have enough time to get his or her work done' (young West Prince male university student).
Rare. *Includes three senior grade-school-educated Tignish men, senior high-school-educated Souris female homemaker, and middle-aged high-school-educated St. Eleanors female nurse.*

busy as a hen picking fly-shit out of pepper
Vulgar. Distracted by innumerable small and useless tasks. Also attested from New York State, by an Island informant who worked there 'on a farm in 1950.' Compare *DSUE*: '*busy as a hen with one chick*. Anxious; fussy; ludicrously proud.'
– 'Extremely active; occupied with many matters. "On Prince Edward Island in the summer, the beaches are as busy as a hen picking fly-shit out of pepper"' (Gojmerac, 'Prince Edward Island Expressions').
Not in Survey II. Probably widespread.

busy as / worse than a fart in a mitt(en) (looking for a thumb-hole)
running around like a fart in a mitt(en)
*Also reported
tearing around like a fart in a mitt
Vulgar. Anxiously working to little

purpose. Also attested from Newfoundland. Compare *CCW*: 'He was all over the place, like a fart in a glove [attested from Castlegar, BC]' (94). Compare also *DSUE*: '*fart in a bottle, or colander, like a.* Restless; jumpy; "rushing around in small circles"'; also *DCP*.
– 'Folk language was full of these apt comparisons. Some of them were ordinary, but the ones which survived the winnowing process of repeated usage were the work of genius, requiring often a real leap of imagination. Consider, for example, the saying, "as busy as a fart in a mitt." I confess I can scarcely imagine anyone clever enough to have thought that up' (Weale, *Them Times*, 62).
– 'In confusion – running around like a fart in a mitt' (senior college-educated Queens male teacher).
– 'That's as much good as a fart in a mitt' (senior female homemaker).
– 'Like a fart in a mitten – won't sit still' (senior high-school-educated male farmer).
Includes middle-aged college-educated Summerside male lawyer, college-educated West Royalty female nursing administrator, and young college-educated Charlottetown female pharmacist's assistant. Not in Survey II. Probably widespread.

to run around like a bee / fly in a bottle
To be frantically busy; parallel to common *busy as a bee, busy as a beaver, run around like a chicken with its head cut off*. The frequency label below may be inflated by the similarity of this saying to *a bee in one's bonnet*. 'an obsession or craze.' Compare *DSUE*: '*busy as a bee in a treacle-pot* ... 1923'; *LD*: '*run around like a blue-arsed fly*';

and *DAPPP*: '*Bee* ... As bisy as bees in a tar-barrel.'
Widespread in Prince, occasional elsewhere; especially rural. *Includes senior college-educated Canoe Cove male teacher.*

*busy as a flea at a dog show
Desperately trying to get everything done while there is still time.
*Late entry, not surveyed. Reported by young university student.

*busy as flies at a meat market
Happily working at many alternatives.
*Late entry, not surveyed. Reported by middle-aged college-educated Kings man.

busy as an accountant at tax-time
Suddenly very busy.
Widespread in Summerside, occasional elsewhere except rare in Kings; significantly urban, especially male, not middle-aged. *Includes young Charlottetown female university student.*

I'm not an eight-day clock or a sewing machine.
I can't go on and on, you know. See also I CAN'T DANCE AND HOLD THE BABY TOO and HAVE A HEAD LIKE A SEWING MACHINE BUT BE NO SINGER. (An eight-day clock is programmed to go for eight days without needing winding, and thus can go on even if the weekly winding is forgotten.)
– 'I can't do everything' (middle-aged college-educated Prince woman).
Rare.

like dog shit, everywhere you go
Vulgar. Some disagreeable person seems to be everywhere. Also attested from New York State, by an Island

98   Busyness

informant who worked there 'on a farm in 1950.'
– 'Like horseshit used to be, all over the place' (anon.).
Includes young Charlottetown female university student. Not in Survey II. Probably occasional.

See also CRAZY AS A CUT CAT.

Money

THRIFT

They'd walk on their heel to save their sole.
Pun on sole/soul. Someone is practising false economy; parallel to standard proverbial saying *rob Peter to pay Paul* (ODEP).
– 'This means especially frugal' (middle-aged college-educated Charlottetown woman).
Rare.

to throw more out the back door than they carry in the front
To be habitually wasteful with money and possessions.
Occasional except rare in Kings. *Includes senior grade-school-educated New Haven male farmer.*

always a day late and a dollar short
Of persons, habitually unreliable, especially with money.
– 'Someone is always late in paying bills or rent, never fixes business' (young college-educated West Prince man).
– 'The interpretation is they're late because the money is gone' (anon.).
Widespread. *Includes middle-aged Montague man, and young college-educated Cornwall man.*

*Don't buy anything on Monday or you will be spending all week.
Extravagance can get to be a habit, if you don't have strict rules. Compare CUT YOUR FINGERNAILS ON SUNDAY AND THE DEVIL WILL BE AFTER YOU ALL WEEK.
– '"Wilful waste makes woeful want," was a principle of life ranking right up there with the golden rule [in rural P.E.I. before the Second World War], and indebtedness a condition more to be feared than a state of mortal sin. "Don't buy anything on Monday or you will be spending all week," was a revered proverb in that kingdom of carefulness, as was the shorter, though no less ominous, 'Waste not, want not'" (Weale, *Them Times*, 68).
*Not surveyed.

*You can only use the eggs you have in the henhouse.
We simply must not overspend this budget.
*Late entry, not surveyed. *Reported by middle-aged Queens female teacher.*

POVERTY

It's easy to pass a poor man's door.
1. It is all too easy to be uncharitable.
2. In playing auction bridge, I can't take this trick; I have a poor hand. One informant added '... when his dog is tied up' (anon.). Williams, *Irish Proverbs*, 132, records: 'It is easy to pass by a dead man's door.'
– 'My father talks / and I listen. / "It's easy to pass / a poor man's door." / I nod from / twenty years away' (Ledwell, *Crowbush and Other Poems*, 20. Rare.

to be **so poor we couldn't pay attention**
... **the garbage man would leave three bags**
... **we couldn't afford to have a father**
... **we drew laces on our feet to walk to town**
... **we had to lace our toes for shoes**
... **we took turns sleeping on the feather (tick)**
*Also reported
to be **so poor that four in the bed meant half the family was away on vacation**
Joking. The family I grew up in was a lot poorer than yours was; somewhat comparable to standard *poor as a church mouse*. This form of humour, involving speakers attempting to top each other in outrageous statements and verbal play, is widespread beyond Prince Edward Island (for example, it features in a well-known *Monty Python* routine). An example in the routine of Lorne Elliot, a Canadian comedian who often plays at the Charlottetown Festival, is 'so poor we had to sleep in the box the satellite dish came in.' Compare *YA*: 'So broke he couldn't even pay attention,' 127.

[*attention:*] Occasional except rare in Kings; [other variants:] Rare. Includes [*bag:*] *young Charlottetown female university student;* [*father:*] *middle-aged grade-school-educated Charlottetown male taxi-driver;* [*town:*] *senior grade-school-educated Miscouche female housekeeper, and middle-aged high-school-educated Bloomfield male mechanic;* [*shoes:*] *middle-aged high-school-educated Queens woman;* [*feather:*] *senior college-educated Montague male artist, middle-aged college-educated Prince woman, and young college-educated Queens man.*

They couldn't afford to pay an instalment on a T D pipe / on a clay pipe.
Archaic. Someone is exceptionally poor. Compare *DNE*: 'T D ... Brand-name of a type of clay tobacco pipe ... [in citation:] These clay pipes cost two cents each.' Note also *DA*: 'T.D. (pipe) ... 1889 ... It is said that they took their name from Timothy Dexter, an eccentric capitalist, who in his will left a large sum of money to be expended in the erection of a factory where cheap clay pipes, such as those that now bear the name of "T.D.'s," were to be manufactured.'
Rare. *Includes senior North Shore woman.*

They couldn't afford the first instalment on a free lunch (for a canary).
They couldn't afford the ticket to a free meal.
They couldn't afford the down payment on a three-cent stamp.
*Also reported
They couldn't afford a feed of oats for a nightmare.
... **a pair of spats for a canary.**
Someone is poor beyond all imagining. In 'Texas Folk Similes,' 254, George Hendricks lists *So poor he*

couldn't make the down payment on a free lunch, which is also attested on Prince Edward Island. 'A *meal ticket* is a ticket given to workers in certain companies ... that allows them to buy a meal without having to pay for it' (*LD*).
Widespread in Summerside, occasional elsewhere; significantly senior, urban, male. *Includes senior grade-school-educated St. Peters female homemaker, senior high-school-educated Lot 37 woman, senior college-educated Charlottetown female homemaker, and middle-aged grade-school-educated Charlottetown male taxi-driver.*

They couldn't afford to call a Ford a Ford.
Someone is so poor as to be unable even to use the word *afford*. Compare A CHEV'S A CHEV AND A FORD'S A FORD.
Rare. *Includes senior grade-school-educated New Haven male farmer.*

If overalls for an elephant cost five cents, they couldn't afford a diaper.
If overalls for an elephant cost five cents, they couldn't afford the buttons for a pismire.
Whatever the price, someone is too poor to pay it. *Pismire*, 'ant,' is increasingly archaic and dialectal; it has also been 'applied contemptuously to a person' (*OED*, 1569–1818; *W3*; *DPEIE*). 'I haven't got enough money to buy a ladybug a wrestling jacket' is attested from Arkansas.
Rare. *Includes middle-aged high-school-educated Charlottetown man, and young college-educated Queens woman.*

to go through the loop
To go bankrupt, to go under the auctioneer's hammer.
Occasional in Prince, Summerside, and Charlottetown, rare elsewhere; especially senior, not high-school and college-educated. *Includes senior college-educated Canoe Cove male teacher.*

to keep their money in a snowbank / sandbank
Ironic. To have no money to keep at all.
Rare. *Includes senior grade-school-educated Queens man.*

to have more troubles than money
Not to have enough money put by.
Occasional in Prince, Queens, and Kings, rare elsewhere; especially rural. *Includes senior grade-school-educated St. Peters female homemaker, and middle-aged high-school-educated St. Eleanors female nurse.*

The flour in the barrel would take a mouse to its knees.
The flour's so low in the barrel a mouse would have to get on its knees.
A mouse wouldn't go up to its ankles in the flour barrel.
The mice come out of the cupboard with tears in their eyes.
Some household is very poor and on an insubstantial diet. Compare *CCW*: 'They were so poor there was nothing on the table but elbows, and the mice in the cellar had tears in their eyes' (attested by an informant in Port Morien, NS). See also MAY THE RATS NEVER LEAVE YOUR FLOUR BARREL WITH A TEAR IN THEIR EYE.
Rare. *Includes middle-aged high-school-educated Charlottetown man, and middle-aged college-educated Summerside man.*

to kill a sheep and to hell with poverty
To have a good time or celebrate, whatever the cost; comparable to standard *kill the fatted calf*.
Rare. *Confirmed by six informants in two surveys, including young female university student.*

Farming and Fishing

land so poor a grasshopper would have to pack / take / carry a lunch (to get across it)
land so poor a grasshopper / mouse would starve to death crossing it
*Also reported
land so poor a mouse would have to pack a lunch
a field so poor a rabbit would shed tears going across it
Very unproductive land; variants of more common exaggeration *land so poor a rabbit would have to carry a lunch*. Also attested from Ontario. Mary Clarke records 'A crow would have to carry his grub over this field of corn ... Land so poor that birds flying across it had to carry rations' in 'Proverbs ... in the Writings of Jesse Stuart' [southern U.S.A.], 149. Compare *DPEIE*: 'grasshopper land ... "Originally grasshoppers swarmed and cleaned the land. After that a rabbit would have to take his lunch to get across ..."' "Land so poor you couldn't raise an umbrella ..."' Compare also *PPS*: '*Crow* ... A crow would shed tears if obliged by its errand to fly across the district ... *Killdeer* ... it makes the tears come into the kildeer's [*sic*] eyes when they fly over the old fields.'
Occasional in Prince and Kings, rare elsewhere; significantly senior (unattested by young). *Includes three senior grade-school-educated Tignish men, senior high-school-educated Long River female homemaker, senior Parkdale woman, and middle-aged high-school-educated Morell male carpenter.*

land so poor it wouldn't grow thistles / grasshoppers / rock
Very unproductive land. See previous entry also. Person records 'Land so poor that it won't even grow weeds' in 'Proverbs from the State of Washington,' 181.
[*thistles, grasshoppers*:] Widespread in Kings, occasional elsewhere except rare in Charlottetown; significantly senior, especially rural. [*rock*:] Occasional except rare in Kings; significantly senior, especially high-school-educated. *Includes senior college-educated Charlottetown male editor, middle-aged high-school-educated St. Eleanors female nurse, and St Georges female teacher.*

land so poor it's on welfare
*Also reported
That land is waiting for the pogie.
Very unproductive land.
– '[I know this saying] but we never heard tell of welfare in my day' (senior college-educated Wheatley River female teacher).

Rare. *Includes three senior grade-school-educated Tignish men, and middle-aged grade-school-educated Charlottetown male taxi-driver.*

dry as a dust storm
dry as snuff
1. Of land or the weather, lacking moisture; variant of standard *dry as dust*. 2. Of persons, very thirsty; see also SO DRY I'M SPITTING SPARKS. Not apparently related to the common adjective phrase *dry-as-dust*, 'dull, lifeless' (as in *NDASCE*).
– 'As a child we were told to go out and play because it was "dry as a dust storm"' (young college-educated Queens man).
[*dust storm:*] Occasional except unattested in Kings; significantly male, especially urban. [*snuff:*] Rare. *Includes* [dust storm] *young Charlottetown female university student; and* [snuff] *senior college-educated Strathgartney female teacher.*

to **fish (on the) half-line**
To fish for half the catch as wages. This catchphrase and the next were not surveyed; the entries are largely repeated from *DPEIE*.

– 'Local lobster packers often owned their own small fleet of fishing boats which they rented out to many fishermen for the season. These "hired" fishermen were also supplied with the necessary equipment, including gasoline, bait and board and lodging. In return for his investment the factory owner received one-half of the season's catch from each boat. This arrangement was commonplace and in some localities was referred to as "fishing half line"' (Morrison, *Along the North Shore*, 70).
– 'If I owned a boat and gear, in order to give you a good break I would fish on the half line with you. That is, we would halve up the catch between the two of us' (anon.).

in / on the round
Of fish, not gutted, salted, or otherwise prepared for market; offered whole. See previous entry.
– '*Selling on the round*: another way of saying selling them green or not salted (Kennedy, 'Visitor's Guide,' 9).
– 'A fish in the round has no gut out. It is not dressed' (anon.).

Weather

THUNDER

God is moving (his) furniture (around).
They're moving the chairs in the Great Hall above.
They're housecleaning up above.
God is taking out the garbage cans.
Probably archaic; potentially offensive. It's thundering. The *furniture* variant is also attested from Moncton and from Ireland. Halpert's *Folklore Sampler from the Maritimes*, 112, has 'Thunder – God's housekeeper cleaning out heaven (housecleaning) and thumping the furniture around' attributed to PEI.
– 'When I was about ten years old we used to say this' (middle-aged grade-school-educated Charlottetown male taxi-driver).
Rare. *Includes senior grade-school-educated Prince woman, senior college-educated Charlottetown male editor, senior Kinkora female nurse, and middle-aged high-school-educated Queens woman.*

God / The old man / Saint Peter / The Devil is rolling (his) barrels (in the sky) / is rolling stones / is rolling barrels over a stone bridge.
Potentially offensive. It's thundering. The variant *God is rolling stones* is also attested from Ontario, and may be relatively common.
– 'Used by my family and friends' (young university student).
[*barrels:*] Occasional in Prince, Kings, and Summerside, rare elsewhere; especially senior. [*stones:*] Occasional except rare in Kings, unattested in Summerside; significantly senior. [*other variants:*] Rare. *Includes senior grade-school-educated Northam male farmer, senior grade-school-educated St. Peters female homemaker, senior high-school-educated St. Eleanors female homemaker, senior high-school-educated Covehead female teacher, and senior Coleman woman.*

The Devil is rolling his oats.
Saint Peter is rolling his turnips.
It's thundering. Compare *The Devil is beating his wife / his mother*, which was formerly standard for sun and rain at the same time (*ODEP*, 1666–1828).
Rare. *Includes young Charlottetown female university student.*

The angels are bowling.
God / The Lord is (gone) bowling (with the angels).
God is dropping bowling balls.
Potentially offensive. It's thundering. Also attested from British Columbia,

Ontario, and New Brunswick. 'Thunder was the angels bowling' is in Halpert's *Folklore Sampler from the Maritimes*, 111, attributed originally to 'Northern Saskatchewan, early 1930's.'
Occasional except rare in Queens; significantly senior. *Includes senior high-school-educated Bedeque female homemaker, middle-aged high-school-educated Prince man, and several young university students.*

God / The Lord is angry tonight.
That's the angry voice of the Lord.
*Also reported
God is mad at the Devil.
The Lord has an upset stomach.
Potentially offensive. It's thundering. Also attested in Halpert, *Folklore Sampler from the Maritimes*, 110. Another meaning suggested was 'an angry squall' (senior grade-school-educated Prince woman).
– '"When I was a boy growin' up, God was something to be feared. Oh yes! The fear of God was drilled into us every chance they got. That's how they kept us on the straight and narrow, by puttin' the fear of hell in us." ... There were, to be sure, elements of the faith which helped to soften somewhat the awful scowl of the Almighty ... But God had the last word, and He was a distant, offended potentate with a propensity to be eternally out of sorts. "I remember," said one woman, "that when it would thunder, some of the old people would say, 'Don't you know, that's the angry voice of our Lord'"' (Weale, *Them Times*, 109).
Widespread in Prince, occasional in Queens, Summerside, and Charlottetown, rare in Kings; especially female.

The clouds are banging into one another.
It's thundering.
Occasional except rare in Queens and Kings; significantly urban.

The boards are falling on Grandpa.
It's thundering.
Rare. *Confirmed by five informants in two surveys.*

RAIN

*It's raining cats and dogs, claws down.
The rain is drilling down especially hard; extension of common *It's raining cats and dogs*.
Late entry, not surveyed. Reported by middle-aged grade-school-educated Prince man.

God is spitting.
God is crying.
Potentially offensive. A fine mist is falling. Halpert, *Folklore Sampler from the Maritimes*, 109, reports *God is crying* from Sydney, Nova Scotia.
Occasional except rare in Kings and Summerside; especially senior, significantly college-educated. *Includes senior college-educated Charlottetown male editor, and young Charlottetown female university student.*

A rooster crowing to bed is sure to rise with a wet head.
Proverb. If a rooster crows in the evening, it will rain by morning; comparable to standard forecast: *Red sky at night, sailors delight; red sky in the morning, sailors take warning*. Confirmed by eight informants in two surveys. One added that 'a rooster crowing in the late morning means a stranger is coming' (anon.).
Rare.

to blow up rain
Of the wind, to grow stronger just before the rain falls. Probably not related to the jazz saying *to blow up a storm* (*DAS*).
— 'It looks like it is going to blow up rain when the weather is getting worse' (middle-aged Belmont male farmer). Widespread in Prince, occasional elsewhere except rare in Queens.

STORM and COLD

Not (too) many flies out today.
At least there's no flies out today.
... blackflies / mosquitoes ...
... around today / right now.
Good weather for flies / blackflies / mosquitoes.
to be **not bothered by flies / blackflies / mosquitoes**
Ironic. It is piercingly cold, especially from strong winds. Also attested from New Brunswick, Ontario, and Newfoundland.
— 'January was a month of storms. It snowed for three weeks on end. The thermometer went miles below zero and stayed there. But, as Barney and Valancy pointed out to each other, there were no mosquitoes. And the roar and crackle of their big fire drowned the howls of the north wind (Montgomery, *The Blue Castle*, 195).
— We are now having lots of snow and it seems that the thermometer has gone miles below zero; however, everyone really seems to be enjoying the weather, making jokes about it and doing fun things to down the howls of the north wind. Of course, even with modern technology and all kinds of pesticides, we still can bring smiles to people's faces by saying there aren't any mosquitoes!' (*Kindred Spirits of P.E.I.*, Winter 1991/92).

— 'I've heard this from Tracadie, PEI. As a child, we used to pick cranberries, and it was here that I heard this saying' (young college-educated Queens man).
— '"At least there's no blackflies" is a way to address a cold day and look at the bright side!' (young university student).
[*flies:*] Common in Kings, widespread elsewhere. [*blackflies, mosquitoes:*] Occasional; *mosquitoes* significantly senior, *blackflies* significantly male. Includes middle-aged college-educated Summerside male lawyer, and middle-aged college-educated Charlottetown man.

a whore of a day
Potentially offensive. A day of terrible weather.
— 'I heard this dialogue in northeast Kings County: "G'day, its a whore of a day." "Yes, a pure slut."' (middle-aged college-educated Queens male teacher).
— 'Used a lot by myself' (young Charlottetown female university student). Not in Survey II. Probably common.

It's chilly eyebrow today.
The weather is rather cold.
— 'Fairly nippy all right – Pisquid area' (university student).
— 'My father, a sailor, would say this' (middle-aged Charlottetown male civil servant).
Rare.

too cold (out) for a fence post
Cold almost beyond standing.
— '*cold for a fence post, too* ... applies to inclement weather involving below average temperatures. "With the wind blowing the way it is, it's too cold for a fence post"' (Gojmerac, 'Prince Edward Island Expressions').

– 'Very popular' (young Charlottetown female university student).
Rare.

not fit for a mailbox (to be out)
not fit for a woodpile
Of the weather, viciously stormy; comparable to conventional *not a fit night out for a dog / for man nor beast*. Along the roads of rural Prince Edward Island in winter, the mailboxes are symbols of endurance.
– 'If it wasn't so nasty, I'd go out and take the mailbox in' (middle-aged high-school-educated Souris male agricultural worker).
– 'Not fit for delivery (weather so bad mail cannot be delivered)' (senior grade-school-educated Tignish male farmer).
Occasional except rare in Summerside and Charlottetown; especially rural. *Includes senior college-educated Summerside male education official, and middle-aged grade-school-educated Queens man.*

a poor day to set a hen
*Also reported
a good day to let the ram go
Ironic understatement. Very nasty weather, a day for staying inside if at all possible. Compare A GOOD DAY TO SET A HEN. Also attested from Ireland.
– '"Hell of a day, ain't she?" says Herman, with a wicked gleam in his eye. Abe gave him a look. "Yes, she's a poor day to set a hen alright"' (Boyles, 'Living in Harmony,' 54).
Widespread in Prince, occasional elsewhere except rare in Summerside; significantly rural, not young.

cold as the horns off the Devil
Very cold. Connecting the Devil with excessive cold, not heat, is common in folklore; a university student supplied *cold as the back door of Hell*.
Rare. *Includes senior grade-school-educated St. Peters female homemaker.*

cold as a widow's breath
Very cold; parallel to more common *cold as a step-mother's / mother-in-law's breath / kiss* (DCP, TTEM).
Rare. *Includes senior high-school-educated Summerside male farmer.*

so cold it would freeze the nuts off a steel / iron bridge
so cold it would freeze the nuts off the Hillsborough Bridge
so cold it would freeze the nuts off a dump cart
Very cold. Probably a euphemism for the common *so cold it would freeze the balls off a brass monkey* (DCP). The Hillsborough Bridge is a much-travelled connection between central Charlottetown and several suburbs.
– 'Heard first [both *bridge* and *cart*] from my father' (young Bonshaw male university student).
Occasional. *Includes [bridge] senior grade-school-educated Prince female homemaker, and senior high-school-educated Queens woman; [cart] senior college-educated Charlottetown female teacher, and senior Vernon Bridge male farmer; and [both] senior high-school-educated Summerside male farmer, and middle-aged high-school-educated St. Eleanors female nurse.*

froze to pokers
Stiffened from a heavy frost. Also attested in Porter, 'Some Newfoundland Phrases,' 297). Compare *ODEP*: 'Stiff as a poker,' 1706–1886.
– 'Well we've got winter up here now and no mistake. All through November we had charming weather, warm clear and bright – but – on my birth-

day night – it came up a snowstorm and when we got up in the morning everything was froze to pokers. Oo-o-o-o-o! (Fancy a dozen shivers now) and hasn't it been cold since' (Montgomery, *Letters* to Penzie MacNeill, 42).
Rare.

to shiver like a dog in a wet blanket
To shiver uncontrollably with cold. Compare *SD*: '*Trembling ...* Shivering like a whippet on a cold day.'
– 'He was shivering like a dog in a wet blanket' (Noonan, 'Irish Expressions,' 14).
Occasional except rare in Queens; significantly senior, especially male.

nine / ten / eleven months of winter and three / two / one month(s) of tough sledding / of poor skating conditions / of (late) fall
The Canadian or Prince Edward Island climate, severe and inhospitable. In *A Treasury of New England Folklore*, 495, B.A. Botkin records 'the New England climate consists of "nine months winter and three months late in the fall."' This catchphrase is possibly a variation of the reported British description of their climate: 'Two months of rain and the rest winter.' Note also *NDFRRS*: '"hard sledding AND tough sledding" a very difficult time.'
– 'Canada's climate has been referred to as nine months of winter and three months of late fall' (MacPhee, 'Along the Rural Routes,' 7).
– 'We can put up with 10 months of winter and two months poor skating conditions and still like it here' ('Ten reasons for pride in Canada,' 1).
Widespread in Prince and Queens, occasional elsewhere; significantly senior, male, especially high-school-educated.

cold as a barn
Of a house, too cold to be comfortable.
– 'Used by my friends and family' (young university student).
Common in Queens and Kings, widespread in Summerside and Charlottetown, occasional in Prince; significantly not young, especially female. *Includes senior West Royalty male farmer, and middle-aged college-educated Charlottetown female secretary.*

See also NOT TOO BAD OF A DAY.

DARKNESS

black as the inside of a black cow
black as two black bears at midnight
black as a blue pig
Exceptionally dark outside, without moon or stars; variants of stock similes *dark as the inside of a cow / of a cow's belly, black as the inside of a cat, black as a crow*. Informants also suggested many traditional, non-animal similes for blackness including *dungeon, pitch, your boot, the bottom of a tea-kettle*, and non-White races. The form *black as the inside of* is also common. Compare *MBP*: 'As dark as the inside of a cow'; *NDFRRS*: '(as) dark as the inside of a cow's belly ... darker than the inside of a cow's belly'; *WPI*: 'I can't see more than if in a black cow's belly'; and *SD*: '(A hall) black as a billy goat's belly.' Note also *DAPPP*: '*Cat ...* All was as dark as a stack of black cats.'
[*cow*:] Occasional except rare in Prince and unattested in Charlottetown. [*bears, pig*:] Rare. *Includes senior high-school-educated Darnley female secretary, senior high-school-educated Lot 37 woman, senior Stanhope man, middle-aged high-school-educated St. Eleanors female nurse, young West Prince male univer-*

sity student, and young Hunter River female university student.

*black as a witch's pocket
Very dark. Probably a euphemism for older, offensive *black as a squaw's pocket*.
*Late entry, not surveyed. *Reported by middle-aged high-school-educated Queen's woman.*

black as arse
Vulgar. As dark as can be, pitch-black. Compare *RH*: 'black as the devil's arse' (1774).
Includes senior high-school-educated St. Catherines female homemaker, and young Stanhope female university student. Not in Survey II. Probably common.

FINE WEATHER

The sun is splitting the trees.
*Also reported
The sun is splitting the sky / heavens.
The sun is splitting the rocks.
The sun has just arisen and it is an exceptionally bright and beautiful morning. Also attested from Ireland. *The sun is splitting the rocks* is also attested from Newfoundland. A few informants restrict this saying to summer mornings only.
– 'You're on vacation and you've just arrived in Charlottetown [on 24 July]. There isn't a cloud in the sky and the sun is splitting the trees, just like the photograph on the travel brochure you picked up at the tourism information centre. So what are you going to do on such a nice day?' (Doug Gallant, 'City offers lots of activities,' 16).
– 'As I write this column [for 5 December] the sun is splitting the trees and the weatherman is saying that before the day is over the temperature will plummet and snow will come' (Blacquiere, 'North Shore News,' 9).
– This, and variations of it, I've often heard as a reference to the first warm days of early March' (anon.).
Common or widespread; significantly college-educated, especially not young. Includes senior college-educated Canoe Cove male teacher, senior college-educated Charlottetown female homemaker, and young college-educated Charlottetown woman.

a good day to set a hen
A good day for activity. See also *a poor day to set a hen*. Also attested from Ireland and Ontario.
– 'Meaning a good day to do this or that' (Weale collection).
Occasional; significantly senior, especially high-school-educated, male.

not too bad of a day
Ironic. A day that is either exceptionally fine or exceptionally foul.
– 'I heard this twice on Friday, June 5, 1992 from the weather reporter on 'Compass' [local CBC program]' (young college-educated Murray Harbour male librarian).
Common or widespread; especially young, college-educated.

smooth as the kitchen table
Of the sea, calm.
– 'My father uses this; he fishes in Savage Harbour' (young male university student).
Rare. Includes senior high-school-educated Parkdale female nurse.

*calm as a cradle
Meaning uncertain: possibly of a boat in a calm sea, rocking only slightly.
*Late entry, not surveyed. *Reported by senior college-educated woman.*

to **hang a powder horn on (a tip of) the moon**
Especially for fall hunting. 1. To have the prospect of fine weather. 2. To have the prospect of poor weather. The two opposite meanings are each confirmed by several informants. The first meaning is also attested from Maine and Massachusetts. Compare IF YOU SEE THE NEW MOON THROUGH GLASS, IT'S TROUBLE WHILE IT LASTS.
– 'The evening star had already set its brightness, and below to the west moved a magic new crescent of moon. Weather-wise, what was the forecast? Rain or sunshine? Could one hang a powder horn on a tip?' (Dixon, *Going Home*, 173).
– 'If the "new moon" hung so that a powder horn (gunpowder container) could be supported (new moon on its back), the hunter stayed home, indicating bad weather. If the new moon shone sideways indicating a powder horn could not hang on (could fall off) the tip of the moon, the hunter could hunt. Good weather indicated' (senior high-school-educated Summerside man).
Rare. *Includes [for sense 1] senior college-educated Charlottetown woman, and middle-aged grade-school-educated Kings woman.*

*The moon is holding water.
The new moon is lying on its side, as if it could hold water in the cup – a portent of fine weather. See previous entry.
*Late entry, not surveyed. *Reported by senior college-educated Charlottetown woman.*

Physical Properties

AGE OF OBJECTS

old enough to vote
old enough to draw a pension
Of any object or creature, much older than others of its kind. Also attested from New Brunswick. See also A COW SO OLD IT MUST HAVE HAD A VOTE.
– 'My grandmother says this about her refrigerator (young college-educated Murray Harbour male librarian). Widespread in Prince and Queens, occasional elsewhere; especially young, female. *Includes senior grade-school-educated Prince woman, middle-aged college-educated Kings woman.*

a song so old it has a grey beard / it has holes in it
A once popular song that is now out of fashion.
Rare. *Confirmed by eleven informants in two surveys, including young male university tudent.*

rotten as dirt
Decayed, worn down. Also listed in Porter, 'Some Newfoundland Phrases, 295. Compare *DARE*: 'dirt: meaner than (or mean as) dirt.'
Widespread in Kings, occasional elsewhere; especially senior.

See also **Old Age**, and A COW SO OLD IT MUST HAVE HAD A VOTE, IT MUST HAVE BEEN OLDER THAN THE FIRST SETTLERS.

EASE OF JOB

slick as a kitten's / cat's wrist
Fitting easily or neatly; parallel to traditional *slick as a whistle*. One informant suggested the meaning "sly, sneaky" (young university student).
– 'An alternate to "as slick as glass." Kittens can get into almost anything. They can slip their paws through small spaces' (young university student).
– 'A cat's paw glides easily' (high-school-educated woman).
Rare. *Includes senior college-educated Strathgartney female teacher.*

slick as a biscuit (with butter on it)
1. Of a job, finished neatly and well.
2. Sly, cunning.
– 'Easy to do, or in some cases sly' (anon.).
– 'Slippery' (senior college-educated Charlottetown male editor).
Rare.

clean as an eggshell
Of an object just worked on, slick and spotless; parallel to traditional *clean as a whistle*.
– '"Will you take me out for a little row in the dory? I haven't been out for so long." "Of course. Come – here's the dory – your namesake, you know. I had her fresh painted last week. She's as clean as an eggshell"' (Montgomery, 'Mackereling out in the Gulf,' 52).
– 'Exaggerating neatness' (young college-educated Queens man).
Rare. *Includes young Charlottetown female university student.*

to **fit like a sock in a pig's ear / nose**
Ironic. Not to fit at all. The proverbial awkwardness of pigs, as in *like a pig on ice*, is commonplace. Compare *SD*: 'Belonging ... Fit (poor fit) like a breeching on a pig.'
– 'I had a grade eight teacher who used this a *lot*' (middle-aged college-educated female teacher).
Rare. *Includes senior grade-school-educated Prince woman, and senior college-educated Montague male artist.*

the cock for Dolly
Coarse and potentially offensive. Just the thing that's appropriate.
– 'The part that is found to fit a mechanism. Usually applies to a nut/bolt combination. "I knew I'd find the cock for Dolly in this box of spare parts"' (Gojmerac, 'Prince Edward Island Expressions).
– 'A good substitute' (Georgetown university student).
Not in Survey II. Probably occasional.

TIGHTNESS

tight as the tail on a cat
*Also reported
tight as a cat's ass
Fixed in place very firmly; parallel to more common *tight as a mouse's ear*.
Rare. *Includes middle-aged Brooklyn man.*

tight as two coats of paint
Of objects, close fitting, secure, inseparable.
Occasional except rare in Prince; especially male. *Includes young Charlottetown female university student.*

tight as a cup
*Also reported
tight as a pop bottle
Of a boat, soundly made.
– 'Silas was talking about a boat someone had made. "She was well put together," he said, "as tight as a cup." I had never heard that saying before, but it seemed to me a stroke of brilliance. Who could ever forget such an apt turn of phrase: "as tight as a cup." It was perfect, immortal' (Weale, *Them Times*, 61).
Occasional in Prince and Kings, rare in Queens and Summerside, unattested in Charlottetown; significantly rural, male. *Includes young grade-school-educated Summerside man.*

***tight as a coot**
Water-tight, able to repel water as easily as an aquatic bird's feathers. (A coot is marsh bird resembling a duck.)
*Late entry, not surveyed. *Reported by senior college-educated Charlottetown woman.*

tight as a fiddlestring
*Also reported
tight as a fiddler's fart
1. Of persons, stingy, tightfisted.

2. Inebriated. 3. Of objects, fully stretched, taut; comparable in this meaning to conventional *tight as a drum*. Unfortunately, this simile was surveyed without a meaning attached; the frequency label thus includes all three meanings together, listed here in their apparent order of popularity in two surveys. Compare *SD*: '(People were as) tense as fiddle strings.'
– 'Heard among carpenters or mechanics when fitting a key part into some assembly, or when stringing a line on a boat, or lashing loads on a truck or wagon' (anon.).
– 'I've heard this meaning that something is fixed firmly in place' (young Stanhope female university student). Widespread in Prince, Queens, and Kings, occasional in Summerside and Charlottetown; significantly senior, rural. *Includes three senior North River women.*

TOUCH

hard as the knockers of hell
Of objects, extremely hard; variant of popular *hard as the hobs of hell* (*DSUE*). Another suggested meaning was 'hard times' (anon.).
Common except widespread in Queens; significantly high-school-educated and not young. *Includes senior grade-school-educated Miscouche female housekeeper.*

soft as porridge
1. Of objects, soft to the touch. 2. Of persons, mentally deficient, 'soft in the head.' Comparable in both senses to more common *soft as mush*.
Occasional except rare in Queens; especially senior. *Includes senior college-educated Queens woman.*

tough as a sow's snout
Of objects, capable of withstanding great pressure.
Rare. *Confirmed by ten informants in two surveys.*

heavy as a man and a boy
Exceptionally heavy.
– 'Silas was a man who would surprise you with his comparisons. He probably had never heard of a simile, but he used them all the time; which, to my way of thinking, is a lot further ahead than knowing what they are but not being able to use them. I confess, for example, that if I were attempting to describe something extra heavy I'd be liable to say, "heavy as a rock." On a bad day, I might even say, "heavy as lead," and be ashamed afterwards. But Silas could always do better than that. I remember once he was describing something he had carried. It was, he said, "as heavy as a man and a boy."' (Weale, *Them Times*, 61).
Rare.

*so sharp you could shave a mouse and never wake him up
Of a knife, incredibly sharp.
*Late entry, not surveyed. Reported by middle-aged grade-school-educated Prince man.

See also YOU'LL NEVER PUT AIR UNDER THAT.

HEAT

The biscuits are done.
The turkey / chicken is cooked / roasted.
*Also reported
The supper's cooked.
Someone has set the temperature in

this place far too high. The frequency label for the *turkey / chicken* variant may be inflated by overlap with the standard *to cook one's goose*, 'to bring on certain trouble.'
– 'He turned the heat down and said, "Whew, the biscuits are done." Usually sarcastically spoken as the heat is turned down or off' (Gojmerac, 'Prince Edward Island Expressions' 1986).
– 'It's hot enough to roast a chicken' (middle-aged high-school-educated St. Eleanors female nurse).
[*biscuits*:] Widespread in Summerside, occasional elsewhere; especially grade-school-educated, urban. [*turkey / chicken*:] Widespread in Prince, occasional elsewhere; especially rural, female. *Includes senior grade-school-educated Northam male farmer, and middle-aged Charlottetown woman.*

You could cook / fry eggs on the floor.
It's really hot inside; variant of established saying (for outside temperature) *You could cook eggs on the sidewalk / pavement / engine bonnet.*
Widespread in Prince and Summerside, occasional elsewhere. *Includes senior high-school-educated Miscouche female teacher.*

DIMENSIONS

so high you have to look twice to see
1. Of any object, extraordinarily high.
2. Of persons, extraordinarily tall.
Compare so THIN THEY HAVE TO WALK BY TWICE TO MAKE A SHADOW.
– 'A New Zealand [PEI] term' (Central Lot 16 man).
Occasional in Prince, Summerside, and Charlottetown, rare in Queens, unattested in Kings.

wide as a fishcake
Meaning unclear; see quotation.
– 'Folk language was full of these apt comparisons. Some of them were ordinary, but the ones which survived the winnowing process of repeated usage were the work of genius, requiring often a real leap of imagination. Consider, for example, ... "as wide as a fishcake"' (Weale, *Them Times*, 62).
– 'Alberton' (Weale collection).
Rare.

wide as the Devil's boots
Of any object, far too wide. Also attested from Newfoundland in Porter, 'Some Newfoundland Phrases, 297.
– 'He needs them wide to catch you' (senior grade-school-educated Prince woman).
Rare.

*so thin it only has one side
Of cake or bread, sliced too thinly for good eating.
Late entry, not surveyed. Reported by young male university student.

straight / long as a sleigh track on the Western Road
Of any line, exceptionally straight or long. See also A FACE AS LONG AS THE WESTERN ROAD. Compare CROOKED AS THE TRANS-CANADA. Two sections of Highway 2, the 'Western Road' from Summerside to Tignish, are exceptionally long and straight by PEI standards. According to Lorne Elliot, a professional comic often in the Charlottetown Festival, 'You know something's wrong when you're looking forward to Kensington! [almost the first stop light]'
– 'As far as Brupp could see the road

was straight behind the truck ...
"*Straight as a sleigh track on the Western Road*. That's how Mrs. Gallant described the road that leads to the western part of Prince Edward Island"' (Kessler, *The Private Adventures of Brupp*, 50).
– 'Something long and unbroken' (anon.).
– 'I agree: how well I know the road!' (anon.).
– 'I've heard of a letter long as a sleigh track, and sometimes a boring story' (senior Coleman woman).
Rare. *Includes middle-aged high-school-educated Kings man, and middle-aged college-educated Prince female broadcaster.*

LOCATIONS

a spit and a jump (away)
a look and a half (away)
half a look (away)
*Also reported
a whipstitch away
At a short, indeterminate distance; variant of popular catchphrases *a skip and a jump away*, *a hop and a skip away*; comparable to popular *a cat('s) jump away*. The *spit* variant is also attested from Newfoundland and Ireland. Lewis Poteet discusses phrases of this kind, where 'a degree of imprecision or rough measure may be helpful,' in 'Rough Measure in Maritime Dialect Research,' appendix 2 of *SSPB*. Compare *DPEIE*: '*look and a half, a.*'
– 'An expression of distance, e.g., "It's a look and a half down the road" or "He lives half a look that way"' (senior St. Theresa male farmer).
– 'Very popular [*spit*]' (young Charlottetown female university student).
[*spit:*] Widespread in Charlottetown, occasional elsewhere; significantly urban, especially senior, college-educated. [*look:*]

Rare. *Includes two middle-aged college-educated male teachers of St. Peters and Charlottetown.*

up west
In or to any part of Prince Edward Island west of Summerside, especially the most western area. The information in this entry is adapted from that in *DPEIE*, which states of *up west*, 'Generally, the further east the speaker, the wider the area covered by this term.'
– 'I have met so many men of his type. I remember one time, when I was teaching school up west I went home to dinner one day and found a "preacher" there who evidently modelled his religion after "Pansy's" fairy tales' (Montgomery, *Green Gables Letters*, 67).
– 'Her daughter Elizabeth moved with husband and children "up west," as Islanders put it, to Enmore, in the western part of Prince Edward Island, a section of the province economically depressed for generations' (Graves, *William Schurman*, I: 54).
– 'Tignish is no longer "away up west" but within driving distance some evening after tea' (Sellick, *My Island Home*, 85).
Common.

down east
In or to any part of Prince Edward Island east of Charlottetown. The information in this entry is adapted from that in *DPEIE*, which states of *down east*, 'The standard Canadian sense, "in or to the Maritimes," is also commonly known, but generally expresses the view of someone in, or coming from, central Canada.'
– 'While it is true that there are often winter conditions that prevail

throughout the whole 140 miles of the Island, there are days in which it is much milder down east' (Sellick, *My Island Home*, 81).
– 'For the early Gowan Brae days I recall a good many differences from the folkways and mores of Victoria [PEI] and environs. "Down East" there were always more children about. It was the pre-pill era in both places but family planning was more obviously coming into vogue in the community farther west' (MacQuarrie, 'Recollections of His Early Childhood,' 2).
Common.

up east
In or to the most easterly part of Prince Edward Island, especially east of St. Peters or Souris. The information in this entry is adapted from that in *DPEIE*, which states of *up east*, 'This term was used primarily by informants who themselves lived "down east," that is, east of Charlottetown.'
– 'Too bad they don't run special trains in from up east and down west any more, like they used to when the Junior Royals were playing. That'd fill the old Forum like it used to then' (Ledwell and Gool, *Portraits and Gastroscopes*, 74).
– 'What if they [the people of St. Peters] object to my binges and my heavy smoking? Will they take it in stride like the people up east?' (Ledwell, *The North Shore of Home*, 39).
– 'If you are from east of Charlottetown and you leave the city you go "up east" but if you are from Charlottetown and west you go "down east."' (anon.).
Common in east Kings, occasional in Charlottetown, rare or unattested elsewhere; significantly male.

down west
In or to any part of Prince Edward Island west of Charlottetown. The information in this entry is adapted from that in *DPEIE*, which states of *down west* ... 'This term was generally used by informants living "up east."'
– 'Too bad they don't run special trains in from up east and down west any more, like they used to when the Junior Royals were playing. That'd fill the old Forum like it used to then' (Ledwell and Gool, *Portraits and Gastroscopes*, 74).
– 'People from up west (Alberton) say "down east," but people from Souris say "up east" and "down west"' (anon.).

(to jump) across the puddle / pond / brook
(To travel) across the Northumberland Strait, to or in New Brunswick or Nova Scotia. *Across the pond* is also used with reference to the Atlantic Ocean, parallel to *DAS* (*big pond, herring pond*), and *IPI* (*across the herring pond*). Compare also *DPEIE*: '*puddle, the* ... Frequent in Egmont and Summerside, infrequent elsewhere; especially younger, male.'
– 'Going "across the puddle" means to move there or emigrate to New Brunswick' (middle-aged college-educated West Prince male teacher).
– 'A trip across the puddle means going to Dorchester to jail' (Brooklyn man).
– 'I have heard this said a few times by older people, but the saying more familiar to me is "across to the other side" or "across the way"' (young Stanhope female university student).
Common in Summerside, widespread in Queens, occasional elsewhere; significantly male, especially college-educated.

Includes middle-aged college-educated Summerside male lawyer.

from across
from over across
From the mainland across the Northumberland Strait, Nova Scotia or New Brunswick. The information in this entry is adapted from that for *across* in *DPEIE*. Research for that work included the survey question 'If someone lives in New Brunswick or Nova Scotia he or she is from ...?' *Across* was favoured by 7 per cent of the informants, chiefly rural users, over such choices as *the other side* or *the mainland*. Typically, *from across* and *from away* are not equated, though they are by the first speaker below.
– 'People here definitely think that, if someone is going to come from across, they've got to be better because they're "from away"' (senior woman).
– 'I have heard this said a few times by older people, but the saying more familiar to me is "across to the other side" or "across the way"' (young Stanhope female university student). Widespread except occasional in Charlottetown. *Includes young college-educated Charlottetown female pharmacist's assistant.*

from away
From any place other than Prince Edward Island or, occasionally, the Maritimes. Also attested from the West Indies, Newfoundland, Nova Scotia, and Maine – with appropriate meaning (as recorded, for example, in *ML*, 37: 'To be *from away* is to be non-native ... There are niceties of distinction in the numerous Maine terms for non-Mainers which are best appreciated after attentive exposure; *from away* does suggest some effort to conform and belong. A man who has lived fifty years in your town and paid his taxes faithfully would hardly be called a *furriner*, and certainly not a *pilgrim*, but he will retain his non-Maine status of being *from away*.'). On Prince Edward Island the outer limit of *away* is not always fixed at the world but may be, in minority usage, North America or the rest of Canada only. People from Ontario are especially said to be *from away*. Non-native Islanders sometimes refer to themselves jokingly as *PFA's*, 'people from away,' or *CFA's*, 'come from away.' Native Islanders who have moved elsewhere are sometimes *home from away*: 'As she was a fond sister and extremely proud of all her brothers it was a joy to her to have one of them "home from away" and available for one of her parties' (Stewart, *Marion Stewart's Journal*, 20). Most of the information in this entry is adapted from *DPEIE*. Compare also *DARE*: '*away* ... Any place other than the place considered home,' 1888–1975 [informants from Maine, Boston, Kentucky, Georgia, all using phrase 'from away'], and *SSPB*: '*away* – any place other than Nova Scotia, usually employed as the direct opposite of "around here": "Are you from 'away'? Ye're not from around here."'
– 'First, it means that the folk tradition was vital enough in this area to make it worth Doyle's while to work within it, and second it shows Doyle preferring what is local and familiar to that which is "from away" and "new" (hence strange)' (Ives, *Lawrence Doyle*, 247).
– 'You can see at once how that magnificent voice, those fast good looks, the casual good humour carried an

outsider from Ontario – someone from "away" with no more than 18 years on the Island – to prominence in Party politics' (Ledwell and Gool, *Portraits and Gastroscopes*, 15).
– 'There are drawbacks in the cultural/social environment for anybody from away because the Islanders do not really accept ideas of people who are not born in Prince Edward Island' (Prince Edward Island Multicultural Council, *Exploratory Survey*, 30).
– '"Anne [of Green Gables] herself has come 'from away' ..." (We can cherish this irony about the most famous "Islander.")' (Lemm, Review of *The Fragrance of Sweet-Grass*, 40).
– 'I know people from away, from down in the States, and they wouldn't come to your home unless they were invited at a certain time' (senior woman).
– 'I hear this saying almost every day' (young Stanhope female university student).
Common.

from the other side
on the other side
From / In New Brunswick or Nova Scotia, on the other side of the Northumberland Strait from Prince Edward Island. The information in this entry is adapted from that for *other side* in *DPEIE*, which states: 'For a small minority this phrase has the meaning of "the British Isles." For prisoners, *the other side* can mean specifically Dorchester Penitentiary in New Brunswick.' Compare *DKS*: '*Other Side, The* Australia, the other side of the water [from New Zealand]; c.1880.'
– 'Old William Palmer, you know, John W.'s father, and I don't know who else was with him, went across to Buctouche, on the other side some place for rum, and they got a supply of it' (Morrison, *Along the North Shore*, 97–8).
– '"... [T]he twins are thinking about going away to work," Ronnie said. "Oh where? Halifax?" Jimmy put in. "Oh somewhere on the other side, I'm not sure where," said Ronnie' (Ledwell, *The North Shore of Home*, 123).
– 'That bear's tracks came up out of the water and he must have swum over from the other side' (senior Belfast woman).
– 'People who say that Anne of Green Gables is an orphan "from away" have it all wrong. She's from the other side [i.e., Nova Scotia]. That's a lot different!' (middle-aged college-educated Queens male teacher).
– 'I was teased as a child because I used to ask my aunt, "The other side of what?"' (young Charlottetown female university student).

*to be stuck home
To have to remain on Prince Edward Island when desperately wanting to join others in emigrating. 'In 1891 the population of Prince Edward Island was 109,000. By 1931, despite the high birth rate, that number had plummeted to 88,000' (Weale [as below], 83).
– 'So many people were emigrating during these years [the late nineteenth and early twentieth centuries] that leaving home became a routine pattern of behaviour ... A man from Kelly's Cross had this recollection: "I was stuck home. My oldest brother came home on holidays, and I coaxed and coaxed to go back with him."
'I am intrigued by the term "stuck home," which I have heard frequently. I believe it suggests

poignantly the feelings of those many Islanders who wanted to get away, but who, for reasons beyond their control, were unable to leave; those who were bound and immobilized by family obligation, like shingles nailed and overlapped on the side of the barn ...

'In all of this it is possible to detect what might be termed an "outmigration trauma." It is the trauma of being left behind or, quite literally, of missing the boat. With so many of their contemporaries leaving for greener pastures, it was easy for the stay-at-homes to feel aggrieved and resentful, to think of themselves deprived, and to regard the Island as a place of entrapment and missed opportunity' (Weale, *Them Times*, 84).
*Late entry, not surveyed.

SPEED

like walking on / through molasses
Of movement, slow and difficult; variant of standard *slow as molasses* and *slow as molasses running uphill (in January / February)*. Compare SD: 'As easy as wading in tar.'
– 'Walking on molasses, like – simile.

tricky. "Trying to get to work through all of the traffic was like walking through molasses"' (Gojmerac, 'Prince Edward Island Expressions'). Occasional. *Includes young Charlottetown female university student.*

to walk back on her
To dance fast and well. Also attested in New Brunswick, by Herb Curtis in *Look What the Cat Drug In!*: 1990: 'What one yells when a fiddler is playing something close to the floor' [i.e., up tempo]).
– 'Refers to dancing – someone really step-dancing fast or swinging fast: "He's really walking back on her"' (senior grade-school-educated Northam male farmer).
– 'I've heard this and remember it being said at a dance. The faster the couple went, they were said to be "walking back on her"' (senior grade-school-educated Northam female homemaker).
– '"Walk back on her" – encouraging one to do good steps (step-dancing, either male or female)' (senior grade-school-educated Summerside female homemaker).
Rare. *Includes St. Georges female teacher.*

Miscellaneous

every hitch and turn
Annoyingly often. Perkins, in 'Vanishing Expressions of the Maine Coast,' 140, provides a parallel in *every hand's turn*.
– 'My mom says this. I've heard others say it too' (anon.).
Occasional; significantly urban.

a touch of the orchard about / in [someone]
*Also reported
a dash of lavender
Of homosexual men, a certain amount of the stereotypical or supposed effeminacy of this group; intended to suggest, euphemistically, the common North American offensive slang word, *fruit*, 'homosexual man.'
– 'He went on for a good few more minutes about the poets he'd bring with him, saying how the fruity fella had actually spent a few summers in Cavendish and so had a sort of claim to be an Islander, and the scruffy one was raised on a fruit farm in the Okanagan Valley or some place, so he could identify with rural life.
"That's funny," says Ray with a loud voice, "I could have swore there was more of a touch of the orchard about the other one, myself"' (Boyles,

'Living in Harmony,' 7).
– 'I like this one – have only heard it in the past few years from some Rustico friends' (anon.).
– 'Augustine Cove' (middle-aged college-educated Summerside male lawyer).
Rare. *Includes middle-aged high-school-educated Charlottetown female secretary, and young Stanhope female university student.*

*yellow as a duck's foot
A horrible yellow colour.
*Late entry, not surveyed. *Reported by senior high-school-educated Lot 37 woman.*

smart as a bee
Quick and alert; probably derived from standard *busy as a bee*. Also attested from Ireland and Newfoundland (see Porter, 'Some Newfoundland Phrases,' 296).
– 'Moves quickly and gets things done quickly' (middle-aged college-educated Prince woman).
– 'I was told that I was "smart as a bee" in mathematics and the sciences' (young college-educated Queens man).
Common in Charlottetown, widespread or occasional elsewhere.

pretty as a red wagon
Of persons, usually female, attractively dressed.
Rare. *Includes senior college-educated Summerside woman.*

long as a wet week
long as a wet Sunday and three times as disagreeable
Of some activity, long and boring; second variant probably an extended blend of more common similes *longer than a month of Sundays, long as a rainy / wet Sunday*. Gaffney and Cashman's *Proverbs and Sayings of Ireland* records *long as a wet Sunday* (18). Compare *DSUE*: '*wet week* In *look like a ... wet week* to look, to feel miserable or wretched: coll[oquial].: C. 20. Obviously because a wet week tends to cause people to look miserable.'
– 'Means a boring party or gathering' (young university student).
Rare.

about as religious as my neighbour's dog
Ironic. Not religious at all.
– 'Used in rural areas' (anon.).
Rare. *Includes senior college-educated Charlottetown male editor.*

long and ever ago
A long time ago, usually beyond memory.
– 'I paid him long and ever ago' (middle-aged high-school-educated Queens male gas station owner).
– 'Means simply "a long time ago" (which could be five minutes or fifty or more years depending on the context) in my family's use' (young college-educated Charlottetown male lawyer).
Common in Kings, widespread in Queens and Charlottetown, occasional in Prince and Summerside; especially senior, not grade-school-educated. *Includes middle-aged high-school-educated Charlottetown female secretary.*

to make full
To answer well (on an examination), to satisfy all requirements.
– 'Made full – received high marks. "I made full on that exam"' (young male university student).
– 'One hundred percent' (young Charlottetown male university student).
Rare.

*to get salve
Ironic. To receive punishment. Compare BE NEAR NOTHING. Note *DPEIE*: 'Tongue-in-cheek words like *chocolates, fudge*, and *weak*, all of which are found in the western end of the province, especially around Tignish ... mean roughly the opposite of what they seem to mean' (174). Compare also *DSUE*: '*chocolate without sugar, give* (a person). To reprove: military' (1785–1890).
*Late entry, not surveyed. *Reported by middle-aged grade-school-educated Prince woman and young West Prince female university student.*

to take pass of
To take notice of (something striking). This catchphrase was not surveyed. The information in this entry is adapted from *DPEIE*.
– 'It's taking notice of anything extraordinary. Anything rare you take pass of' (anon.).
– 'It means to pass your eyes over: "Take pass of that girl." It's usually said of pretty girls or fish or machinery' (anon.).
– 'Did you take pass of the beautiful flowers?' (anon.).

to **rock the roof**

Historical. See quotation; related to common *raise the roof* 'complain vigorously,' and *rock the boat,* 'disturb arrangements.' This saying was not surveyed.

– 'The temperance organization had a strong society in our school, and was strongly supported by the best of our people. The movement was new at the time and elicited great enthusiasm – still there was an element prepared to disturb, and as our school was in such close proximity to the woods it gave great opportunity for annoyance ... [T]he operators were generally those that were black-beaned out of the society. They would feel injured and then perhaps retaliate by – as they used to call it – *rocking* the roof. This trick consisted in someone watching, and, when a person objectionable to the one deposed was up speaking in the meeting, a shower of stones would fall upon the roof with startling effect. This would bring the members out like bees, and cause the offenders to lie low or beat a hasty retreat' (J.J. 'School Days at Long River,' 175).

Includes young Charlottetown female university student.

to **cut the dead man's throat**
to **make a dead man's bubble**

To throw a stone into water without making a splash. Also attested from British Columbia. Compare *DNE*: 'dead-man's dive: method of throwing a stone into the water without making a splash'; and *SND*: '*deid man's dive ... deid man's plunge,* this is made by throwing a stone, so that it enters the surface of water with such force that no splash is made.'

– 'Danny picked up a stone and threw it in a high arc so that, in coming down, and entering the water it barely broke the surface and made only a hollow, quiet sound like a final gasp. "That's called cuttin" the dead man's throat,' he said. "It's easier to do than skippin' stones" ... Dougald picked up a dollar-sized, smooth, black pebble and rolled it slowly between his thumb and fingers, staring out at the water, now rippled and reflectionless. He drew back his arm and hurled the stone in a high, high arc and watched it make a perfect entry into the water. "That's as good a cuttin' a dead man's throat as I ever seen," said Danny' (Ledwell, *The North Shore of Home,* 40–1).

– 'Extremely popular when I was younger. At about ten years old' (young Charlottetown male university student).

– 'Common in Murray Harbour area' (Kings male university student).

Occasional except rare in Queens and unattested in Summerside. *Includes young Charlottetown female university student.*

*They went to school for two days: the first was a holiday and the second the teacher wasn't there.

Someone hasn't had much of an education, that's for sure.

*Late entry, not surveyed. *Reported by middle-aged grade-school-educated Prince man.*

I don't care if school keeps or not.

It's completely a matter of indifference to me; comparable to standard proverbial assertion *I couldn't care less.*

– 'I don't give a hoot' (senior college-educated Summerside male teacher).

– 'I wouldn't miss it if it wasn't there' (senior grade-school-educated St. Peters female homemaker).

– 'It means the person wouldn't care which way something worked out' (senior Parkdale woman).
Rare.

going to the country
Historical. See quotation. This saying was not surveyed.
– 'Peddling in the rural districts of Prince Edward Island was known among the Lebanese as "going to the country" ... In some cases, they [Lebanese peddlers] learned to speak English by going to the country ... By the 1950's, the era of the foot-peddler was over ... No more would it be possible for the emigrant Lebanese to get a start by "going to the country," for the country and the country people were disappearing' (Weale, 'Going to the Country,' 12–16).

When you see a pig, you should kick it.
Meaning unclear. Confirmed by seven informants in two surveys. *DAP* contains this entry solely on the basis of its presence on a list supplied from the present work in manuscript. The definition in that dictionary is 'Some people should be treated like an unruly pig'; however, the present editors cannot say, on their evidence, that this guess is correct. Another possibility is suggested by the folklore of Newfoundland, Nova Scotia, Maine, and Scotland, where *pig* is a taboo word among fishermen. To utter it is thought to bring on bad weather or bad luck (see *ML* and Hiscock, 'Traditional Taboo,' [Nfld.] 11–16).
Rare.

quite a / the [someone's first name]
Someone is quite a memorable character; parallel to standard *quite a / the lad, quite a case / a card.* See also THEY THINK THEY'RE [THE PERSON'S OWN NAME].
– 'Quite a Gerard' (middle-aged college-educated Borden female physiotherapist).
– 'Quite the Shelley. Does something that shocks others' (young university student).
– 'When comparing someone to someone else (young St. Louis male university student).
– 'Quite a McGinnis – [somebody] who gears things up, or can make anything work' (middle-aged grade-school-educated Prince man).
Rare. *Includes middle-aged high-school-educated Kings man, and middle-aged college-educated Kings woman.*

to **never drop [someone] in a hole**
Never to leave one in an embarrassing or difficult situation; comparable to standard *to leave [someone] in the lurch, hang [someone] out to dry.*
– 'We [my employer and I] didn't always agree, but one thing I could be sure of, he never dropped me in a hole' (senior college-educated Kings man).
Rare.

He couldn't beat up a carload of poets.
He is a weakling.
Rare. *Confirmed by seven informants in two surveys.*

There's never an old shoe / slipper but there's an old sock / stocking to fit / match it.
*Also reported
There is a mate for every old sock.
Everyone can find a compatible partner. Also attested from Ireland and Ontario. Compare *IP*: 'There never

was an old slipper but there was an old stocking to match it.' Quoted in *DAP* on this evidence in manuscript.
– 'I suspect that if Danny is looking he will find a wife one of these days.

There never was an old slipper but there was an old stocking to match it' (Noonan, 'Irish Expressions').
– 'Older people' (anon.).
Not in Survey II. Probably widespread.

Bibliography

Aitken, A.J. 'The Extinction of Scotland in Popular Dictionaries of English.' In *Dictionaries of English: Prospects for the Record of Our Language*. Ed. Richard W. Bailey. Cambridge: Cambridge UP, 1987.
Alsopp, Richard. 'Some Parallels to Swift's *Polite Conversation* in Current Caribbean English.' *English Today* 10.1 (1994): 35–40.
Bagnall, Margaret Ruth. 'When I Was Very Young.' Unpublished essay, Public Archives of Prince Edward Island, [1964].
Blacquiere, Paul. 'North Shore News.' *The Guardian* [Charlottetown], 5 Dec. 1991: 9.
Botkin, B.A., ed. *A Treasury of New England Folklore: Stories, Ballads, and Traditions of Yankee Folk*. New York: Crown Publishers, n.d.
Boyles, Anne. 'Living in Harmony.' Diss., U of New Brunswick, 1983.
Brewster, Paul G. 'Folklore Sayings from Indiana.' *American Speech* 14 (1939): 261–8.
Bruce, Harry. *Down Home: Notes of a Maritime Son*. Toronto: Key Porter Books, 1988.
Cameron, Silver Donald. 'Nova Scotia.' *Inflight* [Canadian Airlines]. August 1992: 26.
Champion, Helen Jean. *Over on the Island*. Toronto: Ryerson Press, 1939.
Chesterfield, Philip Dormer Stanhope, Earl of. *Letters of Lord Chesterfield*. Ed. Phyllis M. Jones. London: Oxford UP, 1929.
Clarke, Mary Washington. 'Proverbs, Proverbial Phrases, and Proverbial Comparisons in the Writings of Jesse Stuart.' *Southern Folklore Quarterly* 29.2 (1965): 142–63.
'Climbing the hill to yesterday.' *Globe and Mail*, 29 Sept. 1994: A17–18.
Coulton, Julie. 'Survey of the Effects of Distinctive Dialects.' Unpublished student essay, UPEI, Charlottetown, 1992.
Creighton, Helen. 'Folklore of Victoria Beach, Nova Scotia.' *Journal of American Folklore* 63 (1950): 134.
Curtis, Herb. *Look What the Cat Drug In!: Miramichi Dictionary*. Fredericton, NB: Non-Entity Press, 1990.
– *Slow Men Working in Trees: Fredericton Dictionary*. 3rd concise edition. Fredericton, NB: Non-Entity Press, 1991.
Darrach, Don. 'Portly Mayor on Diet.' *The Guardian* [Charlottetown], 5 Jan. 1989: 1.
Devereux, Joseph. *Looking Backward*. N.p.: n.p., [post 1979?].
Dixon, Margaret. *Going Home: An Autobiography*. Clyde River, PEI: n.p., 1979.
Dunkling, Leslie. *The Guinness Book of Curious Phrases*. London: Guinness Publishing, 1993.

English, L.E.F. *Historic Newfoundland*. St. John's, Nfld.: Newfoundland Tourist Development Division of the Department of Economic Development, 1955.
Frazier, Marshall W. 'Truck Drivers' Language.' *American Speech* 30 (1955): 91–4.
Gaffney, Sean, and Seamus Cashman, eds. *Proverbs and Sayings of Ireland*. Dublin: Wolfhound Press, 1974.
Gallant, Donna. 'What's a Fella Gonna Do?' In *The Maritime Experience*. Ed. Michael O. Nowlan. Toronto: Macmillan, 1975.
Gallant, Doug. 'City offers lots of activities to entertain summer visitors.' *The Guardian* [Charlottetown], 24 July 1987: 16.
– 'Fatherhood brings mixed blessings.' *The Guardian* [Charlottetown], 9 July 1994: 9.
Gojmerac, Anna. 'Prince Edward Island Expressions.' Unpublished student essay, UPEI, Charlottetown, 1986.
Graves, Ross. *William Schurman, Loyalist of Bedeque, Prince Edward Island; and His Descendents*. 2 vols. Summerside, PEI: Harold B. Schurman, 1973.
Gulland, Daphne M., and David Hinds-Howell, eds. *The Penguin Dictionary of English Idioms*. Harmondsworth, Middlesex: Penguin, 1986.
Haber, Tom Burns. 'Canine Terms Applied to Human Beings and Human Events: Part I.' *American Speech* 40 (1965): 83–101.
Hall, Joseph S., ed. *Sayings from Old Smoky: Some Traditional Phrases, Expressions, and Sentences Heard in The Great Smoky Mountains and Nearby Areas*. Asheville, NC: Cataloochee Press, 1972.
Halpert, Herbert. *A Folklore Sampler from the Maritimes*. St. John's, Nfld.: Memorial University of Newfoundland Folklore and Language Publications, for the Centre for Canadian Studies, Mount Allison University, 1982.
Hanford, G.L. 'Metaphor and Simile in American Folk Speech.' *Dialect Notes* 5 (1922): 149–80.
Hendricks, George D. 'Texas Folk Similes.' *Western Folklore* 19 (1960): 245–62.
Hendrickson, Robert. *Whistlin' Dixie: A Dictionary of Southern Expressions*. New York: Facts on File, 1993.
Hennessey, Michael. 'The Trial of Minnie McGee.' Unpublished play, Charlottetown, 1983.
Hiscock, Philip. 'Traditional Taboo on *pig* in Newfoundland.' *Regional Language Studies ... Newfoundland* 15 (1994): 11–16.
Hornby, Susan, ed. *Belfast People: An Oral History of Belfast Prince Edward Island*. Charlottetown: Tea Hill Press, 1992.
Ives, Edward D. *Lawrence Doyle: The Farmer Poet of Prince Edward Island. A Study in Local Songmaking*. Orono: U of Maine P, 1971.
J.J. 'School Days at Long River.' *The Prince Edward Island Magazine* 3.5 (1901): 172–6.
Kennedy, Libby. 'A Visitor's Guide to the Language of the Wharf.' Unpublished student essay. UPEI, Charlottetown, 1985.
Kessler, Deirdre. *The Private Adventures of Brupp*. Charlottetown: Ragweed Press, 1983.
Kindred Spirits of P.E.I. Newsletter, Winter 1991/92.
Lakoff, George, and Mark Johnson. *Metaphors We Live By*. Chicago: U of Chicago P, 1980.
Ledwell, Frank J. *Crowbush and Other Poems*. Charlottetown: Ragweed Press, 1990.
– *The North Shore of Home*. Halifax, NS: Nimbus Publishing, 1986.
Ledwell, Frank, and Reshard Gool. *Portraits and Gastroscopes*. Charlottetown: Square Deal Publications, 1972.

Lemm, Richard. Review of *The Fragrance of Sweet-Grass: L.M. Montgomery's Heroines and the Pursuit of Romance*, by Elizabeth Rollins Epperley. *The Island Magazine* 33 (1993): 39–40.
McArthur, Tom, ed. *Longman Lexicon of Contemporary English*. Harlow, Essex: Longman, 1981.
– *Worlds of Reference: Lexicography, Learning and Language from the Clay Tablet to the Computer*. Cambridge: Cambridge UP, 1986.
McCutcheon, Marc. *Descriptionary: A Thematic Dictionary*. New York: Ballantine, 1992.
MacPhee, Audrey. 'Along the Rural Routes.' *The Guardian* [Charlottetown], 24 Nov. 1989: 7.
MacQuarrie, Heath. 'Recollections of His Early Childhood and Society on Prince Edward Island.' Unpublished compilation, PEI Collection, UPEI, Charlottetown, 1985.
Montgomery, L.M. *Anne of Green Gables*. Boston: L.C. Page & Co., 1908.
– *Anne of Ingleside*. 1939. New York: Grosset & Dunlap, 1970.
– *Anne's House of Dreams*. New York: Frederick A. Stokes Co., 1917.
– *The Blue Castle*. 1926. Toronto: McClelland & Stewart, 1989.
– *Chronicles of Avonlea*. Boston: L.C. Page, 1912.
– *Further Chronicles of Avonlea*. 1920. Toronto: Ryerson Press, 1953.
– *The Green Gables Letters: From L.M. Montgomery to Ephraim Weber 1905–1909*. Ed. Wilfred Eggleston. Toronto: Ryerson Press, 1960.
– *Letters from L.M. Montgomery to Penzie MacNeill, circa 1886–1894*. Photocopy, PEI Collection, UPEI, Charlottetown.
– 'Mackereling out in the Gulf.' Repr. in *Along the Shore*, 51–64. Ed. Rea Wilmshurst. Toronto: McClelland & Stewart, 1989.
– *Rilla of Ingleside*. 1920. Toronto: McClelland & Stewart, 1973.
Morrison, J. Clinton, Jr. *Along the North Shore: A Social History of Township 11, P.E.I. 1765–1892*. St. Eleanors, PEI: n.p., 1983.
Noonan, Jo Anne. 'Irish Expressions: A Mark of My Ancestry.' Unpublished student essay, UPEI, Charlottetown, 1989.
Pendergast, James, and Gertrude Pendergast. *Folklore Prince Edward Island*. N.p.: n.p., [1974].
Perkins, Anne. 'More Notes on Maine Dialect.' *American Speech* 5 (1930): 118–31.
– 'Vanishing Expressions of the Maine Coast.' *American Speech* 3 (1928): 134–41.
Person, Henry A. 'Proverbs and Proverbial Lore from the State of Washington.' *Western Folklore* 17 (1958): 177–85.
Picturesque Expressions: A Thematic Dictionary. Ed. Laurence Urdang, Walter W. Hussinger, and Nancy LaRoche. 2nd edition. Detroit: Gale Research, 1985.
Porter, Bernard H. 'Some Newfoundland Phrases, Sayings, and Figures of Speech.' *American Speech* 41 (1966): 294–7.
Poteet, Lewis J. *Talking Country: The Eastern Townships Phrase Book*. Ayers Cliff, PQ: Pigwidgeon Press, 1992.
Pratt, T.K., ed. *Dictionary of Prince Edward Island English*. Toronto: U of Toronto P, 1988.
– 'The Proverbial Islander.' *The Island Magazine* 10 (1981): 8–11.
Prince Edward Island Multicultural Council of Charlottetown. *An Exploratory Survey of First-Generation Immigrants Living on Prince Edward Island*. Charlottetown: n.p., 1980.
Sellick, Lester. *My Island Home*. Windsor, NS: Lancelot Press, 1973.
Smith, J.B. 'Whim-Whams for a Goose's Bridle: A List of Put-offs and Related Forms in English and German.' *Lore and Language* 3.3 (1980): 32–49.
Spears, Richard A. *Forbidden American English*. Lincolnwood, IL: Passport Books, 1990.

Stevenson, James A.C. *Scoor-Oot: A Dictionary of Scots Words and Phrases in Current Use.* London: Athlone, 1989.
Stewart, Marion Lea. *Marion Stewart's Journal.* N.p.: n.p., 1976.
Stirling, Lilla. *Jockie: A Story of Prince Edward Island.* New York: Charles Scribner's Sons, 1951.
Swift, Jonathan. *A Complete Collection of Genteel and Ingenious Conversation According to the Most Polite Mode and Method now Used at Court, and in the Best Companies in England.* 1738. Ed. Eric Partridge as *Swift's Polite Conversation.* London: Andre Deutsch, 1963.
Tabbert, Russell. *Dictionary of Alaskan English.* Juneau: Denali, 1991.
Taylor, Jay L.B. 'Snake County Talk.' *Dialect Notes* 5 (1923): 197–225.
'Ten reasons for pride in Canada.' *The Guardian* [Charlottetown], 30 June 1994: 1.
Thompson, Harold W. *Body, Boots and Britches.* Philadelphia: J.P. Lippincott Co., 1940.
Walsh, Vicki. 'Trap-smashers possible veteran fisherman says.' *The Guardian* [Charlottetown], 24 April 1984: 3.
Waugh, F.W. 'Canadian Folk-lore from Ontario.' *Journal of American Folk-Lore* 31 (1918): 1–82.
Weale, David. 'The Gloomy Forest.' *The Island Magazine* 13 (1983): 8–13.
– 'Going to the Country: Lebanese Peddlers on Prince Edward Island.' *The Island Magazine* 18 (1985): 11–16.
– 'Them Times.' On *Island Morning.* CBC Radio broadcasts, Charlottetown, 10 March 1987 and 3 Jan. 1990.
– *Them Times.* Charlottetown: Institute of Island Studies, 1992.
Weale collection. David Weale, Department of History, UPEI. Private ms. collection of sayings.
Williams, Fionnuala. *Irish Proverbs.* Swords, Co. Dublin: Poolbeg Press, 1992.
Woofter, Carey. 'Dialect Words and Phrases from West-Central West Virginia.' *American Speech.* 2 (1927): 347–67.

Index

accountant at tax time, busy as an 97
across, from (over) 117
across the puddle / pond / brook 116
afford, They couldn't | *a feed of oats for a nightmare *a pair of spats for a canary *the down payment on a three-cent stamp *the first instalment on a free lunch *the ticket to a free meal *to call a Ford a Ford *to pay an instalment on a clay / T D pipe 100–1
afford a diaper / the buttons for a pismire, If overalls for an elephant cost five cents, they couldn't 101
afford to have a father, so poor we couldn't 100
Africa, dry as an old bucket / a wooden bridge / a wooden leg in 88
age, cow so old it died of old 85
ago, long and ever 121
airmail (with the crows), up on the roof sorting 77
air under that, You'll never put 84
alive, give [someone] flowers while they're still 70
all over the pond 90
All that's left of them is the gear shift 15
alone *black spark 66 *thousands from Tyne Valley 80
always a day late and a dollar short 99
amount to a row of postholes, not 52
angels, God / The Lord is bowling with the 104

angels are bowling, The 104
angry *tonight, God / The Lord is *voice of the Lord, That's the 105
animal, but it led a tough life, This may be a young 85
ankles in the flour barrel, mouse wouldn't go up to its 101
another [something] in for the stranger, put 83
answer, They'd never break your heart with a bad 28
antifreeze (boil over), Don't let your 82
Antigonish, My brother slept with a man who came from 34
anti-grouch pill, They should have taken their 63
ant short of a picnic, one 43
apartment *but there's no one home, have a nice *is vacant, the upstairs 43
appetite with the skin pulled over, like an 84
apple, face like a sour 4
apple through a *picket fence, They could eat an *wire fence, They look like a horse eating an 9
apples *not have the brains God gave little 41 *They couldn't box 45
apples short of a picnic, a few 43
Arabs, They could sell oil / sand to the 73
arm broken? Is your 68
arms, I can't dance with a baby in my 62

around like the button on the outhouse
   door, get 66
arse, not worth *a patch on a good man's
   *the sweat off a dead man's 50–1
arse *black as 109 *drunk as 90
arse *heartburn, Wouldn't that give the
   dog's 61 *or you'd feel it, It's not up
   your 80 *out of an iron pot, talk the 75
arsehole, They know as much about
   [something] as my 45
arse and tearing it, There's a difference
   between scratching your 48
asked if you had a mouth on you, not 67
ass (at fly-time), *dry as a cow's 88 *tight
   as a cat's 112
ass at the same time, You can't sweep the
   floor and wipe your 53
ass *too mean to give the smell off their 31
   *Wouldn't that frost your 61
attention, so poor we couldn't pay 100
attic, There's *a loose board in the *no
   light in the *static in the 38
attic not finished / not plastered, There's
   one room in the 38
automobile, useless as a whipstand on
   an 51
awake, stupid as pissing the bed 44
away, from 117
away, *half a look *look and a half *spit
   and a jump *whipstitch 115
axe *down cellar behind the 80 *two-faced
   as a double-bitted 28
axe handle, ugly as an 4
axehandles, boiled / cooked with 84

baby *in my arms, I can't dance with a
   *too, I can't dance and hold the 62
back, I'd walk a mile if I didn't have to
   walk 91
back barn door, tongue (going) like a button on a 72
back door, homely as ma's 5
back door than they carry in the front,
   throw more out the 99
back of a dump truck, mouth like the 73
back getting around them, snake would
   break its 28

back on her, walk 119
back to look down a well / in the cellar, so
   cross-eyed they have to lie on their 8
backside of a cow, Wouldn't that frost
   the 61
backwards, If you put their brain in a bird,
   the bird would fly 45
back woods they have to come out to
   hunt, live so far in the 67
bacon, Wouldn't that burn your brother's
   60
bad answer, They'd never break your
   heart with a 28
bad of a day, not too 109
badly as, They need [something] as | a
   goat needs a beard / a toad needs a
   tail / they need a second nose 51
bag, hit the flea 92
bag full of hammers / monkeys / mortal
   sins, face like a 6
bag of hammers, deaf as a 18
bag of hammers *clumsy / crazy / dense /
   dumb / stupid as a *dumber than a
   *have as much sense as a 40
bag of nails, have as much sense as a 40
bags, so poor the garbage man would
   leave three 100
bags short of a load, have a few 43
bail the river with a pitchfork, You might
   as well try to 50
baked in the sun 84
bakery, enough crust to start a 34
baking a cake 78
bales short of a load, have a few 43
ball, sharp as a bowling 42
ball, There's more meat on a golf 15
ball bearing, sharp as a 42
balls, God is dropping bowling 104
balls, not worth the sweat off a dead
   man's 51
baloney sandwich, making a 78
balsam on them, They still have the 35
banana *full as a 90 *No thanks, I've just
   had a 81
bananas out of your ears, Clean the 62
banging into one another, The clouds
   are 105

bank a fire, You can 47
barefoot, If clues were shoes, they'd be 45
bargain, as much as a 56
barking at the moon, crazy as Tom's dog and he died 36
barley stack, like a 7
barn *busy as a rooster in a three-storey 96 *cold as a 108 *Down comes your goose house and fifty feet of the 64 *I was thinking I might move the 78 *out behind the 78 *up to the top of the 77 *You might as well try to climb to the top of the 50
barn door *and down the hatch, Open the 86 *enough rouge to paint a 9 *homely / ugly as a 5 *tongue (going) like a button on a back 72
barn full of straw, You might as well spit on a fire in a 50
barnyard, look as if they had been dragged through a 3
barnyard in case there was shit in it, They wouldn't say 36
barnyard owl, crooked as a 28
barrack? Were you born / brought up in a 68
barrel, a mouse would have to get on its knees / wouldn't go up to its ankles, The flour's so low in the 101
barrel *and scale the wall, Get off the flour 91 *behind the piano, in the pig's 80 *between their legs, so bow-legged you could roll a 16 *have a few pickles short of a 43 *of snot, slippery as six fat eels in a 29 *with a tear in their eye, May the rats never leave your flour 82
barrels *down cellar behind the fish 80 *God / The Devil / The old man / Saint Peter is rolling (his) 104 *I'm going downstairs behind the fish 77
barrels of shit, drunk as two / three / four / seven 90
basket *not many eggs in the 43 *The bottom has fallen out of the 48
batteries, not operating on all 37
Bay of Fundy, useless as a snowball in the 51

Beach Grove Johnny, dressed like a 16
beam, cut a notch in the 58
beams, You have your brake lights ahead of your high 74
beans? How's your belly for 75
beans, That'll put different water on the 47
bear *fat as a 11 *full as a teddy 90
beard, They need [something] as badly as a goat needs a 51
bearing, sharp as a ball 42
bears, go for / kill 94
bears at midnight, black as two black 108
beat by an ugly stick, look as if they got 6
beat the feet 67
beat up a carload of poets, He couldn't 123
beautiful blue eyes – one blew east and one blew west, two 8
bed, a lot of bunk, like the elephant's 29
bed, so stupid they'd miss the floor if they fell out of 44
bed awake, stupid as pissing the 44
bed with the hens and get up with the roosters, Go to 92
bed is sure to rise with a wet head, rooster crowing to 105
bed meant half the family was away on vacation, so poor that four in the 100
bedroom, (all) dressed up like a spare 17
bee, smart as a 120
bee in a bottle, run around like a 97
beech nut, as many faces as a 28
bees' knees and fried onions 81
bee's nest, like a 7
behind the *axe, down cellar 80 *the barn, out 78 *the fish barrels, I'm going downstairs 77 *the piano, in the pig's barrel 80
belly *button? How's your *for beans? How's your 75
belly is flapping, so hungry my 84
bent over, so skinny / thin they'd break if they 14
beside the furnace, down cellar 80
bet a sweet cent, I'd 47
better, If I was any | *I couldn't stand it *I'd be bigger / dangerous / twins *I'd be sick 57

better but it (would) cost more 76
better out than a(n) (farmer's) eye 69
better than a cold fog, warm smoke is 67
bewitched barley stack, like a 7
Bibles, I'm going to Jerusalem for a load of 76
big as *a codfish, mouth as 10 *a haystack 11 *a horse, have the Devil in them as 30 *a two-by-four 12 *gingersnaps, freckles as 8 *number nine wire 12
big enough to eat hay / a horse and cart and chase the driver 11
bigger, If I was any better I'd be 57
big wooden hill, It's time to buckle up / climb / hit the 92
bill and coo, There's nothing left of [someone] but the 14
bill of North Cape, old as the 20
billy, old as Methuselah's 20
billy goat, crazy / silly / stupid as a 41
bin, more rolls than a / the bread 10
bird, the bird would fly backwards, If you put their brain in a 45
bird, There's more meat on a little grey 14
bird's nest *empty as last year's 41 *like a 7
biscuit, look like a cream of tartar 16 *slick as a 111
biscuit going down, eat so fast you can see the 86
biscuit *not worth the butter on a 50 *so thirsty I could drink a 88
biscuits? How's your belly for 75
biscuits are done, The 113
biscuits short / shy of a dozen 43
black as *a blue pig *arse *a witch's pocket *the inside of a black cow *two black bears at midnight 108–9
blackflies *Good weather for *not bothered by *not too many 106
black keys *missing, have a few *than white, have more 37–8
black spark alone 66
blade, mouth / tongue like a winding 73
blanket, look like two pigs fighting in a 11

blanket harbour, get to 92
blanket *shiver like a dog in a wet 108 *useless as a pee-hole / piss-hole in a 52
blankets, hit the 92
blew east and one blew west, two beautiful blue eyes – one 8
blind in one eye and can't see out of the other 8
blister a stone, tongue that would 74
blow the hen right off her nest, Wouldn't that 61
blow right through them, so thin the wind could 12
blow up rain 106
blue eyes – one blew east and one blew west, two beautiful 8
blue pig, black as a 108
board, If you can't get a | take a slab 53
board in the attic, There's a loose 38
board fence, homely as a 5
boarding house, dry as the inside of a woodpecker's 88
boards are falling on Grandpa, The 105
boat? Were you born / brought up in a 68
bob when they should have weaved 55
boil over, Don't let your antifreeze 82
boil your britches, Wouldn't that 60
boiled with axehandles 84
boiled worm, stupid as a 41
bold as a country bull / pet pig / ram in a gap 35
book, so hungry I could eat an old 83
boot, so fond of liquor they would drink it out of a(n) (old) rubber 89
boot *drunk as a 89 *dry as a Mountie's 84 *dry / thirsty as a burnt 84 *more tongue than a / tongue like a Mountie's 73
boots, They still have the cowshit on their 35
boots, wide as the Devil's 114
born, Were you | *in a(n) barrack / boat / henhouse / hole / igloo / sawmill? *in the woods with no door on? *on a raft? *under a bridge? 68

born richer and not so good-looking, I wish I was 50
both ends, well-fed at 10
bothered by blackflies / flies / mosquitoes, not 106
bottle *run around like a bee / fly in a 97 *so mean they would save a fart in a gas bottle 31 *tight as a pop 112
bottom has fallen out of the basket / bucket, The 48
bottom of a well, lazy as (a) toad(s) at the 25
bottom of your shoe(s), like shit stuck to the 35
bottom out of an iron pot *eat the 83 *talk the 75
bought me for two cents (half spent), You could have 59
bouncing bricks off, good head for 42
bow to the fiddle, put the 67
bowl, down cellar behind the fish 80
bow-legged as a cowboy after a grasshopper / a pet pig / a six-day ride 16
bow-legged you could roll a barrel between their legs, so 16
bowling, God / The Lord is / The angels are 104
bowling ball, sharp as a 42
bowling balls, God is dropping 104
box, not much feed in the feed 43
box apples / strawberries, They couldn't 45
boy, heavy as a man and a 113
brain, If they had a | *it would be lonesome *it would rattle 45
brain in a bird, the bird would fly backwards, If you put their 45
brain made out of sawdust / Swiss cheese, have a 42
brains *they wouldn't even get wet, If it rained *they would rattle, If they had two *were rubber, they wouldn't have enough to stretch around the hair on a flea's leg, If *were water, they would die of thirst, If 45
brains God gave a goat / a louse / little apples, not have the 41

brake lights ahead of your high beams, You have your 74
branch on the way down, They fell out of an ugly tree and hit every 6
brass enough to make a pot and gall enough to fill it 32
brass were gold, they'd be a millionaire, If their 32
bread *not worth the butter on their *with, not worth the knife they butter their 50
bread bin, more rolls than a / the 10
break a snake's back getting around them, so crooked it would 28
break if they bent over, so skinny / thin they'd 14
break your heart with a bad answer, They'd never 28
breakfast, Their mother gave them ugly pills for 63
breakwater, I'm going to the | to fork off the fog 76
breath, cold as a widow's 107
breathe, too lazy to 26
bricks off, good head for bouncing 42
bridge, God / The Devil / The old man / Saint Peter is rolling barrels over a stone 104
bridge, so cold it would freeze the nuts off a steel / iron 107
bridge? Were you born under a 68
bridge in Africa, dry as a wooden 88
bridle, doodle-daddle for a goose's 79
bright as a burnt-out / two-watt (light) bulb 42
bring grandmother back from the dead, Wouldn't that 61
britches, Wouldn't that boil / burn / fester your 60
broke off where you cracked, you'd be damn short, If you 32
broken? Is your arm 68
brook, across the 116
brook for drink, crazy as Tom's dog who would put his ass in the 36
broom handle, There's more meat on a 14
broomstick, so thin they *could hide behind a *couldn't be shot behind a 12

134   Index

brother slept with a man who came from Antigonish, My 34
brother's bacon, Wouldn't that burn your 60
brought up in a barrack / boat / sawmill? Were you 68
brown felt? How's your old straw hat – or would you rather have your 75
brush, There's a difference between scratching your arse and tearing it all to pieces with a wire 48
brush fence *homely / ugly as a 5 *ignorant as a 70
bubble, make a dead man's 122
buck, old as Methuselah's 20
bucket, dry as an old wooden 88
bucket *bottom has fallen out of the 48 *dance around like a fish in a 57
bucket of *(squashed) worms, face like a 4 *steam, I'm going to get a 76
bucket under a bull, useless as a 51
buckle up the wooden hill, It's time to 92
bug, Someone got hit with the ugly 6
bulb, bright as a burnt-out / two-watt (light) 42
bull, useless as a bucket under a 51
bull in a gap, bold as a country 35
bunch of starving Russians, hungry as a 83
Bun King, more rolls than 10
bunky harbour, go to 92
buns, Wouldn't that cook your 60
buoys by them, They set the 26
burned down, Some place must have 16
burnt *boot / potato, dry / thirsty as a 84 *cake, like frosting on a 29
burnt-out (light) bulb, bright as a 42
burn your britches / brother's bacon, Wouldn't that 60
bush (in a) barley stack, like a 7
busier than a *cat having kittens *cow calving *toad eating grubs / lightning 95
business, busier than a cat in a round room trying to find a corner to do his 96

business, Eaton's / Simpson's don't tell Simpson's / Eaton's their 29
busy as a(n) *accountant at tax time *fart in a mitt *flea at a dog show *hen picking fly-shit out of pepper *rat in a shed with three lofts *rooster in a three-storey barn *squint-eyed cat trying to catch all the mice it sees 96–7
busy as a cut cat 37
busy as flies at a meat market 97
butter on *a biscuit / on their bread, not worth the 50 *it, slick as a biscuit with 111
butter their bread with, not worth the knife they 50
butter *three mosquitoes fried in 81 *tongue as oily as a churnful of 73
button? How's your belly 75
button on *a back barn door, tongue like a 72 *the outhouse door, get around like the 66
button holes / buttons, make 60
buttons, all in but the 91
buttons for a pismire, If overalls for an elephant cost five cents, they couldn't afford the 101
buy anything on Monday or you will be spending all week, Don't
by the *(holy) (Lord) liftins *end of the stick *liftin George / Jehosaphat *living John Bull / cripple 64–5

C, up in high 96
cabbage, good head if you like 42
cabbage twice, not sell the 71
cake *baking a 78 *like frosting on a burnt 29
calendar, so slow you have to time them on a 26
calf at a new gate, stubborn as a 34
call a Ford a Ford, They couldn't afford to 101
calm as a cradle 109
Calm your hormones 59
calving, busier than a cow 95
canary, They couldn't afford *a pair of

Index   135

spats for a *the first instalment on a free lunch for a 100–1
cans, God is taking out the garbage 104
can of snakes / (squashed) worms, face like a 4
care if school keeps or not, I don't 122
carload of poets, He couldn't beat up a 123
carrot *cut [someone] off like a 69 *short as a 10
carry *a lunch, land so poor a grasshopper would have to 102 *a tune if it had handles, They couldn't 18 *in the front, throw more out the back door than they 99
carrying last year's fun 11
cars, face like someone who was chasing parked 6
cart, so cold it would freeze the nuts off a dump 107
cart and chase the driver, big enough to eat a horse and 11
Carter has liver pills, more [something] than 52
case of the pollywoggles of the diaphobickalorium 24
case without a lid, They're a 37
cat, kick the 72
cat? Who's killing the 18
cat *beside an open hearth, nervous as a long-haired 58 *caught in a (screen) door, like a 18 *having kittens, busier than a 95 *trying to catch all the mice it sees, busy as a squint-eyed
cat *homely as a wet 4 *lazy as a pet 25 *lonesome as a pole 66 *old as Methuselah's 20 *running around like a cut 37 *tight as the tail on a 112
cat in a *round room trying to find a corner to do his business, busier than a 96 *sandbox, sitting like a 59
cat who can't climb a tree, stupid as a 41
cat with *its tail caught in a wringer, like a 18 *someone standing on its tail, like a 18
catch all the mice it sees, busy as a squint-eyed cat trying to 96

catch some rabbit tracks, I'm going to 76
catch twice, not sell the 71
catching, not know if they're pitching or 55
catching eels / flies, nooden-nadden / oodle-addle / for 79
catching pigs, no good at 16
cat's *ass, tight as a 112 *nest, like a 7 *wrist, slick as a 111
cats and dogs, claws down, It's raining 105
caught the fox / the rabbit, If that dog hadn't stopped to shit he would've 26
caught in a (screen) door / wringer, like a cat (with its tail) 18
causes, cow so old it died of natural 85
Cawnpore, When you die, you go to Heaven, Hell, or 21
ceiling of one room not finished, There's the 38
cellar, so cross-eyed they have to lie on their back to look in the 8
cellar behind / beside the axe / the fish barrels / the fish bowl / the furnace, down 80
cellar picking chickens out of feathers, upstairs in the 77
cent, I'd bet a sweet 47
cent head, wear a ten dollar hat on a ten 33
centre to either end, twice as long as from the 81
cents (half spent), You could have bought me for two 59
cents short of a dollar, have a few 43
chairs in the Great Hall above, They're moving the 104
chamber pot, so fond of liquor they would drink it out of a 89
charm the heart (out) of, They could 73
charming likely, not 48
chase a crow a mile for [something], I'd 86
chase the driver, big enough to eat a horse and cart and 11
chasing parked cars, face like someone who was 6

Index

cheap they wouldn't give you the smell off their last year's shit, so 31
cheeks and call me cute, Well, pinch my 65
cheese *have a brain made out of Swiss 42 *I'm going to the moon to get some green 76
cherries, dry as a mouthful of choke 89
Chev and a Ford's a Ford, Chev's a 74
chicken coop, They could eat corn / corn on the cob / straw through a 9
chicken house, I was thinking I might move the 78
chicken is cooked / roasted, The 113
chicken's forehead, There's more meat on a 14
chickens out of feathers, upstairs in the cellar picking 77
chilly eyebrow today, It's 106
chimney just the same, The smoke goes up the 47
China, I'm going to | Want to come? 76
choke cherries, dry as a mouthful of 89
churnful of butter, tongue as oily as a 73
circus horse, all dressed up like a 17
claws down, It's raining cats and dogs 105
clay pipe, They couldn't afford to pay an instalment on a 100
Clean the bananas / dirt / hay / straw out of your ears 62
clean as an eggshell 112
click, If they had two clues, they'd make a 44
clicks in a clue, and they haven't even got a click, There's two 44
climb Mount Everest / to the top of the barn, You might as well try to 50
climb a tree, stupid as a cat who can't 41
climb the wooden hill, It's time to 92
clock or a sewing machine, I'm not an eight-day 97
close to the trough, go too 10
cloth, You need a cold 59
clothesline in the rain, dressed like a 17

clouds are banging into one another, The 105
club, There's more meat on a golf 14
cluck(ing) out, take the 62
clue, and they haven't even got a click, There's two clicks in a 44
clue, it would be lonesome, If they had a 45
clue, not have an inkling and that's only a tenth of a 45
clues – one's lost, the other's looking for it, They've got two 44
clues, they'd be out looking for one another / they'd make a click, If they had two 44
clues were shoes, they'd be barefoot, If 45
clumsy as a bag / sack of (claw) hammers 40
coals to the Devil, They could sell 73
coat on the dog's nail, hang their 68
coats of paint, tight as two 112
cob through a chicken coop / picket fence, They could eat corn on the 9
cobwebs, so hungry I could eat 83
cock for Dolly, the 112
codfish *dead as a 41 *mouth as big as a / mouth like 10
cold, face that would knock a dead man 6
cold as *a barn *a widow's breath *the horns off the Devil 107–8
cold cloth, You need a 59
cold fog, warm smoke is better than a 67
cold for a fence post, too 106
cold it would freeze the nuts off a bridge / a dump cart / the Hillsborough Bridge, so 107
cold up there? Is it 10
Coleman tea, I'm going to the 76
come from, but you're not where you come from, You may be a good man where you 34
concrete, You can't grow grass on 7
coo, There's nothing left of [someone] but the bill and 14
cook eggs on the floor, You could 114
cook your buns, Wouldn't that 60

cooked, The chicken / turkey / supper is 113
cooked with axehandles 84
cookies on [someone], We'll soon be having the 21
cookies short of a dozen, have a few 43
coon, lazy as a pet 25
coop, They could eat corn / corn on the cob / straw through a chicken 9
coot *dizzy as a 89 *tight as a 112
cork leg, dry as a 88
corn, talk the ear off a stalk of 73
corn (on the cob) through a picket fence / chicken coop, They could eat 9
corner to do his business, busier than a cat in a round room trying to find a 96
cost five cents, they couldn't afford a diaper / the buttons for a pismire, If overalls for an elephant 101
cost more, I've been better but it 76
count the steps 92
country, going to the 123
country bull in a gap, bold as a 35
cow, Wouldn't that frost the backside of a 61
cow *black as the inside of a black 108 *lot of miles on that old 85 *make as much sense as a dead 56
cow calving, busier than a 95
cow *as a horse, They must have used that *to death, They must have run that 85
cow's ass at fly-time, dry as a 88
cow so old *it died of old age / of natural causes *it must have had a vote *she had to be lifted when she lay down *the rings were falling off its horns 85
cows vote, when 53
cow track, so fond of liquor they would drink it out of a 89
cow-turd, flat as a June 15
cowboy after a six-day ride, bow-legged as a 16
cowhide to the hemlock, lay 67
cowshit on their boots, They still have the 35
crack of crow piss, up at the 93

cracked, you'd be damn short, If you broke off where you 32
cracking, I'm so dry I'm 89
cracks worse than a shingle, if nothing 53
cradle, calm as a 109
crate, hit the 92
crazy as a bag / sack of (claw) hammers / a billy goat / a cut cat / a marsh hen / the crows / Tom Clark's (old) dog 36–41
cream of tartar biscuit, look like a 16
cripple, by the living 109
crooked, so | *it would break a snake's back getting around them *that they could be screwed into the ground *they could swallow a nail and pass a screw *they have to screw their socks on in the morning 27–8
crooked as a barnyard owl / crowbar / (fence) post / fiddler's elbow / pole fence / rooster / stove pipe 27–8
crooked as the *Sherbrooke Road going into Summerside *Trans-Canada 28
cross between a door sill and a door mat 27
cross-eyed they have to lie on their back to look in the cellar / down a well, so 8
crossing it, land so poor a grasshopper / mouse would starve to death 102
crotch at fly-time, dry as a crow's 88
crow, lucky as a pet 57
crow a mile for [something], I'd chase a 86
crow piss (time), up at (the crack of) 93
crowbar, crooked as a 27
crowbar, so thin they couldn't be hit with a shotgun behind a 12
crowing to bed is sure to rise with a wet head, rooster 105
crow's crotch at fly-time, dry as a 88
crows *crazy / queer / odd as the 36 *too mean to give their shit to the 31 *up on the roof sorting airmail with the 77
crucifix, There's more meat on a 14
crust to start a bakery, enough 34
crying, God is 105

cup, tight as a 112
cup of tea, strange 37
cupboard with tears in their eyes, The mice come out of the 101
cut cat, crazy as a / busy as a / running around like a / worse than a 37
cut *it with the knife itself, You couldn't 85 *sets, You have to plant or 53 *the trees off an Island penny, They would 31 *their hair, You have to stand them in the well to 19
cut *a notch in the beam 58 *the dead man's throat 122
cut [someone] off like a carrot 69
Cut your fingernails on Sunday and the Devil will be after you all week 56
cute, Well, pinch my cheeks and call me 65
cutter, mouth / tongue like a hay 73

dance, They could charm the heart of a grindstone and make a wheelbarrow 74
dance around like a fish in a bucket 57
dance and hold the baby too / with a baby in my arms, I can't 62
dance in the rain to get wet, so thin they have to 13
dangerous, If I was any better I'd be 57
darning needle, shit through the eye of a 23
dash of lavender 120
dash in a 90-yard gym, face like someone who won the 100-yard 6
dashboard on an old wagon, look like a new 16
day after tomorrow will be the middle of the week and no work done yet 94
day *is long, wide as the 10 *keeps everyone away, onion a 24 *late and a dollar short, always a 99
day *lazy as a pet 25 *not too bad of a 109 *There's nowhere that'll go in a 50 *whore of a 106
day to let the ram go, a good 107
day older than the tides 20

day to set a hen *a good 109 *a poor 107
days: the first was a holiday and the second the teacher wasn't there, They went to school for two 122
days older than the fog / Island, three / two 20
dead, Wouldn't that bring grandmother back from the 61
dead as a codfish 41
dead cow, make as much sense as a 56
dead duck(s), happy as a / two 57
dead man cold, face that would knock a 6
dead man's *arse / balls, not worth the sweat off a 51 *bubble / throat, make a / cut the 122
dead in Rustico, Someone is 71
deaf as a (bag of) hammer(s) 18
death, They must have run that cow to 85
death crossing it, land so poor a grasshopper / mouse would starve to 102
deep as the grave 29
dense as a *bag / sack of (claw) hammers *sack of wet mice 40
deuce in a jackpot, useless as a 51
Devil *cold as the horns off the 107 *God is mad at the 105 *They could sell coals / a heating pad to the 73
Devil in *a gale of wind, like the 8 *them as big as a horse, have the 30
Devil is rolling barrels (over a stone bridge) / oats / stones, The 104
Devil will be after you all week, Cut your fingernails on Sunday and the 56
Devil's boots, wide as the 114
diaper, If overalls for an elephant cost five cents, they couldn't afford a 101
diaphobickalorium, case of the pollywoggles of the 24
Did you get any on you? 69
die, you go to Heaven, Hell, or Cawnpore, When you 21
die they could be screwed into the ground, so crooked that when they 27
die of thirst, If brains were water, they would 45

Index   139

died of old age / of natural causes, cow so old it 85
difference between scratching your arse and tearing it, There's a 48
different direction every morning, He's like a tom-cat, coming home from a 68
different water on the beans, That'll put 47
dig postholes 60
dinner, worked up like a dog's 59
dipstick, so thin they could be used as a 14
direction every morning, He's like a tom-cat, coming home from a different 68
dirt *ignorant as 70 *rotten as 111
dirt out of your ears, Clean the 62
dirty straw, so fond of liquor they would drink it out of a 89
disagreeable, long as a wet Sunday and three times as 121
disappear, so thin if they turn sideways they 13
dizzy as a coot 89
doctor slapped their mother, so ugly that the 7
dodge between the raindrops, so thin they could 13
dog *about as religious as my neighbour's 121 *crazy as Tom's | and he died howling / barking at the moon / who would put his rear in the brook for a drink 36 *eat as much as two men and a 86 *face like a 4 *old as Methuselah's 20 *They could sell fleas to a 73
dog hadn't stopped to shit he would've won the race / caught the fox / the rabbit, If that 26
dog house, Down comes your 64
dog piss on her pups, Wouldn't that make an old 61
dog shit, everywhere you go, like 97
dog show, busy as a flea at a 97
dog in a wet blanket, shiver like a 108
dog when we get there, I'm taking you nowhere and treating you like a 81
dog off your leg, You can't keep a good 35
dog's arse heartburn, Wouldn't that give the 61

dog's dinner, be worked up like a 59
dog's nail, hang their coat on the 68
dogs, claws down, It's raining cats and 105
dollar, have a few cents short of a 43
dollar hat on a ten cent head, wear a ten 33
dollar short, always a day late and a 99
dolled up *like a teddy bear *with a teddy in their hand 16
dolls, make paper 60
Dolly, the cock for 112
done, The biscuits are 113
donkey, They could sell fleas to a 73
donut, Hoot and holler and wave your 58
doodle-daddle for a duck's / goose's / horse's saddle / waddle 79
door and down the hatch, Open the barn 86
door *as if a pot were emptied through a screen 8 *enough rouge to paint a barn 9 *get around like the button on the outhouse 66 *homely as ma's back 5 *homely / ugly as a barn 5 *It's easy to pass a poor man's 100 *tongue like a button on a back barn 72
door mat, cross between a door sill and a 26
door sill and a door mat, cross between a 26
door on a submarine, useless as a screen 51
door than they carry in the front, throw more out the back 99
door when a horse farted / a manure spreader went by / the sun was shining, standing by a screen 8
doorknob, stunned / stupid as a 42
double-bitted axe, two-faced as a 28
down cellar behind / beside the axe / the fish barrels / the fish bowl / the furnace 80
Down comes your dog / goose house (and fifty feet of the barn) 64
down *cow so old she had to be lifted when she lay 85 *eat so fast you can see the biscuit going 86 *have their mouth

turned upside 58 *head so high a martingale wouldn't bring it 33 *It's raining cats and dogs, claws 105
down *east 115 *west 116
down the *hatch, Open the barn door and *little red lane 86
down payment on a three-cent stamp, They couldn't afford the 100
downstairs behind the fish barrels, I'm going 77
dozen, short / shy of a | *a few cookies *twelve biscuits / eggs *two biscuits 43
dragged through a barnyard, look as if they had been 3
draw a pension, old enough to 111
dressed (up) like a *Beach Grove Johnny *circus horse *clothesline in the rain *Protestant priest *spare bedroom 16–17
drew laces on our feet to walk to town, so poor we 100
drink, crazy as Tom's dog who would put his ass in the brook for a 36
drink a biscuit, so thirsty I could 88
drink it out of a(n), so fond of liquor they would | chamber pot / dirty straw / sheep('s) / cow('s) track / (old) sock / rubber boot / wagon track 89
drink of water *With a face like that, they'd have to sneak up on a 6 *You might as well take a 52
driver, big enough to eat a horse and cart and chase the 11
driveway doesn't quite meet the road, Their 43
drop [someone] in a hole, never 123
dropping bowling balls, God is 104
drown if they walked in the rain, They would 33
drunk, so | *they couldn't hit the ground if they fell on it *they couldn't hit the ground with their hat *they'd spit and miss the ground, so 89
drunk as a boot / a fart / arse / barrels of shit / 89–90

drunk on the wagon for a month, dry as a 88
drunker than two barrels of shit 90
dry, I'd rather watch paint 52
dry, I'm so | *I can't/couldn't spit *I feel like a raisin / a prune *I'm cracking / squeaking *I'm spitting dust / sparks 88–9
dry as a(n) *burnt boot / potato 84 *cork leg 88 *cow's ass / crow's crotch at fly-time 88 *drunk on the wagon for a month 88 *dust storm 103 *Mountie's boot 84 *mouthful of choke cherries 89 *old bucket *strap 84 *wooden bridge in Africa / wooden leg / wooden spoon 88
dry as *snuff 103 *the inside of a woodpecker's boarding house 88
duck, happy as a dead 57
duck's foot, yellow as a 120
duck's saddle, doodle-daddle for a 79
ducks, happy as two dead 57
dumb as / dumber than a *bag / sack of (claw) hammers *frog on a log *left-handed hammer 40–1
dump cart, so cold it would freeze the nuts off a 107
dump truck, mouth like the back of a 73
Dundee, I'm going to 76
dust, I'm so dry I'm spitting 89
dust storm, dry as a 103

ear, fit like a sock in a pig's 112
ear off an elephant, talk the 73
eardrums, Wouldn't that frost your 61
early, It's not late until it's twelve and then it's getting 67
ears, Clean the bananas / dirt / hay / straw / potatoes out of your 62
ears? *Are you growing potatoes in your 62 *How's your feet and 75
east, down / up 115–16
east and one blew west, two beautiful blue eyes – one blew 8
east end of a *horse / skunk going west,

Index   141

so hungry I could eat the 83 *train going west, face like the 6
easy, make 59
easy to pass a poor man's door, It's 100
eat, big enough to | a horse and cart and chase the driver / hay 11
eat, so hungry I could | an old book / cobwebs / leftover leftovers / my spats / the bottom out of an iron pot / the east end of a horse / skunk going west / the plate / the table 83
eat an apple / corn (on the cob) / pretzels / straw through a chicken coop / picket fence, They could 9
eat as much as two men and a dog 86
eat so fast you can see the biscuit going down 86
eating, busier than a toad | grubs / lightning 95
Eaton's don't tell Simpson's their business 29
eel, They couldn't even skin an 45
eels, nooden-nadden / oodle-addle for catching 79
eels in a barrel of snot, slippery as six fat 29
egg, There's more meat on a poached 15
eggs, painful as a hen laying square 23
eggs and on to the potatoes / onions / straw, off their 74
eggs in the basket, not many 43
eggs on the floor, You could cook / fry 114
eggs shy of a dozen, twelve 43
eggs you have in the henhouse, You can only use the 99
eggshell, clean as an 112
eight-day clock or a sewing machine, I'm not an 97
elbow, crooked as a fiddler's 27
elephant, talk the ear off an 73
elephant cost five cents, they couldn't afford a diaper / the buttons for a pismire, If overalls for an 101
elephant's bed, a lot of bunk, like the 29
eleven months of winter and one month of (late) fall / of poor skating conditions / of tough sledding 108
emptied through a screen door, as if a pot were 8
empty as last year's bird's nest 41
end, twice as long as from the centre to either 81
end of a *horse / skunk going west, so hungry I could eat the east 83 *train going west / north, face like the east / south 6
end of the stick, by the 65
end of your nose, silver know-nothing / new nothing to hang on the 79
ends, well-fed at both 10
enough *crust to start a bakery 34 *meat on you to make a sandwich, There's not 15 *on to flag a train / a wheelbarrow, not 17 *rouge to paint a barn door 9 *to draw a pension, old 111 *to vote, old 111
Eskimo, They could sell snow to an 73
Eskimos, I'm going north for a load of 76
every hitch and turn 120
every old sock, There is a mate for 123
everywhere you go, like dog shit 97
excited, Don't get your hormones all 59
expect the tide to wait while you paint the sand, You might as well 49
eye, better out than a farmer's / an 69
eye, May the rats never leave your flour barrel with a tear in their 82
eye and can't see out of the other, blind in one 8
eye of a (darning) needle (at forty / fifty paces), shit through the 23
eyeballs, Wouldn't that frost your 61
eyebrow today, It's chilly 106
eyebrows, fat as a hen between the 14
eyes – one blew east and one blew west, two beautiful blue 8
eyes, The mice come out of the cupboard with tears in their 101
eyes for looking at [someone], hate my 63
eyes out of your head, so greedy they would steal the 30

Index

face, fly-shit on the 9
face, mouth (going) five miles faster than their 72
face, right tight in the 63
face as long as the Western Road 58
face like a *bag full of hammers / monkeys / mortal sins *bucket / can of snakes (squashed) worms *dog *horse *plowshare *skate *sour apple *twisted sneaker 3–6
face like someone who was chasing parked cars / won the 100-yard dash in a 90-yard gym 6
face like that, they'd have to sneak up on a drink of water, With a 6
face like the east / south end of a train going west / north 6
face so ugly it *must be painful / hurt *would run a train off the tracks 6–7
face that would knock a dead man cold 6
faces as a beech nut, as many 28
fact, That's a God's 47
factory *gall enough to start a vinegar 32 *nervous as a hemophiliac in a razor-blade 59
Fair weather to you and snow to your heels 82
fallen out of the basket / bucket, The bottom has 48
falling off its horns, cow so old the rings were 85
falling on Grandpa, The boards are 105
family was away on vacation, so poor that four in the bed meant half the 100
fanny, Wouldn't that frost your 61
far in the back woods they have to come out to hunt, live so 67
farm to do that, I wouldn't take a 48
farmer's eye, better out than a 69
Fart, the Messenger, They think they're King Shit, but they're only 34
fart *drunk as 90 *tight as a fiddler's 112
farted, standing by a screen door when a horse 8
fart in a *gas bottle, so mean they would save a 31 *mitt, tearing around like a 96

*mitt(en) (looking for a thumbhole), busy as / tearing around like a / worse than a 96
fart sack, hit the 92
fast you can see the biscuit going down, eat so 86
faster than their face, mouth (going) five miles 72
fat as *a bear / a lump on a stump / a runny loaf 11 *a hen between the eyebrows 14 *grannie's goose 11
fat eels in a barrel of snot, slippery as six 29
fat pig, lazy as a 25
father, so poor we couldn't afford to have a 100
feather (tick), so poor we took turns sleeping on the 100
feathers *upstairs in the cellar picking chickens out of 77 *Wouldn't that fluff your 61
fed, They would shit (too) if they were well 32
feed box, not much feed in the 43
feed of oats for a nightmare, They couldn't afford a 100
feel it, It's not up your arse or you'd 80
feel like a shit house mouse / rat 23
feet, beat the 67
feet and ears? How's your 75
feet to walk to town, so poor we drew laces on our 100
fell down they'd be half way home, so tall if they 10
fell on it, so drunk they couldn't hit the ground if they 89
fell out of an ugly tree and hit every branch on the way down, They 6
fell out of bed, so stupid they'd miss the floor if they 44
felt? How's your old straw hat – or would you rather have your brown 75
fence *They could eat an apple / corn (on the cob) / straw through a picket *They look like a horse eating an apple through a wire 9

Index   143

fence *crooked as a pole 27 *homely / ugly as a board / brush / picket / stump / wire 5 *ignorant as a brush 42
fence post *crooked as a 27 *too cold for a 106
fester your britches, Wouldn't that 60
few apples / bags / bales / cents / cookies / nuts / pickles short of a barrel / dollar / dozen / full jar / load / picnic 43
fiddle, put the bow to the 67
fiddler's *elbow, crooked as a 27 *fart, tight as a 112
fiddlestring, tight as a 112
field so poor a rabbit would shed tears going across it 102
fifty feet of the barn, Down comes your goose house and 64
fill it, brass enough to make a pot and gall enough to 32
find the gaps, It's time to 91
fingernails on Sunday and the Devil will be after you all week, Cut your 56
finished, There's one room in the attic / one room upstairs / the ceiling of one room not 38
fire, You can bank a 47
fire in a barn full of straw, You might as well spit on a 50
first instalment on a free lunch, They couldn't afford the 100
first settlers, It must have been older than the / one of the 85
fish barrels / fish bowl, down cellar / downstairs behind the 80
fish in *a bucket, dance around like a 57 *Saturday's market, I'm going to get Friday's 77
fish (on the) half-line 103
fish *homely as an ugly 4 *I'm going to Souris / Tignish for a load of (rotten) 76
fishcake, wide as a 114
fishing, I'm going | Do you want to build the boat? 76

fit for a mailbox / woodpile (to be out), not 107
fit like a sock in a pig's ear / nose 112
fit it, There's never an old shoe / slipper but there's an old sock / stocking to 123
five miles faster than their face, mouth (going) 72
flag a train / a wheelbarrow, not enough on to 17
flapping, so hungry my belly is 84
flashlight, You could X-ray them with a 13
flat as a June cow-turd 15
flea bag / pen, hit the 92
flea at a dog show, busy as a 97
flea's leg, If brains were rubber they wouldn't have enough to stretch around the hair on a 45
fleas to a dog / to a donkey, They could sell 73
flesh on a fly's / robin's leg, There's more 14
flies *Good weather for *not bothered by 106
flies at a meat market, busy as 97
flies out today, At least there's no / Not (too) many 106
flim-flam for a goose's necktie 79
floor *They didn't take that off the 4 *You could cook / fry eggs on the 114
floor if they fell out of bed, so stupid they'd miss the 44
floor and wipe your ass at the same time, You can't sweep the 53
floored me with a pitchfork, You could have 61
flour *barrel, mouse wouldn't go up to its ankles in the *in the barrel would take a mouse to its knees, The 101
flour barrel with a tear in their eye, May the rats never leave your 82
flour barrel and scale the wall, Get off the 91
flowers while they're still alive, give [someone] 70
fluff your feathers, Wouldn't that 61

fly backwards, If you put their brain in a bird, the bird would 45
fly in a bottle, run around like a 97
fly's leg, There's more flesh / meat on a 14
fly-shit *on the face 9 *out of pepper, busy as a hen picking 96
fly-time, dry as a cow's ass / crows crotch at 88
fog *I'm going to the breakwater to fork off the 76 *old as the / three days older than the 20 *warm smoke is better than a cold 67
fog locker for a can of green paint, I'm going to the 76
foolish it would trip a goat, so 55
foolish as a rooster with a sock on its head 56
foot *twelve inches shy of a 43 *yellow as a duck's 120
Ford, Chev's a Chev and a Ford's a 74
Ford a Ford, They couldn't afford to call a 101
forehead *have a vacancy in one's 44 *There's more meat on a chicken's 14
fork, You might as well try to keep Niagara Falls back with a 50
fork off the fog, I'm going to the breakwater to 76
fox, If that dog hadn't stopped to shit he would've caught the 26
freckles as big as gingersnaps 8
free lunch (for a canary), They couldn't afford the first instalment on a 100
free meal, They couldn't afford the ticket to a 100
freeze, so cold it would | the nuts off a dump cart / an iron/steel bridge / the Hillsborough Bridge 107
Friday's fish in Saturday's market, I'm going to get 77
fried in butter, three mosquitoes 81
fried onions, bees' knees and 81
frog, make as much sense as a three-legged 56
frog on a log, dumb as a 41

from across / away / the other side 117–18
front, throw more out the back door than they carry in the 99
frost your ass / eardrums / eyeballs / fanny / preserves / socks / the backside of a cow, Wouldn't that 61
frosting on a burnt cake, like 29
froze to pokers 107
fry eggs on the floor, You could 114
full, make 121
full as a banana / teddy bear 90
full jar, have pickles short of a 43
fun *carrying / paying for last year's 11 *night owl has the 67
furnace, down cellar beside the 80
furniture (around), God is moving (his) 104

gale of wind, like the Devil in a 8
gall enough to *fill it, brass enough to make a pot and *start a vinegar factory 32
gall than a snake, more 34
gap, bold as a country bull / ram in a 35
gaps, It's time to find the 91
garbage cans, God is taking out the 104
garbage man would leave three bags, so poor the 100
gas bottle, so mean they would save a fart in a 31
gate, stubborn as a calf at a new 34
gatepost, look like the skin of a nightmare pulled over a 15
gear, nothing left but the running 15
gear shift, All that's left of them is the 15
geese, Shoot 71
George, by the liftin 65
get to blanket harbour 92
Get off the flour barrel and scale the wall 91
get salve 121
ghost, old as Methuselah's 20
ghost on toast, roast 81
gingersnaps, freckles as big as 8
gingersnaps last night, (have) too many 90

Index   145

give [someone] flowers while they're still alive 70
glass, it's trouble while it lasts, If you see the new moon through 54
go for bears 94
Go to bed with the hens and get up with the roosters 92
go to bunky harbour 92
go once too often to / close to the trough 10
go quick and stay long 24
go and snare a rabbit, I've got to 82
go through the loop 101
goat, old as Methuselah's 20
goat needs a beard, They need [something] as badly as a 51
goat *crazy / silly / stupid as a billy 41 *not have the brains God gave a 41 *so foolish it would trip a 55
God gave a goat / a louse / little apples, not have the brains 41
God is *angry tonight *bowling with the angels *crying *dropping bowling balls *mad at the Devil *moving (his) furniture (around) *rolling his barrels in the sky *spitting *taking out the garbage cans 104–5
God made only a few perfect heads; the rest he put hair on 7
God's fact, That's a 47
going around worse than a cut cat 37
going to [nonsensical locations] 76–7
going to the country 123
gold, they'd be a millionaire, If their brass were 32
goldfish, I was about to walk the 78
golf ball / club, There's more meat on a 14–15
good *day to let the ram go / set a hen 107 *dog off your leg, You can't keep a 35 *head for bouncing bricks off / if you like cabbage 42 *man where you come from, but you're not where you come from, You may be a 34 *man's arse, not worth a patch on a 50 *twist, in 23

Good Friday, There's more meat on (the Pope's plate on) 15
good-looking, I wish I was born richer and not so 50
Good weather for blackflies / flies / mosquitoes 106
goose, fat as grannie's 11
goose house (and fifty feet of the barn), Down comes your 64
goose's bridle / necktie / saddle / waddle, for a 79
graceful as a sack of hammers 40
grain, short in the 62
grandmother back from the dead, Wouldn't that bring 61
Grandpa, The boards are falling on 105
grannie's goose, fat as 11
grass *and twice as spry, green as 19 *make it to the 21 *on concrete, You can't grow 7
grasshopper, bow-legged as a 16
grasshopper would have to pack a lunch crossing it / starve to death, land so poor a 102
grasshoppers, land so poor it wouldn't grow 102
grave, deep as the 29
Great Hall above, They're moving the chairs in the 104
greedy, so | they would *save the tallow from a mosquito *steal swill from an orphan pig / the eyes out of your head 30
green *cheese, I'm going to the moon to get some *paint, I'm going to the fog locker for a can of 76
green as grass and twice as spry 19
grey beard, song so old it has a 111
grey bird, There's more meat on a little 14
grindstone, They could charm the heart out of a 73
ground if they fell on it, so drunk they couldn't hit the 89
ground *so crooked that (when they die) they could be screwed into the 27 *so drunk they'd spit and miss the 89

ground with their hat, so drunk they couldn't hit the 89
grow grass on concrete, You can't 7
grow grasshoppers / rock / thistles, land so poor it wouldn't 102
growing on you? What's 76
growing potatoes in your ears? Are you 62
grubs, busier than a toad eating 95
gull on a rock, lonesome as a 66
gums, look out stomach, here it comes, Over the lips and over the 86
gunney sack, look like two pigs fighting in a 11
guppers, stuffed to the 87
gym, face like someone who won the 100-yard dash in a 90-yard 6

hair *They have straw in their 35 *You have to stand them in the well to cut their 19
hair on, God made only a few perfect heads; the rest he put 7
hair on a flea's leg, If brains were rubber they wouldn't have enough to stretch around the 45
half *a look (away) *(away), look and a 115
half the family was away on vacation, so poor that four in the bed meant 100
half-line, fish (on the) 103
half way home, so tall if they fell down they'd be 10
ham sandwich, not worth the mustard / salt on a 50
hammer, dumb as a left-handed 40
hammers, as a bag / sack of | *clumsy *crazy *dense *dumb *graceful *stupid 40
hammers, deaf as a bag of 18
hammers, dumber than / have as much sense as a bag / sack of (claw) 40
hammers, face like a bag full of 6
hamster gets off the wheel sometimes, The 39
handle *off an iron pot, talk the 75

*There's more meat on a broom 14
*ugly as an axe 4
handles, They couldn't carry a tune if it had 18
hang on the end of your nose, silver know-nothing / new nothing to 79
hang a powder horn on (a tip of) the moon 110
hang their coat on the dog's nail 68
hanging since they were [some stated age], I wouldn't like to be 21
happier, If I was any | I wouldn't be working *there would be two of me 57
happy as a dead / two dead duck(s) 57
happy as if they were wise 36
harbour, get to blanket / bunky 92
hard as the knockers of hell 113
hard with the ugly stick, look as if they were hit too 6
hardwood, lay leather to the 67
hardwood stump, homely as a 5
harrow *the headlands of what I've plowed, You couldn't *what I plowed, if they 95
hat? How's your old straw 75
hat, so drunk they couldn't hit the ground with their 89
hat on a ten cent head, wear a ten dollar 33
hatch, Open the barn door and down the 86
hate my eyes for looking at [someone] 63
hats, so two-faced they should wear two 28
hauling wood, sweat like a hen 94
hay, big enough to eat (a round ball of) 11
hay cutter, mouth / tongue like a 73
hay out of your ears, Clean the 62
haystack, big as a 11
head, so greedy they would steal the eyes out of your 30
head *foolish as a rooster with a sock on its 56 *rooster crowing to bed is sure to rise with a wet 105 *wear a ten dollar hat on a ten cent 33
head *for bouncing bricks off, good *if you

Index   147

like cabbage, good *like a (thumb)tack 42
head like a sewing machine but be no singer 18
head so high a martingale wouldn't bring it down 33
head toad in the puddle 76
headlands of what I've plowed, You couldn't harrow the 95
heart with a bad answer, They'd never break your 28
heart of a grindstone and make a wheelbarrow dance, They could charm the 74
heart and soul, hole 86
heartburn, Wouldn't that give the dog's arse 61
hearth, nervous as a long-haired cat beside an open 58
heating pad to the Devil, They could sell a 73
Heaven, Hell, or Cawnpore, When you die, you go to 21
heavens, The sun is splitting the 109
heavy as a man and a boy 113
hedgehog *lazy as a 25 *stupid as a 41
heel to save their sole, They'd walk on their 99
heels, Fair weather to you and snow to your 82
Hell, or Cawnpore, When you die, you go to Heaven, 21
hell, hard as the knockers of 113
hemlock, lay cowhide to the 67
hemophiliac in a razorblade factory, nervous as a 59
hen *between the eyebrows, fat as a 14 *crazy / stupid as a marsh 41 *good day to set a 109 *hauling wood, sweat like a 94 *laying square eggs, painful as a 23 *picking fly-shit out of pepper, busy as a 96 *right off her nest, Wouldn't that blow the 61
henhouse, You can only use the eggs you have in the 99
henhouse? Were you born in a 68

hens and get up with the roosters, Go to bed with the 92
hide behind a broomstick, so thin they could 12
high beams, You have your brake lights ahead of your 74
high C, up in 58
high a martingale wouldn't bring it down, head so 33
high you have to look twice to see, so 114
hill, It's time to climb the wooden 92
Hillsborough Bridge, so cold it would freeze the nuts off the 107
hit *a wire, They could shit through a screen door and never touch a 23 *every branch on the way down, They fell out of an ugly tree and 6 *the blankets / crate / fart sack / flea bag / flea pen 92 *the ground if they fell on it / with their hat, so drunk they couldn't 89 *the wooden hill, time to 92 *too hard with the ugly stick, look as if they were 6 *with a shotgun behind a broomstick / behind a crowbar, so thin they couldn't be 12 *with the ugly bug, Someone got 7 *[someone] but they say manure splatters, I'd 64
hitch and turn, every 120
hockey stick, There's more meat on a 14
hold the baby too, I can't dance and 62
hold me till you get a rope, That will 87
holding water, The moon is 110
hole, heart, and soul 86
hole, never drop [someone] in a 123
hole? Were you born in a 68
hole in a lead pot / an iron pot / a tin pot, talk / wear a 75
holes, make button 60
holes in it, song so old it has 111
holiday and the second the teacher wasn't there, They went to school for two days: the first was a 122
holler and wave your donut, Hoot and 58
holy (Lord) liftins, by the 65
Holy wick 65
home, stuck 118

148   Index

home *from a different direction every morning, He's like a tom-cat, coming 68 *have a nice apartment but there's no one 43 *so tall if they fell down they'd be half way 10
homely as a(n) *barn door / ma's back door *board / brush / picket / stump / wire fence *hardwood stump *ugly fish *wet cat 4–5
honest as the sun 29
hoodle-haddle / hoodle-laddle / hoody-addle for a goose's necktie 79
Hoot and holler and wave your donut 58
hormones *all excited, Don't get your *Calm your 59
horn on (a tip of) the moon, hang a powder 110
horns, cow so old the rings were falling off its 85
horns off the Devil, cold as the 107
horse *all dressed up like a circus 17 *face like a 4 *have the Devil in them as big as a 30 *like Pontius Pilate's 4 *They must have used that cow as a 85
horse and cart and chase the driver, big enough to eat a 11
horse eating an apple through a wire fence, They look like a 9
horse farted, standing by a screen door when a 8
horse going west, so hungry I could eat the east end of a 83
horse's saddle, doodle-daddle for a 79
hot, Don't get your water (all) 60
house, I was thinking I might move the 78
housecleaning up above, They're 104
howling at the moon, crazy as Tom's dog and he died 36
How's your belly button / belly for beans / belly for biscuits / feet and ears / old straw hat? 75
hundred, not a 43
hungry, so | I could eat an old book / cobwebs / leftover leftovers / my spats / the bottom out of an iron pot / the east end of a horse / skunk going west / the plate / the table 83
hungry as a bunch of starving Russians 83
hungry my belly is flapping, so 84
hunt, live so far in the back woods they have to come out to 67
hurt, face so ugly it must 6

igloo? Were you born in an 68
ignorant as a brush fence / as dirt 42
in the round 103
inches shy of a foot, twelve 43
Indian, They could sell toothpicks to a wooden 73
inkling and that's only a tenth of a clue, not have an 45
inside of a *black cow, black as the 108 *woodpecker's boarding house, dry as the 88
instalment on a free lunch (for a canary) / on a clay pipe / T D pipe, They couldn't afford the first / They couldn't afford to pay an 100
invisible, so thin if they turn sideways they're 13
Irish lick and a Scotch promise / rub 9
iron bridge, so cold it would freeze the nuts off an 107
iron pot *so hungry I could eat the bottom out of an 83 *talk the bottom / handle / lid off an 75
Island, two days older than the 20
Island penny, They would cut the trees off an 31
Island was when they were up a tree, The only time they were off the 35
itchy prick, have an 62

jackpot, useless as a deuce in a 51
jagged, jig when they should have 55
jar, have a few / seven pickles short of a full 43
jaws of her, pound of paint on the 9
Jehosaphat, by the liftin 65
jellybeans, I'm going to Souris for a load of 76

Index   149

Jerusalem for a load of Bibles, I'm going 76
jig when they should have jagged 55
John Bull, by the living 64
judgment, tough as leather 85
Jumbo's hole to see the moon rising, I'm going up 76
jump (away), spit and a 115
June cow-turd, flat as a 15

keep, You might as well try to | *Niagara Falls back with a fork / teaspoon *the tide out with a pitchfork 50
keep their money in a snowbank / sandbank 101
keeps or not, I don't care if school 122
keys *missing, have a few 37 *than white, have more black 38
kick the cat 72
kick it, When you see a pig, you should 123
kill *(a) bear(s) 94 *a sheep and to hell with poverty 101
killing the cat? Who's 18
king of the trough 76
King Shit, They think they're | but they're only Fart, the Messenger 34
kitchen table, smooth as the 109
kittens, busier than a cat having 95
kitten's wrist, slick as a 111
knees, The flour so low in the barrel a mouse would have to get on its 101
knees and fried onions, bees' 81
knife, I'd stab [someone] but I'd be sorry for the 63
knife itself, You couldn't cut it with the 85
knife they butter their bread with, not worth the 50
knit, learning to 78
knock a dead man cold, face that would 6
knockers of hell, hard as the 113
knocking nails 91
knot, get their neck / pantyhose / shorts in a 62
know, not | *if they're pitching or catching 55 *whether to shit or wind one's watch 53
know as much about [something] as my arsehole 45
know-nothing to hang on the end of your nose, silver 78

lace our toes for shoes, so poor we had to 100
laces on our feet to walk to town, so poor we drew 100
land is waiting for the pogie, That 102
land so poor *a grasshopper / mouse would have to pack a lunch / starve to death crossing it *it wouldn't grow grasshoppers / rock / thistles *it's on welfare 102
landmark to see them moving, It takes a 26
lane, down the little red 86
last night, too many gingersnaps 90
last year (and piling it up), the same thing I did 78
last year's *bird's nest, empty as 41 *shit, so cheap they wouldn't give you the smell off their 31 *snowbank, useless as a pee-hole/piss-hole in 52
late and a dollar short, always a day 99
late until it's twelve, not 67
lavender, dash of 120
lay cowhide to the hemlock / leather to the hardwood 67
laying square eggs, painful as a hen 23
lazy to breathe / live / spit, too 26
lazy as a fat pig / hedgehog / pet cat / pet coon / pet day / pet pig / toad 25
lazy to walk back, I'd stretch a mile but I'm too 91
lead pot, talk / wear a hole in a 75
lean up against the wall to squeal, so thin they have to 14
learning to knit 78
leather judgment, tough as 85
leather to the hardwood, lay 67
left (of them) *but the bill and coo /

150 Index

running gear, nothing *is the gear shift, All that's 14–15
left-handed hammer, dumb as a 40
left long enough in the oven, not 37
leftover leftovers, so hungry I could eat 83
leg *dry as a cork / wooden 88 *If brains were rubber they wouldn't have enough to stretch around the hair on a flea's 45 *There's more flesh / meat on a fly's / robin's 14 *You can't keep a good dog off your 35
legs, so bow-legged you could roll a barrel between their 16
lick and a Scotch promise / rub, Irish 9
lid, They're a case without a 37
lid off an iron pot, talk the 75
lie – I swallowed it, It must have been a 72
lie on their back to look in the cellar, so cross-eyed they have to 8
life, This may be a young animal, but it led a tough 85
lifted when she lay down, cow so old she had to be 85
liftin George / (holy) (Lord) / Jehosaphat, by the 65
light(s) (on) upstairs / in the attic / upper storey, There's no 38
light bulb, bright as a burnt-out / two-watt 42
lightning, busier than a toad eating 95
lights ahead of your high beams, You have your brake 74
likely, not charming 48
links missing, have a few 37
lips and over the gums, look out stomach, here it comes, Over the 86
liquor, so fond of I they would drink it out of a chamber pot / cow / dirty straw / old sock / rubber boot / sheep / wagon track 89
liquor store, You might as well go to the 52
listened, talk when they should have 55
little *apples, not have the brains God gave 41 *grey bird, There's more meat on a 14 *rally, thresh a 95 *red lane,

down the 86 *wooden hill, It's time to buckle up / climb / hit the 92
live, too lazy to 26
live so far in the back woods they have to come out to hunt 67
liver pills, more [something] than Carter has 52
living John Bull, by the 64
load *have a few bags / bales / nuts short of a 43 *three sticks short of a 37
load of jellybeans / postholes / rotten fish / smelts, going for a 76
loaf, fat as a runny 11
lodging, If you were singing for a night's I you'd be sleeping outside 18
lofts, busy as a rat in a shed with three 96
log, dumb as a frog on a 41
lonesome, If they had a brain / clue, it would be 45
lonesome as a gull on a rock / a pole cat 66
long *go quick and stay 24 *wide as the day is 10
long and ever ago 121
long as *a sleigh track on the Western Road 114 *a wet Sunday / week and three times as disagreeable 121 *from the centre to either end, twice as 81 *the Western Road, face as 58
long enough in the oven, not left 37
long streak of misery 58
long-haired cat beside an open hearth, nervous as a 58
loodle-laddle for a goose's necktie 79
look *and a half (away) *(away), half a 115
look as if *one was thrown in the ugly pond *their mother beat them with an ugly stick *they got beat by / took a beating from / were hit too hard with an / the ugly stick 6–7
look as if they had been dragged through a barnyard 3
look down a well, so cross-eyed they have to lie on their back to 8
look like *a cream of tartar biscuit 16 *a new dashboard on an old wagon 16

*the skin of a nightmare pulled over a gatepost 15 *two pigs fighting in a blanket / gunney sack 11
look twice to see, so high you have to 114
looking at [someone], hate my eyes for 63
looking for *it, They've got two clues – one's lost, the other's *one another, If they had two clues, they'd be out 44
looking glass, two-faced as a 28
loop, go through the 101
loose board in the attic, There's a 38
Lord, The | *has an upset stomach *is angry tonight *is (gone) bowling (with the angels) 104
Lord liftins, by the (holy) 65
lost, the other's looking for it, They've got two clues – one's 44
lot more, I could be better but it would cost a 76
lot of miles on that old cow 85
louse, not have the brains God gave a 41
lovely staircase but no upstairs, have a 43
low in the barrel a mouse would have to get on its knees, The flour's so 101
lucky as a pet crow 57
lump on a stump, fat as a 11
lunch, land so poor a grasshopper / mouse would have to pack / take / carry a 102
lunch (for a canary), They couldn't afford the first instalment on a free 100

ma's back door, homely as 5
machine *but be no singer, have a head like a sewing 18 *I'm not an eight-day clock or a sewing 97 *mouth / tongue like a threshing / hay 73
mad at the Devil, God is 105
Magdalen Islands for a load of postholes, I'm going to the 76
mailbox (to be out), not fit for a 107
make a dead man's bubble 122
make *as much sense as a dead cow / sucking turkey / three-legged frog 56 *buttons / button holes and sew them on 60 *easy 59 *full 121 *it to the grass 21 *paper dolls 60
making a baloney sandwich 78
man *and a boy, heavy as a 113 *cold, face that would knock a dead 6 *where you come from, but you're not where you come from, You may be a good 34 *who came from Ántigonish, My brother slept with a 34 *would leave three bags, so poor the garbage 100
man's *arse / balls, not worth a patch on a good / the sweat off a dead 50–1 *bubble, make a dead 122 *door, It's easy to pass a poor 100 *throat, cut the dead 122
manure splatters, I'd hit [someone] but they say 64
manure spreader went by, standing by a screen door when a 8
marble, sharp as a 42
market, busy as flies at a meat 97
marsh hen, crazy / stupid as a 41
martingale wouldn't bring it down, head so high a 33
mat, cross between a door sill and a door 26
match it, There's never an old shoe / slipper but there's an old sock / stocking to 123
mate for every old sock, There is a 123
May the rats never leave your flour barrel with a tear in their eye 82
meal, They couldn't afford the ticket to a free 100
mean *as / meaner than second skimmings *they would save a fart in a gas bottle, so *to give the smell off their ass / their shit to the crows, too 31
mean when we get there, I'll give you nothing, take you nowhere, and treat you 81
meat, There's more | on a broom handle / chicken's forehead / crucifix / fly's leg / golf ball / golf club / hockey stick / little grey bird / poached egg / on (the Pope's plate on) Good Friday 14–15

152 Index

meat market, busy as flies at a 97
meat on you to make a sandwich, There's not enough 15
meatloaf, Don't let your 82
meet the road, Their driveway doesn't quite 43
men and a dog, eat as much as two 86
Messenger, They think they're King Shit, but they're only Fart, the 34
Methuselah's billy / buck / cat / dog / ghost / goat / nanny, old as 20
mice come out of the cupboard with tears in their eyes, The 101
mice *dense as a sack of wet 40 *it sees, busy as a squint-eyed cat trying to catch all the 96
middle of the week and no work done yet, The day after tomorrow will be the 94
midnight, black as two black bears at 108
mile but I'm too lazy to walk back, I'd stretch / walk a 91
mile for [something], I'd chase a crow a 86
miles faster than their face, mouth (going) five 72
miles on that old cow, lot of 85
millionaire, If their brass were gold, they'd be a 32
misery, long streak of 58
miss the floor if they fell out of bed, so stupid they'd 44
miss the ground, so drunk they'd spit and 89
missing, have a few black keys / links / pegs / slats / sticks 37
mitt, fart in a | *busy as a / running / tearing around like a / worse than a 96
molasses, like walking on / through 119
Monday or you will be spending all week, Don't buy anything on 99
money, have more troubles than 101
money in a sandbank / snowbank, keep their 101
monkey, talk the ear off a 73
monkeys, face like a bag full of 6
month, dry as a drunk on the wagon for a 88
months of winter and three / two / one month(s) of (late) fall / of poor skating conditions / tough sledding, nine / ten / eleven 108
moon *hang a powder horn on (a tip of) the 110 *I was thinking I might move the 78 *is holding water, The 110 *rising, I'm going up Jumbo's hole to see the 76 *to get some green cheese, I'm going to the 76
moon through glass, it's trouble while it lasts, If you see the new 54
more, I could be better but it would cost a lot 76
more, This tastes like 86
morning, so crooked they have to screw their socks on in the 27
mortal sins, face like a bag full of 6
mosquito, so greedy they would save the tallow from a 30
mosquitoes *At least there's no *good weather for *not bothered by 106
mosquitoes fried in butter, three 81
mother *beat them with an ugly stick, look as if their 6 *gave them ugly pills for breakfast, Their 63 *so ugly that the doctor slapped their 7
Mount Everest, You might as well try to climb 50
Mountain, King Shit from Turd 34
Mountie's boot *dry as a 84 *more tongue than a / tongue like a 73
mouse *and never wake him up, so sharp you could shave a 113 *feel like a shit house 23 *land so poor a | would have to pack a lunch / starve to death crossing it 102 *sly / slick as a 29 *to its knees, The flour in the barrel would take a 101 *wouldn't go up to its ankles in the flour barrel 101
mouth *as big as a codfish 10 *(going) five miles faster than their face 72 *like a codfish 10 *like a hay cutter / sewing machine / the back of a dump truck / threshing machine / winding blade 73 *on you, not asked if you had a 67 *turned upside down, have their 58
mouthful of choke cherries, dry as a 89

Index 153

move the barn / the chicken house / the moon, I was thinking I might 78
moving *(his) furniture (around), God is *the chairs in the Great Hall above, They're 104
moving, It takes a landmark to see them 26
mustard on a ham sandwich, not worth the 50

nail *and pass a screw, so crooked they could swallow a 27 *hang their coat on the dog's 68
nails, have as much sense as a bag of 40
name it after you, If there's anything slower than stopped, we'll 26
nanny, old as Methuselah's 20
natural causes, cow so old it died of 85
near nothing 49
neck in a knot, get their 62
necktie, a flim flam / hoodle-haddle / hoodle-laddle / hoody-addle / nooden-nadden / oodle-addle / wiggle-waggle for a goose's 79
need a cold cloth, You 59
need [something] as badly as, They | *a goat / toad needs a beard / tail *they need a second nose 51
needle at ninety yards, thread the 23
neighbour's dog, about as religious as my 121
neighbours that needed it, It wasn't the 49
nerve than a sore tooth, have more 33
nervous as a *hemophiliac in a razorblade factory *long-haired cat beside an open hearth 58–9
nest *empty as last year's bird's 41 *like a cat's / bird's / bee's 7 *Wouldn't that blow the hen right off her 61
never *drop [someone] in a hole 123 *put air under that, You'll 84 *wake him up, so sharp you could shave a mouse and 113
new *dashboard on an old wagon, look like a 16 *gate, stubborn as a calf at a 34 *moon through glass, it's trouble while it lasts, If you see the 54 *nothing, silver | *to hang on the end of your nose / wind up the sun / with a whistle on it 79
Newfoundland for a load of postholes, I'm going to 76
Niagara Falls back with a fork / teaspoon, You might as well try to keep 50
nice apartment but there's no one home, have 43
night, too many gingersnaps last 90
night owl has the fun, (But) the 67
nightmare *pulled over a gatepost, look like the skin of a 15 *They couldn't afford a feed of oats for a 100
nine wire, big as number 12
ninety yards, thread the needle at 23
no good at catching pigs 16
No sweetbreads yet 21
No thanks, I've just had a banana 81
nooden-nadden for a goose's necktie / catching eels / flies 79
north, face like the south end of a train headed 6
North Cape, old as the bill of 20
north for a load of Eskimos, I'm going 76
nose *fit like a sock in a pig's 112 *silver know-nothing / new nothing to hang on the end of your 79
not a hundred 43
not too *bad of a day 109 *many flies out today 106
notch in the beam, cut a 58
nothing, near 49
nothing, take you nowhere, and treat(ing) you mean / like a dog when we get there, I'll give you 81
nothing to hang on the end of your nose / to wind up the sun / with a whistle on it, silver know- / new 79
nothing left but the bill and coo / running gear 14–15
nothing and saw wood, Say 71
nowhere, and treat you mean / like a dog when we get there, I'll (give you nothing,) take you 81
nowhere that'll go in a day, There's 50
nut, as many faces as a beech 28

154   Index

nuts off a dump cart / an iron bridge / a steel bridge / the Hillsborough Bridge, so cold it would freeze the 107
nuts short of a load, have a few 43

oats *for a nightmare, They couldn't afford a feed of 100 *The Devil is rolling his 104
odd as the crows 36
off the walk 23
oil to the Arabs, They could sell 73
oily as a churnful of butter, tongue as 73
old, cow so | *it died of natural causes / old age *it must have had a vote *she had to be lifted when she lay down *the rings were falling off its horns 85
old *age, cow so old it died of 85 *as Methuselah or his billy / buck / cat / dog / goat / ghost / nanny 20 *as the bill of North Cape 20 *as the fog 20 *book / cobwebs / my spats, so hungry I could eat an 83 *bucket, dry as an 88 *chamber pot / rubber boot / sock, so fond of liquor they would drink it out of an 89 *cow, lot of miles on that 85 *dog piss on her pups, Wouldn't that make an 61 *enough to draw a pension / to vote 111 *it has a grey beard / it has holes in it, song so 111 *people go queer, Wouldn't that make the 61 *shoe / slipper but there's an old sock / stocking to fit / match it, There's never an 123 *sock, There is a mate for every 123 *straw hat – or would you rather have your brown felt? How's your 75 *straw hat? How's your 75 *tin can, If you can't get a board, take a slab, and if you can't get a slab, take an 53 *wagon, look like a new dashboard on an 16 *wooden hill, It's time to buckle up / climb / hit the 92
older than the *first settlers, It must have been 85 *fog / Island / tides, day(s) 20 *Stone Age 20
one couldn't be that stupid, There must be two of them because 44

one *shot at a shell-bird, You only get 48 *side, so thin it only has 114
onion a day keeps everyone away 24
onions *bees' knees and fried 81 *off their eggs and on to the 74
only *get one shot at a shell-bird, You 48 *one speed and that's slow / two speeds, slow and stop 26
oodle-addle for a goose's necktie / for catching eels / flies 79
Open the barn door and down the hatch 86
open hearth, nervous as a long-haired cat beside an 58
operating on all batteries, not 37
orchard about / in [someone], touch of the 120
orphan pig, so greedy they would steal swill from an 30
other side, from / on the 118
out *behind the barn 78 *roading 19 *today, At least there's no / Not (too) many flies 106
out *not fit for a mailbox to be 107 *The tide's gone 9
out of [someone], pick the talk 72
out than a farmer's eye / an eye, better 69
outhouse door, get around like the button on the 66
outside, If you were singing for a night's lodging, you'd be sleeping 18
oven, not left long enough in the 37
over across, from 117
Over the lips and over the gums, look out stomach, here it comes 86
over the pond, all 90
overalls for an elephant cost five cents, If | they couldn't afford a diaper / the buttons for a pismire 101
owl, crooked as a barnyard 28
owl has the fun, (But) the night 67

paces, shit through the eye of a (darning) needle at forty / fifty 23
pack a lunch, land so poor a grasshopper / mouse would have to 102

Index   155

pad to the Devil, They could sell a heating 73
painful *as a hen laying square eggs 23 *face so ugly it must be 6
paint *a barn door, enough rouge to 9 *the sand, You might as well expect the tide to wait while you 49
paint *dry, I'd rather watch 52 *on the jaws of her, pound of 9 *tight as two coats of 112
pair of spats for a canary, They couldn't afford a 100
pants, not worth a patch for your 50
pantyhose in a knot, get their 62
paper dolls, make 60
paper in the parlour / on the wall, tight / close as the 32
parked cars, face like someone who was chasing 6
parlour, close / tight as the paper in the 32
pass a poor man's door, It's easy to 100
pass a screw, so crooked they could swallow a nail and 27
pass of, take 121
patch for your pants / on a good man's arse, not worth a 50
pay *an instalment on a clay pipe / on a T D pipe, They couldn't afford to *attention, so poor we couldn't 100
paying for last year's fun 11
payment on a three-cent stamp, They couldn't afford the down 100
pea through them, so thin you could shoot a 12
peanut would stick out in their stomach, so thin a 13
pee-hole in a blanket / in the snow / in a snowbank / in last year's snowbank, useless as a 52
pegs missing, have a few 37
pen, hit the flea 92
penny, They would cut the trees off an Island 31
penny until the water runs out of the Queen's eyes, They would squeeze a 31
pension, old enough to draw a 111

people, think they are the 33
people go queer, Wouldn't that make the old 61
pepper, busy as a hen picking fly-shit out of 96
perfect heads, God made only a few | the rest he put hair on 7
pet *cat / coon / day / hedgehog / pig, lazy as a 25 *cat / goat, old as Methuselah's 20 *crow, lucky as a 57 *pig, bold as a 34 *pig, bow-legged as a 16
piano, in the pig's barrel behind the 80
pick that up off the street, They didn't 3
pick the talk out of [someone] 72
picket fence *homely as a 5 *They could eat an apple / corn / corn on the cob / straw through a 9
picking chickens out of feathers, upstairs in the cellar 77
picking fly-shit out of pepper, busy as a hen 96
pickles short of a barrel / of a full jar, have a few / seven 43
picnic, few apples / one ant short of a 43
pieces, There's a difference between scratching your arse and tearing it all to 48
pig *black as a blue 108 *bold as a pet 34 *bow-legged as a pet 16 *lazy as a fat / pet 25 *so greedy they would steal swill from an orphan 30 *you should kick it, When you see a 123
pig's barrel behind the piano, in the 80
pig's ear / nose, fit like a sock in a 112
pigs, no good at catching 16
pigs fighting in a blanket / gunney sack, look like two 11
piling it up, the same thing I did last year and 78
pill, They should have taken their anti-grouch 63
pills, more [something] than Carter has liver 52
pills for breakfast, Their mother gave them ugly 63
pinch my cheeks and call me cute 65

pipe, crooked as a stove 27
pipe, They couldn't afford to pay an instalment on a clay / T D 100
pismire, If overalls for an elephant cost five cents, they couldn't afford the buttons for a 101
piss (time), up at (the crack of) crow 93
piss on her pups, Wouldn't that make an old dog 61
piss-hole in a blanket / in a snowbank / in the snow / in last year's snowbank, useless as a 52
pissing the bed awake, stupid as 44
pitches and sloughs ahead, have 52
pitchfork *You might as well try to bail the river / keep the tide out with a 50 *You could have floored me with a 61
pitching or catching, not know if they're 55
plaid shirts, I'm going to sell some 76
plant or cut sets, You have to 53
plastered, There's one room in the attic / upstairs not 38
plate, so hungry I could eat the 83
Playing with the plugs again? 8
plowed, harrow (the headlands of) what I('ve) 95
plowshare, face like a 4
plugs again? Playing with the 8
poached egg, There's more meat on a 15
pocket, black as a witch's 109
pocket on a Sunday shirt, useful as a second 51
poets, He couldn't beat up a carload of 123
pogie, That land is waiting for the 102
pokers, froze to 107
pole cat, lonesome as a 66
pole fence, crooked as a 27
pollywoggles of the diaphobickalorium, case of the 24
pond *all over the 90 *(jump) across the 116 *look as if one was thrown in the ugly 6
Pontius Pilate's horse, face like 4
poor, land so | *a grasshopper / mouse would have to carry/pack a lunch / starve to death *a rabbit would shed tears going across it, field so *it wouldn't grow rock / thistles *it's on welfare 102
poor, so | that *four in the bed meant half the family was away on vacation *the garbage man would leave three bags *we couldn't afford to have a father *we couldn't pay attention 100 *we drew laces on our feet to walk to town *we had to lace our toes for shoes *we took turns sleeping on the feather (tick) 100
poor day to set a hen 107
poor man's door, It's easy to pass a 100
pop bottle, tight as a 112
Pope's plate on Good Friday, There's more meat on the 15
porridge, soft as 113
post *crooked as a (fence) 27 *too cold for a fence 106
postholes *dig / sell 60 *I'm going to Newfoundland / Souris / Tignish / to the Magdalen Islands for a truck / wagon load of 76 *not amount to a row of 52
pot *so fond of liquor they would drink it out of a chamber 89 *so hungry I could eat the bottom out of an iron 83
pot, talk *a hole in an iron *the arse / bottom / handle / lid off an iron 75
pot and gall enough to fill it, brass enough to make a 32
pot were emptied through a screen door, as if a 8
potato, dry / thirsty as a burnt 84
potatoes *in / out of your ears 62 *off their eggs and on to the 74
pound of paint on the jaws of her 9
poverty, kill a sheep and to hell with 101
powder horn on (a tip of) the moon, hang a 110
prayers, They'd hear more than my 64
preserves, Wouldn't that frost your 61
pretty as a red wagon 121
prick, have an itchy 62
priest, dressed up like a Protestant 17
promise, Irish lick and a Scotch 9

Index

Protestant priest, dressed up like a 17
prune, I'm so dry I feel like a 89
puddle *head toad in the 76 *(jump) across the 116
pulled over *a gatepost, look like the skin of a nightmare 15 *like an appetite with the skin 84
pump, You might as well take water from the 52
pups, Wouldn't that make an old dog piss on her 61

Queen's eyes, They would squeeze a penny until the water runs out of the 31
queer, Wouldn't that make the old people go 61
queer as *the crows 36 *Tom Peck's bulldog 36
quick, too slow to stop 26
quick and stay long, go 24
quite a / the [someone's first name] 123

rabbit *If that dog hadn't stopped to shit he would've caught the 26 *I've got to go and snare a 82 *They couldn't even skin a 45 *tracks, I'm going to sell / catch some 76 *We'll soon see the 94 *would shed tears going across it, field so poor a 102
race, If that dog hadn't stopped to shit he would've won the 26
raft? Were you born on a 68
rain *blow up 106 *dressed like a clothes-line in the 17 *They would drown if they walked in the 33 *to get wet, so thin they have to dance in the 13
raindrops, so thin they could dodge between the 13
raining cats and dogs, claws down, It's 105
raisin, I'm so dry I feel like a 89
rally, thresh another 95
ram *go, good day to let the 107 *in a gap, bold as a 34
rat *feel like a shit house 23 *in a shed with three lofts, busy as a 96

rats never leave your flour barrel with a tear in their eye, May the 82
rattle, If they had a brain it would 45
razorblade factory, nervous as a hemophiliac in a 59
red lane, down the little 86
red wagon, pretty as a 121
religious as my neighbour's dog, about as 121
rent, have space for 44
richer and not so good-looking, I wish I was born 50
ride, bow-legged as a cowboy after a six-day 16
right tight in the face 63
rings were falling off its horns, cow so old the 85
rise with a wet head, rooster crowing to bed is sure to 105
river with a pitchfork, You might as well try to bail the 50
road, Their driveway doesn't quite meet the 43
roading, out 19
roast ghost on toast 81
roasted, The chicken / turkey is 113
robin's leg, There's more flesh / meat on a 14
rock *land so poor it wouldn't grow 102 *lonesome as a gull on a 66
rock the roof 122
rocks, The sun is splitting the 109
roll a barrel between their legs, so bow-legged you could 16
rolling his *barrels, God is *oats, The Devil is *turnips, Saint Peter is 104
rolls than a bread bin / Bun King, more 10
roof, rock the 122
roof sorting airmail (with the crows), up on the 77
room *in the attic not finished, There's one *not finished, There's the ceiling of one 38
room trying to find a corner to do his business, busier than a cat in a round 96
rooms to let in the upper storey 44
rooster *crooked as a 28 *in a three-storey

barn, busy as a 96 *with a sock on its head, foolish as a 56
rooster crowing to bed is sure to rise with a wet head 105
roosters, Go to bed with the hens and get up with the 92
rope, That will hold me till you get a 87
rotten as dirt 111
rotten fish, I'm going to Tignish for a load of 76
rouge to paint a barn door, enough 9
round room trying to find a corner to do his business, busier than a cat in a 96
row of postholes, not amount to a 52
rub, Irish lick and a Scotch 9
rubber, If brains were | they wouldn't have enough to stretch around the hair on a flea's leg 45
rubber boot, so fond of liquor they would drink it out of a 89
run around *in the shower to get wet, so thin they have to 13 *like a bee / fly in a bottle 97
run that cow to death, They must have 85
running around like a *cut cat 37 *fart in a mitt 96
running gear, nothing left but the 15
running the roads 19
runny loaf, fat as a 11
Russians, hungry as a bunch of starving 83
Rustico, Someone is dead in 71

sack, hit the fart 92
sack of hammers *clumsy / crazy / dense / dumb / graceful / stupid as a *have as much sense as a 40
sack of wet mice, dense as a 40
saddle, doodle-daddle for a duck's / goose's / horse's 79
Saint Peter is rolling barrels / stones / turnips 104
salt on a ham sandwich, not worth the 50
salve, get 121
same, The smoke goes up the chimney just the 47

sand *to the Arabs, They could sell 73 *You might as well expect the tide to wait while you paint the 49
sandbox, sitting like a cat in a 59
sandwich *making a baloney 78 *not worth the mustard / salt on a ham 50 *There's not enough meat on you to make a 15
Saturday's market, I'm going to get Friday's fish in 77
save *a fart in a gas bottle, so mean they would 31 *their sole, They'd walk on their heel to 99 *the tallow from a mosquito, so greedy they would 30
saw wood, Say nothing and 71
sawdust, have a brain made out of 42
sawmill? Were you born brought up in a 68
Say nothing and saw wood 71
scale the wall, Get off the flour barrel and 91
school *for two days: the first was a holiday and the second the teacher wasn't there, They went to *keeps or not, I don't care if 122
Scotch promise / rub, Irish lick and a 9
scratching your arse and tearing it, There's a difference between 48
screen door *as if a pot were emptied through a 8 *on a submarine, useless as a 51 *like a cat caught in a 18 *They could shit through a 23
screen door, standing by a | *when a horse farted *when a manure spreader went by *when the sun was shining 8
screw, so crooked they could swallow a nail and pass a 27
screw their socks on in the morning, so crooked they have to 27
screwed into the ground, so crooked that (when they die) they could be 27
second *nose, They need [something] as badly as they need a 51 *pocket on a Sunday shirt, useful as a 51 *skimmings, mean as 31
second the teacher wasn't there, They

went to school for two days: the first was a holiday and the 122
see *a bit of [some person], not 23 *out of the other, blind in one eye and can't 8
sell, They could | *a heating pad / coals to the Devil *fleas to a dog / donkey *oil / sand to the Arabs *snow to an Eskimo *toothpicks to a wooden Indian 73
sell *plaid shirts 76 *postholes 60 *rabbit tracks 76 *the catch / their cabbage twice, not 71
sense as a bag of nails / hammers, have as much 40
sense as a, make as much | *dead cow *three-legged frog / sucking turkey 56
set the buoys by them, They 26
set a hen *good day to 109 *poor day to 107
sets, You have to plant or cut 53
settlers, It must have been older than the / one of the first 85
sew them on, make button holes and 60
sewing machine *but be no singer, to have a head like a 18 *I'm not an eight-day clock or a 97 *mouth/tongue like a 73
shadow, so thin they have to stand twice in the same spot / walk by twice to make a 13
sharp as a bowling ball / as a ball bearing / as a marble 42
sharp you could shave a mouse and never wake him up, so 113
shave a mouse and never wake him up, so sharp you could 113
shed tears going across it, field so poor a rabbit would 102
shed with three lofts, busy as a rat in a 96
sheep and to hell with poverty, kill a 101
sheep track, so fond of liquor they would drink it out of a 89
shell-bird / shell-duck, You only get one shot at a 48
Sherbrooke Road going into Summerside, crooked as the 28
shift, All that's left of them is the gear 15

shingle, if nothing cracks / splits worse than a 53
shining, standing by a screen door when the sun was 8
shit *he would've won the race, If that dog hadn't stopped to 26 *if they were well fed, They would 32 *or wind one's watch, not to know whether to 53 *through a screen door / a straw / the eye of a (darning) needle 23
Shit, King | *but they're only Fart, the Messenger, They think they're *from Turd Island / Mountain 34
shit *drunk as two / three / four / seven barrels of 90 *everywhere you go, like dog 97 *so cheap they wouldn't give you the smell off their last year's *to the crows, too mean to give their 31
shit house mouse / rat, feel like a 23
shit *in it, They wouldn't say 'barnyard' in case there was 36 *stuck to the bottom of your shoe, like 35
shitting yellow, still 35
shiver like a dog in a wet blanket 108
shoe *like shit stuck to the bottom of your 35 *There's never an old | but there's an old sock to match it 123
shoelaces, all in but the 91
shoes *so poor we had to lace our toes for 100 *they'd be barefoot, If clues were 45
Shoot geese 71
shoot a pea through them, so thin you could 12
short *always a day late and a dollar 99 *If you broke off where you cracked, you'd be damn 32
short *as a carrot 10 *in the grain 62
short of a *barrel, a few pickles *dollar, a few cents *dozen, a few cookies *dozen, two biscuits *full jar, seven pickles *load, a few bags / bales / nuts *picnic, a few apples / one ant 43
short of a load, three sticks 37
shorts in a knot, get their 62
shot behind a broomstick, so thin they couldn't be 12

shot at a shell-bird / shell-duck, You only get one 48
show, busy as a flea at a dog 97
shower *today, Thanks, but I had a 69 *to get wet, so thin they have to run around in the 13
showers? Do you supply towels with your 69
shy of a *dozen, twelve biscuits *foot, twelve inches 43
sick, If I was any better I'd be 57
side *from / on the other 118 *so thin it only has one 114
sideways, so thin if they turn | *they disappear *they're invisible 13
sieve, thin as a 12
sill and a door mat, cross between a door 26
silly as a billy goat 41
silver know-/new nothing *to hang on the end of your nose *to wind up the sun *with a whistle on it 79
Simpson's don't tell Eaton's their business 29
sing, when cows 53
singer, to have a head like a sewing machine but be no 18
singing for a night's lodging, If you were | you'd be sleeping outside 18
sins *face like a bag full of mortal 6 *on their soul, so thin you could see the 15
sitting like a cat in a sandbox 59
six-day ride, bow-legged as a cowboy after a 16
skate, face like a 4
skating conditions, nine / ten / eleven months of winter and three / two / one month(s) of poor 108
skimmings, mean as / meaner than second 31
skin an eel / a rabbit, They couldn't even 45
skin of a nightmare pulled over a gatepost, look like the 15
skin pulled over, like an appetite with the 84

skinny, they'd break if they bent over, so 14
skunk going west, so hungry I could eat the east end of a 83
sky, God / Saint Peter / The Devil / The old man is rolling barrels in the 104
sky, The sun is splitting the 109
sky over them before, I never saw the 49
slab, If you can't get a board, take a 53
slapped their mother, so ugly that the doctor 7
slats missing, have a few 37
sledding, nine / ten / eleven months of winter and three / two / one month(s) of tough 108
sleeping outside, If you were singing for a night's lodging, you'd be 18
sleigh track on the Western Road, straight / long as a 114
slept with a man who came from Antigonish, My brother 34
slick as a *biscuit 111 *cat's / kitten's wrist 111 *mouse 29
slipper but there's an old sock / stocking to fit / match it, There's never an old 123
slippery as six fat eels in a barrel of snot 29
sloughs ahead, have pitches and 52
slow *and stop, only two speeds *only one speed and that's *to stop quick, too *you have to time them on a calendar, so 26
slower than stopped, we'll name it after you, If there's anything 26
sly as a mouse 29
smart, Young steps are 19
smart as a bee 120
smell off their ass / last year's shit, too mean to give the / so cheap they wouldn't give you the 31
smelts, I'm going to Tignish for a load of rotten 76
smoke goes up the chimney just the same, The 47
smoke is better than a cold fog, warm 67
smooth as the kitchen table 109

snake *more gall than a 34 *would break its back getting around them 28
snake's back getting around them, so crooked it would break a 28
snakes, face like a can of 4
snare a rabbit, I've got to go and 82
sneak up on a drink of water, With a face like that, they'd have to 6
sneaker, face like a twisted 5
snipe shooting, They know as much about [something] as my arsehole knows about 45
snot, slippery as six fat eels in a barrel of 29
snow, useless as a pee-hole / piss-hole in the 52
snow to *an Eskimo, They could sell 73 *your heels, Fair weather to you and 82
snowball in the Bay of Fundy, useless as a 51
snowbank *keep their money in a 101 *useless as a pee-hole / piss-hole in a 52
snuff, dry as 103
soap-blowing, They know as much about [something] as my arsehole knows about 45
sock *in a pig's ear / nose, fit like a 112 *on its head, foolish as a rooster with a 56 *so fond of liquor they would drink it out of a(n) (old) 89 *There is a match / mate for every old 123
socks *on in the morning so crooked they have to screw their 27 *Wouldn't that frost your 61
soft as porridge 113
sole, They'd walk on their heel to save their 99
Solomon's mule, stubborn as 34
somersaults in their suit, so thin they can turn 14
song so old it has a grey beard / it has holes in it 111
soon be having the cookies on [someone], We'll 21
sore tooth, have more nerve than a 33

sorry for the knife, I'd stab [someone] but I'd be 63
sorting airmail (with the crows), up on the roof 77
soul alone, all 66
soul *hole, heart, and 86 *so thin you could see the sins on their 15
sour apple, face like a 4
sour twenty-one, Sweet sixteen 19
Souris for a load of jellybeans / fish / postholes, I'm going to 76
south end of a train headed north, face like the 6
sow's snout, tough as a 113
space for rent, have 44
spare bedroom, (all) dressed up like a 17
spark alone, black 66
sparks, I'm so dry I'm spitting 89
spats *for a canary, They couldn't afford a pair of 100 *so hungry I could eat my 83
speed and that's slow, only one 26
speeds, slow and stop, only two 26
spending all week, Don't buy anything on Monday or you will be 99
spit and a jump (away) 115
spit *and miss the ground, so drunk they'd 89 *I'm so dry I can't /couldn't 89 *I wouldn't waste my 64 *on a fire in a barn full of straw, You might as well 50 *through them, so thin you could 12 *too lazy to 26
spitting *God is 105 *sparks, I'm so dry I'm 89
splatters, I'd hit [someone] but they say manure 64
splits worse than a shingle, if nothing 53
splitting the heavens / rocks / sky / trees, The sun is 109
spoon, dry as a wooden 88
spot to make a shadow, so thin they have to stand twice in the same 19
spreader went by, standing by a screen door when a manure 8
spry, green as grass and twice as 19
square eggs, painful as a hen laying 23

squeaking, I'm so dry I'm 89
squeal, so thin they have to lean up against the wall to 14
squeeze a penny until the water runs out of the Queen's eyes, They would 31
squint-eyed cat trying to catch all the mice it sees, busy as a
stab [someone] but I'd be sorry for the knife, I'd 63
stack, like a (bush in a) barley 9
staircase but no upstairs, have a lovely 43
stalk of corn, talk the ear off a 73
stamp, They couldn't afford the down payment on a three-cent 100
stand it, If I was any better I couldn't 57
stand them in the well to cut their hair, You have to 19
stand twice in the same spot to make a shadow, so thin they have to 13
standing by a screen door when *a horse farted *a manure spreader went by *the sun was shining 8
standing on its tail, like a cat with someone 18
starve to death crossing it, land so poor a grasshopper / mouse would 102
starving Russians, hungry as a bunch of 83
static in the attic, There's 38
stay long, go quick and 24
steal swill from an orphan pig / the eyes out of your head, so greedy they would 30
steam, I'm going to get a bucket of 76
steel bridge, so cold it would freeze the nuts off a 107
steps *are smart, Young 19 *count the 92
stick, look as if *their mother beat them with an ugly *they got hit too hard with the ugly *they took a beating from / got beat (bad) by an ugly 6–7
stick *There's more meat on a hockey 14 *by the end of the 65
stick out in their stomach, so thin a peanut would 13

sticks *missing, have a few *short of a load, three 37
still *have the balsam / cowshit on *shitting yellow 35
stocking to fit / match it, There's never an old shoe / slipper but there's a 123
stomach, Over the lips and over the gums, look out | here it comes 86
stomach *so thin a peanut would stick out in their 13 *The Lord has an upset 105
stone, tongue that would blister a 74
Stone Age, older than the 20
stones, God / Saint Peter / The Devil / The old man is rolling is rolling 104
stop, only two speeds, slow and 26
stop quick, too slow to 26
stopped, If there's anything slower than | we'll name it after you 26
store, You might as well go to the liquor 52
storey, in the upper | *rooms to let 44 *There's no light(s) (on) 38
storm, dry as a dust 103
stove pipe, crooked as a 27
straight / long as a sleigh track on the Western Road 114
strange cup of tea 37
stranger, put another [something] in for the 83
strap, dry as a 84
straw, They could shit through a 23
straw *in their hair, They have 35 *off their eggs and on to the 74 *out of your ears, Clean the 62 *so fond of liquor they would drink it out of a dirty 89 *through a chicken coop / picket fence, They could eat 9 *You might as well spit on a fire in a barn full of 50
straw hat? How's your old 75
strawberries, They couldn't box 45
streak of misery, long 58
street, They didn't pick that up off the 3
stretch a mile but I'm too lazy to walk back, I'd 91
stretch around the hair on a flea's leg, If

brains were rubber they wouldn't have enough to 45
stubborn as *a calf at a new gate 34 *Solomon's mule 34
stuck home 118
stuck to the bottom of your shoe(s) / to the wall, like shit 35
stuffed to the guppers 97
stump, fat as a lump on a 11
stump (fence), homely as a (hardwood) 5
stunned as a doorknob 42
stupid, one [person] couldn't be that 1 *There must be two of them because *They must have had a twin because 44
stupid as a *bag / sack of (claw) hammers *billy goat *boiled worm *cat who can't climb a tree *doorknob *hedgehog *marsh hen 40–2
stupid as pissing the bed awake 44
stupid they'd miss the floor if they fell out of bed, so 44
submarine, useless as a screen door on a 51
sucking turkey, make as much sense as a 56
suit, so thin they can turn somersaults in their 14
Summerside, crooked as the Sherbrooke Road going into 28
sun, the 1 *baked in 84 *honest as 29
sun *is splitting the heavens / rocks / sky / trees, The 109 *silver new nothing to wind up the 79 *was shining, standing by a screen door when the 8
sunburned, talk so much that their tongue gets 72
Sunday *and the Devil will be after you all week, Cut your fingernails on 56 *and three times as disagreeable, long as a wet 121 *shirt, useful as a second pocket on a 86
supper's cooked, The 113
supply towels with your showers? Do you 69
swallow a nail and pass a screw, so crooked they could 27
swallowed it, It must have been a lie – I 72
sweat *like a hen hauling wood 94 *off a dead man's arse / balls, not worth the 51
sweep the floor and wipe your ass at the same time, You can't 53
sweet cent, I'd bet a 47
Sweet sixteen, sour twenty-one 19
sweetbreads yet, No 21
swill from an orphan pig, so greedy they would steal 30
Swiss cheese, have a brain made out of 42

table, smooth as the kitchen 109
table, so hungry I could eat the 83
tail *caught in a wringer, like a cat with its 18 *like a cat with someone standing on its 18 *on a cat, tight as the 112 *They need [something] as badly as a toad needs a 51
take *pass of 121 *the cluck(ing) out of 62
take *that off the floor, They didn't 3 *water, You might as well 52
taking you nowhere and treating you like a dog when we get there, I'm 81
talk the *arse / bottom / handle / lid out of / off an iron pot 75 *ear off a(n) elephant / monkey / stalk of corn 73
talk a hole in a(n) iron / lead / pot 75
talk out of [someone], pick the 72
talk *so much that their tongue gets sunburned 72 *when they should have listened 55
tall if they fell down they'd be half way home, so 10
tallow from a mosquito, so greedy they would save the 30
tap, You might as well take water from the 52
tartar biscuit, look like a cream of 16
tastes like more, This 86
tax time, busy as an accountant at 97
tea, strange cup of 37
teacher wasn't there, They went to school for two days: the first was a holiday and the second the 122

Index

tear in their eye, May the rats never leave your flour barrel with a 82
tearing around like a fart in a mitt 96
tearing it, There's a difference between scratching your arse and 48
tears *going across it, field so poor a rabbit would shed *in their eyes, The mice come out of the cupboard with 101–2
teaspoon, You might as well try to keep Niagara Falls back with a 50
teddy bear *dolled up like a 16 *full as a 90
teddy in their hand, dolled up with a 16
tenth of a clue, not have an inkling and that's only a 45
Thanks, but I had a shower today 69
thanks, No | I've just had a banana 81
thin, so | *a peanut would stick out in their stomach *if they turn sideways they disappear *if they turn sideways they're invisible *the wind could blow right through them *they'd break if they bent over *you have to look twice to see them 12–14
thin, so | it only has one side 114
thin, so | they can *be used as a dipstick *dodge between the raindrops *hide behind a broomstick *turn somersaults in their suit 12–14
thin, so | they couldn't be shot / hit with a shotgun behind a broomstick / crowbar 12
thin, so | they have to *dance in the rain to get wet *lean up against the wall to squeal *run around in the shower to get wet *stand twice in the same spot to make a shadow *turn sideways to be seen *walk by twice to make a shadow 13–14
thin, so | you could *see the sins on their soul 15 *shoot a pea through them 12 *spit through them 12
thin as a *drink of water 11 *sieve 12
think they are *the people *the train, They sure don't *[the person's own name], They 33

thinking I might move the barn / the chicken house / the moon, I was 78
thirst, If brains were water, they would die of 45
thirsty as a burnt boot / potato 84
thirsty I could drink a biscuit, so 88
thistles, land so poor it wouldn't grow 102
thousands from Tyne Valley alone 80
thrash the turnips, when I 53
thread the needle at ninety yards 23
three *bags, so poor the garbage man would leave 100 *days older than the fog 20 *lofts, busy as a rat in a shed with 96 *mosquitoes fried in butter 81 *sticks short of a load 37 *times as disagreeable, long as a wet Sunday and 121
three-cent stamp, They couldn't afford the down payment on a 100
three-legged frog, make as much sense as a 56
three-storey barn, busy as a rooster in a 96
thresh a little / another rally 95
threshing machine, tongue like a 73
throat, cut the dead man's 122
through the loop, go 101
throw more out the back door than they carry in the front 99
thrown in the ugly pond, look as if one was 6
thumbhole, busy as / worse than a fart in a mitt(en) looking for a 96
thumbtack, have a head like a 42
tick, so poor we took turns sleeping on the feather 100
ticket to a free meal, They couldn't afford the 100
tide *out with a pitchfork, You might as well try to keep the *to wait while you paint the sand, You might as well expect the 49–50
tide's gone out, The 9
tides, day older than the 20
tight as *a cat's ass / coot / cup / fiddler's fart / fiddlestring / pop bottle *the tail on a cat *two coats of paint 112

tight in the face, right 63
tight as the paper on the wall / in the parlour 32
Tignish for a load of postholes / rotten fish / smelts, I'm going to 76
time *busy as an accountant at tax 97 *up at crow piss 93
time, You can't sweep the floor and wipe your ass at the same 53
time to *buckle up / climb / hit the (big / little) (old) wooden hill *find the gaps 91–2
time them on a calendar, so slow you have to 26
times as disagreeable, long as a wet Sunday and three 121
tin can, If you can't get a board, take a slab, and if you can't get a slab, take an old 53
tin pot, talk / wear a hole in a 75
tip of the moon, hang a powder horn on a 110
toad *at the bottom of a well, lazy as a 25 *eating grubs / lightning, busier than a 95 *in the puddle, head 76 *needs a tail, They need [something] as badly as a 51
toast, roast ghost on 81
today *It's chilly eyebrow 106 *no blackflies / flies / mosquitoes out 106 *Thanks, but I had a shower 69
toes for shoes, so poor we had to lace our 100
tom-cat, coming home from a different direction every morning, He's like a 68
Tom Clarke's / Creed's / Dooley's / Dort's / Duke's / Peck's / Pepper's dog, crazy as 36
tomorrow will be the middle of the week and no work done yet, The day after 94
tongue *as oily as a churnful of butter *gets sunburned, talk so much that their *like a button on a back barn door *like a Mountie's boot *like a threshing machine / hay cutter / sewing machine / winding blade *than a Mountie's boot, more *that would blister a stone 72–4
tonight, God / The Lord is angry 105
too cold for a fence post 106
too lazy to breathe / to live / to spit 26
too mean to give *their shit to the crows *the smell off their ass 31
too slow to stop quick 26
took turns sleeping on the feather (tick), so poor we 100
tooth, have more nerve than a sore 33
toothpicks to a wooden Indian, They could sell 73
top of the barn *up to the 77 *You might as well try to climb to the 50
touch of the orchard about / in [someone] 120
touch a wire, They could shit through a screen door and never 23
tough as *a sow's snout 113 *leather judgment 85
tough life, This may be a young animal, but it led a 85
tough sledding, nine / ten / eleven months of winter and three / two / one month(s) of 108
towels with your showers? Do you supply 69
town, be so poor we drew laces on our feet to walk to 100
track so fond of liquor they would drink it out of a cow('s) sheep('s) / wagon 89
track on the Western Road, long / straight as a sleigh 114
tracks, face so ugly it would run a train off the 6
train *going west, face like the east end of a 6 *headed north, face like the south end of a 5 *not enough on to flag a 17 *off the tracks, face so ugly it would run a 6 *They sure don't think they are the 33
traipsing the roads 19
Trans-Canada, crooked as the 28
treat you mean when we get there, I'll give you nothing, take you nowhere, and 81

tree *and hit every branch on the way down, They fell out of an ugly 6 *stupid as a cat who can't climb a 41 *The only time they were off the Island was when they were up a 35 *up a 77

trees *off an Island penny, They would cut the 31 *The sun is splitting the 109

trip a goat, so foolish it would 55

try to, You might as well | bail the river / climb Mount Everest / climb to the top of the barn / keep Niagara Falls back / keep the tide out (with a fork / pitchfork / teaspoon) 50

trouble while it lasts, If you see the new moon through glass, it's 54

troubles than money, have more 101

trough, the | *go once too often to *go too close to *half an hour earlier, They should push away from 10

trough, king of the 76

truck, mouth like the back of a dump 73

truck / wagon load of postholes, I'm going to Souris for a 76

tune if it had handles, They couldn't carry a 18

Turd Island / Mountain, King Shit from 34

turkey, make as much sense as a sucking 56

turkey is cooked / roasted, The 113

turn, every hitch and 120

turn sideways *they disappear, so thin if they *they're invisible, so thin if they *to be seen, so thin they have to 13

turnips *Saint Peter is rolling his 104 *when I thrash the 52

twelve *biscuits / eggs shy of a dozen *inches shy of a foot 43

twelve and then it's getting early, It's not late until it's 67

twelve and then it's too late, It's not late until it's 67

twenty-nine, They're a 63

twenty-one, Sweet sixteen, sour 19

twice *in the same spot to make a shadow, so thin they have to stand *to make a shadow, so thin they have to walk by 13

twice, not sell the catch / their cabbage 71

twice as *long as from the centre to either end 81 *spry, green as grass and 19

twice to see *so high you have to look 114 *so thin you have to look 13

twin because one person couldn't be that stupid, They must have had a 44

twins, If I was any better I'd be 57

twist, in good 23

twisted sneaker, face like a 5

twister, take a 62

two *beautiful blue eyes – one blew east and one blew west 8 *of me, If I was any happier there would be 57 *of them because one couldn't be that stupid, There must be 44 *pigs fighting in a blanket / gunney sack, look like 11

two and then it's too late, It's not late until it's 67

two-by-four *big / wide as a 12 *stretcher, I'm going to get a 76

two-faced *as a double-bitted axe / looking glass 28 *or I wouldn't be wearing the one I have, I'm not 7 *they should wear two hats, so 28

two-watt (light) bulb, bright as a 42

Tyne Valley alone, thousands (and thousands) from 80

ugly *bug, someone got hit with the *it must hurt, face so *it would run a train off the tracks, face so *pond, look as if one was thrown in the *that the doctor slapped their mother, so *tree and hit every branch on the way down, They fell out of an 6–7

ugly as a(n) axe handle / barn door / brush fence 4–5

ugly fish, homely as an 4

ugly pills for breakfast, Their mother gave them 63

ugly stick, look as if *their mother beat them with an *they took a beating

Index   167

from / got beat bad by an *they were hit too hard with the 6–7
under a bridge? Were you born 68
up *a tree 77 *a tree, The only time they were off the Island was when they were 35 *at crow piss 93 *in high C 58 *on the roof sorting airmail (with the crows) 77 *rain, blow 106 *there? Is it cold 10 *to the top of the barn 77 *with the roosters, Go to bed with the hens and get 92 *your arse or you'd feel it, It's not 80
up *east 116 *west 115
upper storey *rooms to let in the 44 *There's no light(s) (on) in the 38
upset stomach, The Lord has an 105
upside down, have their mouth turned 58
upstairs *apartment is vacant, the 43 *have a lovely staircase but no 43 *not plastered, There's one room 38 *There's no light(s) (on) 38
upstairs in the cellar picking chickens out of feathers 45
useful as a second pocket on a Sunday shirt 51
useless as / a bucket under a bull / a deuce in a jackpot / a pee-hole/piss-hole in a blanket / in a snowbank / in last year's snowbank / in the snow / a screen door on a submarine / a snowball in the Bay of Fundy / a whipstand on an automobile 51–2

vacancy in one's forehead, have a 44
vacant, the upstairs apartment is 43
vacation, so poor that four in the bed meant half the family was away on 100
vinegar factory, gall enough to start a 32
voice of the Lord, That's the angry 105
vote *cow so old it must have had a 85 *old enough to 111 *when cows 53

waddle, doodle-daddle for a goose's 79
wagon *look like a new dashboard on an old 16 *pretty as a red 121

wagon for a month, dry as a drunk on the 88
wagon load of postholes, I'm going to Souris for a 76
wagon track, so fond of liquor they would drink it out of a 89
wait while you paint the sand, You might as well expect the tide to 49
waiting for the pogie, That land is 102
wake him up, so sharp you could shave a mouse and never 113
walk *a mile if I didn't have to walk back, I'd 91 *back on her 119 *by twice to make a shadow, so thin they have to 13 *on their heel to save their sole, They'd 99 *the goldfish, I was about to 78 *to town, so poor we drew laces on our feet to 100
walk, off the 23
walked in the rain, They would drown if they 33
walking on / through molasses, like 119
wall *Get off the flour barrel and scale the 91 *like shit stuck to the 35 *tight / close as the paper on the 32
warm smoke is better than a cold fog 67
waste my spit, I wouldn't 64
watch, not to know whether to shit or wind one's 53
water *(all) hot, Don't get your 60 *from the pump / the tap, You might as well take 52 *on the beans, That'll put different 47 *runs out of the Queen's eyes, They would squeeze a penny until the 31 *The moon is holding 110 *they would die of thirst, If brains were 45 *thin as a drink of 11 *With a face like that, they'd have to sneak up on a drink of 6 *You might as well take a drink of 52
wave your donut, Hoot and holler and 58
wear a *hole in a(n) iron / lead / tin pot 75 *ten dollar hat on a ten cent head 33
wearing the one I have, I'm not two-faced or I wouldn't be 7

weather *for blackflies / flies / mosquitoes, Good 106 *to you and snow to your heels, Fair 82
weaved, bob when they should have 55
week, The day after tomorrow will be the middle of the | and no work done yet 94
week *Cut your fingernails on Sunday and the Devil will be after you all 56 *Don't buy anything on Monday or you will be spending all 99 *long as a wet 121
welfare, land so poor it's on 102
well *lazy as (a) toad(s) at the bottom of a 25 *so cross-eyed they have to lie on their back to look down a 8
well-fed *at both ends 10 *They would shit (too) if they were 32
west, down 116 *up 115
west *face like the east end of a train going 6 *so hungry I could eat the east end of a horse / skunk going 83 *two beautiful blue eyes – one blew east and one blew 8
Western Road *face as long as the 58 *straight / long as a sleigh track on the 114
wet *blanket, shiver like a dog in a 108 *cat, homely as a 4 *head, rooster crowing to bed is sure to rise with a 105 *If it rained brains, they wouldn't even get 45 *mice, dense as a sack of 40 *so thin they have to dance in the rain to get 13 * so thin they have to run around in the shower to get 13 *Sunday and three times as disagreeable, long as a 121 *week, long as a 121
What's growing on you? 76
wheel sometimes, The hamster gets off the 39
wheelbarrow *not enough on to flag a 17 *They could charm the heart out of a 74
wheelbarrow dance, They could charm the heart of a grindstone and make a 74
when *cows vote / sing 89 *I thrash the turnips 52 *you die, you go to Heaven, Hell, or Cawnpore 21 *you see a pig, you should kick it 123
whipstand on an automobile, useless as a 51
whipstitch away 115
whistle on it, silver know-/new nothing with a 79
white, have more black keys than 38
Who's killing the cat? 18
whore of a day 106
wick, Holy 65
wide as *a fishcake 114 *a two-by-four 12 *the day is long 10 *the Devil's boots 114
widow's breath, cold as a 107
wiggle-waggle for a goose's necktie 79
wind, like the Devil in a gale of 8
wind could blow right through them, so thin the 12
wind one's watch, not to know whether to shit or 53
wind up the sun, silver know-/new nothing to 79
winding blade, mouth / tongue like a 73
winter, nine / ten / eleven months of | and three / two / one month(s) of tough sledding / of poor skating conditions / of (late) fall 108
wipe your ass at the same time, You can't sweep the floor and 53
wire, big as number nine 12
wire, They could shit through a screen door and never hit / touch a 23
wire brush, There's a difference between scratching your arse and tearing it all to pieces / all to hell with a 48
wire fence *homely as a 5 *They look like a horse eating an apple through a 9
wise, happy as if they were 36
witch's pocket, black as a 109
won the 100-yard dash in a 90-yard gym, face like someone who 6
wood *Say nothing and saw 71 *sweat like a hen hauling 94
wooden *hill, It's time to buckle up /

climb / hit the (big/little) (old) 92
*Indian, They could sell toothpicks to a 73
wooden bridge in Africa / bucket / leg / spoon, dry as a(n) (old) 88
woodpecker's boarding house, dry as the inside of a 88
woodpile, not fit for a 107
woods *they have to come out to hunt, live so far in the back 67 *with no door on? Were you born in the 68
work done yet, The day after tomorrow will be the middle of the week and no 94
worked up like a dog's dinner 59
working, If I was any happier I wouldn't be 57
worm, stupid as a boiled 41
worms, face like a bucket / can of (squashed) 4
worse than a *cut cat, going around 37 *fart in a mitt(en) (looking for a thumb-hole) 96
worse than a shingle, if nothing splits / cracks 53
worth, not | *a patch for your pants / on a good man's arse *the butter on a biscuit / on their bread *the knife they butter their bread with *mustard / salt on a ham sandwich *the sweat off a dead man's arse / balls 50–1
wouldn't be [some adjective], They 49
Wouldn't that *blow the hen right off her nest *boil / burn / fester your britches *bring grandmother back from the dead *burn your brother's bacon *cook your buns *fluff your feathers *frost your ass / eardrums / eyeballs / fanny / preserves / socks *frost the backside of a cow *give the dog's arse heartburn *make an old dog piss on her pups *make the old people go queer 60–1
wringer, like a cat with its tail caught in a 18
wrist, slick as a kitten's / cat's 111

X-ray them with a flashlight, You could 13

yards, thread the needle at ninety 23
year (and piling it up), the same thing I did last 78
year's bird's nest, empty as last 41
yellow, still shitting 35
yellow as a duck's foot 120
You'll never put air under that 84
young animal, This may be a | but it led a tough life 85
Young steps are smart 19